Y0-CBH-672

The Interest Group Society

The Interest Group Society

THIRD EDITION

Jeffrey M. Berry
Tufts University

 LONGMAN

An imprint of Addison Wesley Longman, Inc.

New York • Reading, Massachusetts • Menlo Park, California • Harlow, England
Don Mills, Ontario • Sydney • Mexico City • Madrid • Amsterdam

Acquisitions Editor: Margaret Loftus
Project Coordination and Text Design: York Production Services
Supervising Production Editor: Lois Lombardo
Cover Design: Scott Russo
Manufacturing Manager: Hilda Koparanian
Electronic Page Makeup: ComCom
Printer and Binder: RR Donnelley & Sons Company
Cover Printer: Phoenix Color Corp.

Library of Congress Cataloging-in-Publication Data

Berry, Jeffrey M., 1948–
    The interest group society / Jeffrey M. Berry.—3rd ed.
    p. ; cm.
    Previously published: Glenview, Ill.: Scott, Foresman, c1989.
    Includes bibliographical references and index.
    ISBN 0-673-52511-2
    1. Pressure groups—United States.   I. Title.
JK1118.B395   1996
322.4/3/0973—dc20   96-2313
                                                              CIP

Copyright © 1997 by Jeffrey M. Berry

All rights reserved. No part of this publication may be reproduced, stored in a retrieval system, or transmitted, in any form or by any means, electronic, mechanical, photocopying, recording, or otherwise, without the prior written permission of the publisher. Printed in the United States.

ISBN 0-673-52511-2

    45678910—DOC—99

For Jessica and Rachel

Contents

Preface

The Interest Group Society, in its three editions, has tracked changes in both the interest group world and in interest group scholarship. In the early 1980s when I wrote the first edition, I was convinced that the number of interest groups had grown dramatically and that the role of interest groups in the policymaking process had expanded. In the intervening years nothing has happened to change my mind. Although they are an enduring part of American political life, interest groups today have more resources, represent more constituencies, and do more lobbying than ever before. We depend on them to speak for us before government and to ensure that legislators and administrators understand our needs and preferences. When we stop to think about the political issue that we care most about, we usually think of it in terms of interest group dynamics. We are truly an interest group society.

Chapter Two, "The Advocacy Explosion," addresses the question of whether interest groups are continuing to expand in number, and analysis has been added to examine the consequences of the growth that has taken place since the 1960s. Chapter Nine, for example, examines the development of issue networks and tries to make sense of dense policymaking environments that include literally hundreds of different lobbies, all of whom are trying to influence the same government officials. Other changes in the interest group world that receive expanded coverage in this edition include the rise of the Christian right, the growing prominence of think tanks, and high-tech lobbying tactics.

The most significant additions in this revision are two new chapters. Chapter Three, "The Party Connection," actually brings back to life a chapter on parties and interest groups that appeared in the first edition. In order to create room for some new chapters in the second edition, I dropped the parties chapter. However, it was never far from my mind, and some new research I was doing led me to think about some of the recent developments in the relationship between parties and groups. Not much of what appeared in that chapter in the first edition has survived, and the focus has shifted from party decline to the means by which interest groups try to influence the direction of the two major parties.

A new Chapter Ten, "Bias and Representation," builds on a chapter entitled "The Power of Business" that appeared in the second edition. Here I move beyond the description and analysis of business lobbying to more directly address the central question concerning the role of business in politics: To what extent is business unfairly advantaged in the democratic process? In trying to answer this question, I offer a broad assessment of what constitutes bias in the interest group system.

As with the research for the two previous editions, for this edition I relied heavily on interviews with Washington lobbyists. Over the three editions of *The Interest Group Society* approximately 130 interviews have been done with Washington representatives of all major types of interest groups. I'm deeply appreciative of the time these lobbyists gave out of their hectic schedules to speak with us about their jobs and the role of interest groups in the governmental process. I've quoted freely from these interviews, but they inform the text even where they are not being quoted.

I've also been fortunate that so much significant research has been published since the second edition of this book. Many new, sophisticated studies have added to our knowledge of interest groups in American politics. Like the number of interest groups, the number of interest group scholars seems to have increased sharply. Unlike interest groups, they all contribute to the common good.

Over the years I have piled up no shortage of debts to people who have helped me in one way or another. I initially began writing *The Interest Group Society* while I was in residence at the Lincoln Filene Center for Citizenship and Public Affairs at Tufts University. I am grateful to Stuart Langton, who served as the director of the center at the time, for his support. I could not have completed any of the editions of this book without the hard work of a number of research assistants. Jan Meriwether and Merilee Mishall helped with the interviews for the first and second editions respectively. They were invaluable colleagues. This time around, Pam Slipakoff assisted with the interviews, and she did an exceptional job in the work she took on. From time to time I was able to call on a number of other Tufts students for their help. Thanks to Debra Candreva, Michael Devigne, Anne Doyle, Bill Fisher, Valerie Goff, Meggan Gondek, Rob Horn, Ann Kelly, Charles Rosenberg, and David Wolin.

I feel very fortunate that so many fine scholars have been willing to take time away from their own work to read and comment on mine. The following people were kind enough to critique chapters or entire drafts of the earlier editions: Christopher Bosso, Vincent Buck, James Ennis, Jerry Goldman, Janet Grenzke, Richard Harris, Gary Jacobson, Burdett Loomis, Sidney Milkis, Kent Portney, Steven Rosenstone, Kay Lehman Schlozman, Frank Sorauf, John Tierney, Jack Walker, and Graham Wilson. For this edition: Sara A. Grove, Darrell M. West, Alan L. Clem, and Marjorie Hershey. I profited greatly from the many suggestions that all of these excellent political scientists made.

Finally, thanks to the many editors who handled the various versions of the manuscript with the care and attention every author hopes for. On the earlier editions I was lucky to work with John Covell, Will Ethridge, Dave Lynch, Don Palm, Traci Sobocinski, and Sally Stickney. For this edition, I'm grateful for the help I received from Margaret Loftus, Leo Weigman, and Angela Finnen.

Jeffrey M. Berry

The Interest Group Society

Chapter
1

Madison's Dilemma

$\mathcal{A}$ troubling dilemma lies at the core of the American political system. In an open and free society in which people have the right to express their political views, petition their government, and organize on behalf of causes, some segments of the population are likely to pursue their own selfish interests. Dairy farmers will push Congress to adopt price subsidies even though it means families will have to pay more at the grocery store. Manufacturers and labor unions will press for tariffs and other trade barriers to protect profits and jobs. Consumers, however, will be saddled with higher prices as a result. Environmentalists will fight for increasing the number of parks and wilderness preserves, though development of those lands might provide jobs for some who are out of work. In short, people will pursue their self-interest even though the policies they advocate may hurt others and may not be in the best interest of the nation.

The dilemma is this: If the government does not allow people to pursue their self-interest, it takes away their political freedom. When we look at the nations of the world in which people are forbidden to organize and to freely express their political views, we find that there the dilemma has been solved by authoritarianism. Although the alternative—permitting people to advocate whatever they want—is far more preferable, it carries dangers. In a system such as ours, interest groups constantly push government to enact policies that benefit small constituencies at the expense of the general public.

This dilemma is as old as the country itself, yet never more relevant than today. As lobbying has grown in recent years, anxiety has mounted over the consequences of interest group politics. Political action committees (PACs) threaten the integrity of congressional elections. Liberal citizen groups are blamed for slowing economic development with the regulatory policies they have fought for. Labor unions are held responsible because America fails to compete effectively in many world markets, while tax cuts granted to businesses seem to increase their profits at the expense of huge federal budget deficits. Beyond the sins allegedly committed by sectors of the interest group community is a broader worry. Are the sheer number of interest groups and their collective power undermining American democracy?

Many agree that interest groups are an increasingly troublesome part of American politics, yet there is little consensus on what, if anything, ought to be done about it. The dilemma remains: Interest groups are no less a threat than they are an expression of freedom.

CURING THE MISCHIEFS OF FACTION

Is there no middle ground between these two alternatives? Must a government accept one or the other? Contemporary discussions of this question inevitably turn to *The Federalist*, for James Madison's analysis in essay No. 10 remains the foundation of American political theory on interest groups.[1] With great foresight, Madison recognized the problem that the fragile new nation would face. Although at the time he was writing the country had no political parties or lobbies as we know them, Madison correctly perceived that people would organize in some way to further their common interests. Furthermore, these groupings, or "factions" as he called them, were a potential threat to popular government.

Factions were not anomalies, nor would they be occasional problems. Rather, as Madison saw it, the propensity to pursue self-interest was innate. The "causes of faction," he concluded, are "sown in the nature of man."[2] As any society develops, it is inevitable that different social classes will emerge, that competing interests based on differing occupations will arise, and that clashing political philosophies will take hold among the populace. This tendency was strong in Madison's eyes: He warned that free men are more likely to try to oppress each other than they are to "co-operate for their common good."[3]

---

[1]*The Federalist Papers* (New York: New American Library, 1961), pp. 77–84.
[2]*Federalist Papers,* p. 79.
[3]*Federalist Papers,* p. 79.

Madison worried that a powerful faction could eventually come to tyrannize others in society. What, then, was the solution for "curing the mischiefs of faction"? He rejected out of hand any restrictions on the freedoms that permitted people to pursue their own selfish interests, remarking that the remedy would be "worse than the disease."[4] Instead, he reasoned that the effects of faction must be controlled rather than eliminating factions themselves. This control could be accomplished by setting into place the structure of government proposed in the Constitution.

In Madison's mind, a republican form of government, as designed by the framers, would provide the necessary checks on the worst impulses of factions. A republican form of government gives responsibility for decisions to a small number of representatives who are elected by the larger citizenry. Furthermore, for a government whose authority extends over a large and dispersed population, the effects of faction would be diluted by the clash of many competing interests across the country. Thus, Madison believed that in a land as large as the United States, so many interests would arise that a representative government with its own checks and balances would not become dominated by any faction. Instead, government could deal with the views of all, producing policies that would be in the common good.

Madison's cure for the mischiefs of faction was something of a leap of faith.[5] The structure of American government has not, by itself, prevented some interests from gaining great advantage at the expense of others. Those with large resources have always been better represented by interest groups, and the least wealthy in society have suffered because of their failure to organize. Still, even though the republican form of government envisioned by Madison has not always been strong enough to prevent abuse by factions, the beliefs underlying *Federalist* No. 10 have endured.

This view that the natural diversity of interests would prevent particular groups from dominating politics found a later incarnation in American social science of the 1950s and 1960s. *Pluralist* scholars argued that the many (that is, plural) interests in society found representation in the policymaking process through lobbying by organizations.

---

[4]*Federalist Papers,* p. 78.
[5]There is an extensive literature on *Federalist* No. 10, but probably no analysis is more important than Robert Dahl's *A Preface to Democratic Theory* (Chicago: University of Chicago Press, 1956).

The bargaining that went on between such groups and government led to policies produced by compromise and consensus. Interest groups were seen as more beneficial to the system than Madison's factions, with emphasis placed on the positive contributions made by groups in speaking for their constituents before government. Although the pluralist school was later discredited for a number of reasons (these will be outlined shortly), it furthered the Madisonian ideal: groups freely participating in the policymaking process, none becoming too powerful because of the natural conflict of interests, and government acting as a synthesizer of competing interests. This ideal remains contemporary America's hope for making interest group politics compatible with democratic values.

INTEREST GROUPS AND THEIR FUNCTIONS

One purpose in this book is to reexamine the fundamental questions raised by *Federalist* No. 10. Can an acceptable balance be struck between the right of people to pursue their own interests and the need to protect society from being dominated by one or more interests? Can we achieve true pluralism, or is a severe imbalance of interest group power a chronic condition in a free and open society?

Our means of answering this question will be to look broadly at behavior among contemporary interest groups. We will often follow research questions that political scientists have asked about the internal and external operations of lobbying organizations. Data for this study come not only from the literature on interest groups, but also from interviews with Washington lobbyists.[6] Although the topics addressed are varied, one argument runs throughout: Important changes have taken place in interest group politics in recent years, because of which renewed thought must be given to controlling the effects of faction.

 On the simplest level, when we speak of an interest group we are referring to an organization that tries to influence government. Some elaboration is necessary to clarify what we mean. Interest groups are organizations that are not part of the government they are trying to in-

---

[6]Unless otherwise cited, quotations in the text are taken from these interviews.

fluence.[7] It is often the case that interest groups are equated with voluntary organizations, membership groups composed of people with similar interests or occupations who have joined together to gain some benefits. Yet the lobbying world is full of organizations that do not have memberships. Corporations and public-interest law firms, for example, have no memberships, although they have constituencies they represent before government. Our focus here includes lobbying organizations regardless of whether they have memberships. Interest groups are distinct from political parties because political parties run candidates for office under their banner, whereas interest groups do not. On the other hand, it is difficult to distinguish between interest groups and social movements because social movements are composed of interest groups.[8]

Another distinction we must make is between *interests* and *interest groups*. Farmers do not constitute an interest group, yet the National Association of Wheat Growers, the American Farm Bureau Federation, and the National Milk Producers Federation are all bona fide interest groups. The critical distinction between farmers and any one of these groups is *organization*. Farmers are people in a similar occupation and they may share some views on what the government's farm policy should be. Farmers, however, do not all belong to an organization that acts on their behalf in attempting to influence public policy. People may share an interest, a common concern, without belonging to the same interest group.

The distinction may seem like an exercise in semantics; members of Congress may be worried about how "farmers" (rather than any particular organization) will react to legislative proposals. Political reality is that most interest groups represent only a part—possibly a very small part—of their potential membership. Government officials rightly care about what the larger constituency feels on policy issues as well as being attentive to specific interest group organizations. Just why it is that

---

[7]However, one level of government may organize a lobbying office or join a trade association trying to influence another level of government. In Washington we find lobbying offices for states and cities whose job it is to get more money out of the federal government.

[8]See Paul Burstein, "What Do Interest Groups, Social Movements, and Political Parties Do? A Synthesis," paper delivered at the annual meeting of the American Political Science Association, Chicago, September, 1995.

not all people who share an interest join an organization representing that interest is an important question, which we will address at length in Chapter 4. Interest groups are thus important not only because of their actual memberships, but because they may represent the views of even larger constituencies.

When an interest group attempts to influence policymakers, it can be said to be engaging in *lobbying*. (The word comes from the practice of interest group representatives standing in the lobbies of legislatures so that they could stop members on their way to a session and plead their case. In earlier times, when many legislators had no offices of their own, the lobbies or anterooms adjoining their chambers were a convenient place for a quick discussion on the merits of a bill.) Although lobbying conjures up the image of an interest group representative trying to persuade a legislator to vote in the group's favor, we should see it in a broader context. Lobbying can be directed at any institution of government—legislative, judicial, or executive. Interest groups can even try to influence those institutions indirectly by attempting to sway public opinion, which they hope in turn will influence government. Lobbying also encompasses many tactics: initiating a lawsuit, starting a letter-writing campaign, filing a formal comment on a proposed regulation, talking face-to-face with a member of Congress or bureaucrat—just about any legal means used to try to influence government can be called lobbying.

Roles

In their efforts to influence government, interest groups play diverse roles in American politics. First and foremost, interest groups act to *represent* their constituents before government. They are a primary link between citizens and their government, forming a channel of access through which members voice their opinions to those who govern them. The democratic process can be described in the most eloquent language and be based on the noblest intentions, but in the real world of politics it must provide some means by which manufacturers, environmentalists, construction workers, or whoever can speak to government about their specific policy preferences and have the government listen. For many people, interest groups are the most important mechanism by which their views are represented before the three branches of government.

Interest groups also afford people the opportunity to *participate* in the political process. American political culture leads us to believe that participation is a virtue, apathy a vice. A person who wants to influence public policymaking may not find voting or other campaign-related activity to be enough. Elections come only at intervals and do not render decisive judgments on most issues. If one wants a larger role in the governmental process, other ways of participating must be found. A major reason for the popularity of prolife and prochoice groups, for example, is that they offer members a chance to do something on an issue about which they feel strongly. If you care deeply about abortion, voting by itself is not likely to make you feel that you've done much to resolve the question. By contributing money to a lobbying organization, and possibly participating through it to do other things such as writing letters or taking part in protests, members come to feel they have a more significant role in the political process. Yet interest groups do more than facilitate participation. They actively try to promote it by stimulating members or potential supporters to take action on behalf of a particular lobbying cause.

Interest groups *educate* the American public about political issues. With their advocacy efforts, publications, and publicity campaigns, interest groups can make people better aware of both policy problems and proposed solutions. An inherent trait in interest groups is that they present only their side of an issue to the public, offering facts and interpretations most favorable to their position. When the Food and Drug Administration (FDA) proposed regulations aimed at cutting down on teenage smoking, tobacco companies launched a counteroffensive. The FDA rules were designed to stop vending machine sales, limit billboard advertising, and prohibit cigarette company sponsorship of sporting and entertainment events. Cigarette manufacturer Philip Morris ran a series of full-page ads in leading newspapers that warned people that these regulations were symptomatic of a federal bureaucracy growing bigger rather than smaller. (One ad showed two policemen next to a squad car marked "Federal Anti-Smoking Police" placing handcuffs on a middle-aged man.)[9] One reason tobacco companies are on the defensive, of course, is the role that anti-smoking groups have

---

[9]Timothy Noah, "Tobacco-Marketing Rules Anger Many Non-Tobacco Industries," *Wall Street Journal*, October 17, 1995.

played in educating people about the link between cigarette smoking and lung cancer.

A related activity is *agenda building*. Beyond educating people about the sides of an issue, interest groups are frequently responsible for bringing the issue to light in the first place. The world has many problems, but not all are political issues being actively considered by government. Agenda building turns problems into issues, which become part of the body of policy questions that government feels it must deal with. Manufacturers and distributors of CDs, videocassettes, and computer software worked to get the government to pay attention to the problem of piracy of such goods in foreign countries. Their efforts paid off as the government began working on the issue and negotiated a major agreement with China in 1995, which promised to crack down on factories that illegally duplicated American goods.[10]

Finally, interest groups are involved in *program monitoring*. Lobbies closely follow programs affecting their constituents and will often try to draw attention to shortcomings through such tactics as issuing evaluative reports and contacting people in the media. They may also lobby agency personnel directly to make changes in program implementation or even go to court in an effort to exact compliance with a law. After the United States agreed to the North American Free Trade Agreement (NAFTA) with Canada and Mexico, one of the groups that fought against NAFTA, Public Citizen, monitored how well the agreement was faring. It found that 20 months after the agreement, most American companies that had promised to hire more workers to expand their export capacity if NAFTA passed had not done so. Thus job creation did not balance the job losses expected in industries exposed to more foreign competition under NAFTA.[11]

Understanding Interest Groups

Important as these roles are, interest groups remain misunderstood and maligned organizations. Americans distrust interest groups in gen-

---

[10]Seth Faison, "U.S. and China Sign Accord to End Piracy of Software, Music Recordings and Film," *New York Times,* February 27, 1995.
[11]Bob Herbert, "Nafta's Bubble Bursts," *New York Times,* September 11, 1995.

eral but value the organizations that represent them. People join an interest group not simply because they agree with its views but because they equate those views with the "public interest." Groups that stand on opposite sides of the same issues are regarded with disdain. Intellectually we accept the legitimacy of all interest groups; emotionally we separate them into those we support and those we must view with suspicion.

The basis of any reasoned judgment about interest groups is a factual understanding of how they operate. This is not easy, for though interest groups all have the same goal—to influence government—organizationally and politically they seem endlessly diverse. Yet patterns are recognizable, and throughout this book such factors as size, type of membership, and resources are used to distinguish basic forms of interest group behavior.

To place this analysis in perspective, we must step back to see how perceptions and attitudes of political scientists toward interest groups have changed in the latter part of the twentieth century. This is more than an interesting piece of intellectual history: A critical change in the thinking of political scientists helped broaden acceptance of the role of interest groups in public policymaking. That change, in turn, helped spur the growth of interest groups.

THE RISE AND FALL OF PLURALISM

The early forerunner of pluralism in political science was known as "group theory," most widely associated with David Truman's *The Governmental Process*, published in 1951.[12] Truman makes a simple assertion: Politics can be understood only by looking at the interaction of groups. He casts his lot with Madison, agreeing that "tendencies toward such groupings are 'sown in the nature of man.'" He also draws on cultural anthropology and social psychology to prove his case that political man is a product of group influences. "In all societies of any

---

[12]David B. Truman, *The Governmental Process* (New York: Knopf, 1951). Truman traces the roots of a group theory of politics to Arthur F. Bentley's *The Process of Government* (Chicago: University of Chicago Press, 1908).

degree of complexity the individual is less affected directly by the society as a whole than differentially through various of its subdivisions, or groups."[13]

The pluralist influence in political science reached its zenith a decade later when Robert Dahl published *Who Governs?*, a study of local politics in New Haven, Connecticut.[14] Dahl examined three areas of local politics to see just who influenced policy outcomes. His crucial finding was that in the three areas—political party nominations, urban redevelopment, and public education—different groups of people were active and influential. New Haven did not have a small, closed circle of important people who together decided all the important issues in town politics.

Dahl found policymaking in New Haven to be a process by which loose coalitions of groups and politicians would become active on issues they cared about. Although most citizens might be apathetic about most issues, many do get interested in the issues that directly affect them. Businessmen were very active in urban redevelopment; teachers, school administrators, and the Parent-Teacher Association (PTA) were involved in school politics. Politicians, always on the lookout for supporters, would court groups, hoping to build their own resources. Consequently, groups representing different interests were not only active, but their support was sought and their views carried weight.

Dahl argued that a realistic definition of democracy was not 50 percent plus one getting their way on each and every issue. Rather, as he wrote in an earlier work, the " 'normal' American political process [is] one in which there is a high probability that an active and legitimate group in the population can make itself heard effectively at some crucial stage in the process of decision."[15] Through bargaining and compromise between affected groups and political elites, democratic decisions are reached, with no one group consistently dominating.

The influence of pluralist thought, and Dahl's writings in particular, was enormous. He had gone a step further than Truman by putting his findings in such an approving light. That is, he not only seemed to be saying this is the way things are, but this is the way things should be.

---

[13]Truman, *The Governmental Process,* p. 15.

[14]Robert A. Dahl, *Who Governs?* (New Haven: Yale University Press, 1961).

[15]Dahl, *A Preface to Democratic Theory,* p. 145. He later reflects on this sentence in *Dilemmas of Pluralist Democracy* (New Haven: Yale University Press, 1982), pp. 207–209.

Policymaking through group interaction is a positive virtue, not a threat to democracy.[16] Placing interest groups at the center of policymaking revived democratic theory by offering an explicit defense of the American political process.

Elegantly and systematically, pluralism made sense of the bargaining between interest groups and government officials. There was a reason to it beyond the selfishness of individual groups. To most social scientists who stood in the ideological mainstream of their disciplines, pluralism was an attractive counterpoint to radical critiques of American society. Books like C. Wright Mills's *The Power Elite* (1956) had gained a good deal of attention with the claim that America was ruled by a small stratum of wealthy and powerful individuals.[17] Members of this power elite were said to be the true decision makers in society, "democracy" being an effective illusion perpetrated on the masses. But if the power elite thesis was false, as most social scientists believed it was, what was the counter theory?

Pluralism thus became the refutation of this damning interpretation of American politics. *Who Governs?* acknowledged that political elites had disproportionate amounts of resources but said that the use of these resources in ways inimical to the system was reasonably well countered by the natural working of interest group politics. Elected officials responded to different groups on different issues, seeking out groups to enhance their own power. Group politics forced elites to be responsive to a broad range of constituencies rather than to a small group of powerful individuals.

Dahl's considerable reputation as a scholar and the book's brilliant documentation of New Haven politics raised the pluralist case to preeminence in political science. At the same time, the unquestioned importance of the book marked the beginning of pluralism's decline. It is

---

[16]Responding to a critique by Jack Walker, Dahl denied that pluralism was intended to be read in such a normative vein. Whatever Dahl's intentions, *Who Governs?* was widely interpreted as praise and defense of the system as well as a description of reality. See Jack L. Walker, Jr., "A Critique of the Elitist Theory of Democracy," *American Political Science Review* 60 (June 1966), pp. 285–295; Robert A. Dahl, "Further Reflections on the Elitist Theory of Democracy," *American Political Science Review* 60 (June 1966), pp. 296–303; and G. David Garson, *Group Theories of Politics* (Beverly Hills, Calif.: Sage, 1978), pp. 119–152.

[17]C. Wright Mills, *The Power Elite* (New York: Oxford University Press, 1956). See also, Floyd Hunter, *Community Power Structure* (Chapel Hill: University of North Carolina Press, 1953).

the natural progression of scientific inquiry for an accepted model of some social, biological, or physical system to come under close scrutiny, to have its faults exposed, and eventually to be replaced with a new model. The attention paid to *Who Governs?* quickened this process as social scientists began to examine the underlying assumptions that guided the pluralists. Two main lines of scholarly criticism soon came to the fore, one *methodological* and the other *normative.*

The methodological criticism of pluralism was that studies like *Who Governs?* focused on too narrow a set of questions.[18] Wanting to know who actually made policy decisions, social scientists using a pluralist framework would do research on selected issues being debated by the relevant government authorities. On those issues, there may well have been participation by a number of affected interest groups, but critics argued that this did not mean that the governmental process was truly democratic. What of the larger issues, such as relative distribution of wealth among different segments of society, that really are never directly addressed by governmental bodies? The issues Dahl analyzed did not threaten to change the basic structure of New Haven society or its economy, no matter how they were resolved. In this view, only issues that do not fundamentally alter the position of elites enter the political agenda and become subject to interest group politics. In sum, critics of the methodology said that pluralists asked biased questions and therefore received misleading answers.[19]

A second strain of criticism stressed the consequences of pluralist theory rather than the research questions that guided it. Critics like Jack Walker[20] and Theodore Lowi[21] attacked pluralism because it justified the status quo. In *The End of Liberalism,* Lowi concludes that government through interest groups is conservative because it creates resistance to change.[22] He points out that lobbying groups arise to protect the interests of some segment of society. Once government be-

---

[18]The methodology of pluralism is best defended by Nelson W. Polsby, *Community Power and Political Theory* (New Haven: Yale University Press, 1980).

[19]A forceful statement of this position is in Peter Bachrach and Morton S. Baratz, "Two Faces of Power," *American Political Science Review* 56 (December 1962), pp. 947–952. A further elaboration is provided by John Gaventa, *Power and Powerlessness* (Urbana: University of Illinois Press, 1980).

[20]Walker, "A Critique of the Elitist Theory of Democracy."

[21]Theodore J. Lowi, *The End of Liberalism,* 2nd ed. (New York: Norton, 1979).

[22]Lowi, *The End of Liberalism,* p. 60.

gins to make policies by bargaining with those groups, it then acts to favor them at the expense of others. This privileged access of groups even favors them against newly organizing interests from the same strata of society, such as business competitors trying to enter a tightly regulated market.

These critics were not making the more radical argument of those who, like Mills, said America was governed by a small ruling class. Rather, they were saying that there was disproportionate privilege, and that privilege was rationalized by pluralism. Not all relevant interests were adequately represented by interest groups, and pluralism falsely suggested that all those significantly affected by an impending decision were taken into the policymaking process.

The validity of pluralism was thrown open to question not only by scholars but by real-world events as well. The civil rights movement that began in the early 1960s made it all too clear that blacks were wholly outside the normal workings of the political system. As the marches, protests, and occasional violence continued during the decade, the inadequacy of pluralist theory to explain the position of blacks in society became increasingly evident. On top of the civil rights movement came the anti–Vietnam War movement. Spreading disillusionment with the war increased alienation toward the federal government. Questions arose in people's minds not only about the wisdom of the war but about the way the government was run. By the end of the 1960s, neither intellectuals nor ordinary citizens were likely to believe contemporary interest group politics was the basis for democratic policymaking.

PLURALISM AS A GOAL

Although pluralism was no longer considered accurate, it nonetheless remained desirable. Dahl's vision of what American politics should look like was still appealing. Pluralism could not simply be discarded like a rejected hypothesis in a small research project; to admit that it could never be an accurate theory of American politics would call into question the legitimacy of interest groups in a democracy. Either a new theory had to rationalize the role of interest groups in a democracy, or the system had to be changed to make pluralism come true.

It is difficult and inherently imprecise to try to trace the force of an idea. How did Keynesian economics come to be dominant for so many years? The exact force of pluralist thinking is impossible to measure directly. Yet in examining the modern behavioral period (roughly since World War II) in political science, there seems little doubt that pluralism has been the most widely debated theory of American politics. At a time when the discipline was so preoccupied with the methodology of political inquiry, pluralism combined an empirical "scientific" approach to the study of power with a broad theory of democracy.

Why has this theory, no longer considered to be true, had such an important legacy? First, no new theories of comparable scope that give broadly accepted explanations of American politics have been advanced. This may seem a damning critique of the social sciences and political science in particular. Since the publication of *Who Governs?* in 1961, why has no new theory replaced pluralism? The reason, in short, is that the task of formulating one is extremely difficult. The new theory would need to provide an all-encompassing explanation and an integrated framework for understanding American government. The American political system is extremely complex, with highly differentiated actors and institutions. To create a theory that would explain American government and the relationships among its parts, and would combine empirical verification and normative assumptions, is a truly herculean task. It is almost pretentious for a social scientist to try. Most political scientists find it more fruitful to work on narrower and, in their minds, more realistic research problems.

A second reason for the pluralist legacy's continued significance is that the Madisonian dilemma remains unresolved. Pluralists adapted Madison's leap of faith to modern American politics by stressing the natural opposition of competing interest groups within the policymaking process. With pluralism declining as an accepted interpretation of American politics, the problem of how to rationalize interest group participation in a democracy had to be addressed again. If interest groups are not part of some type of balance in society, they present dangers. Failing a new resolution to the Madisonian dilemma, the solution has been to try to make pluralism a reality. Scholars, political activists, and policymakers have tried to justify interest group politics by proposing means to make it more balanced.

Some of those who have written about how to make America a true, pluralist democracy have focused on curbing what they see as excessive privilege and influence of certain kinds of interest groups. Most conspicuous have been the arguments for reducing the role of political action committees in the financing of political campaigns. Yet few be-

lieve that the power of business and trade groups is going to be brought
into balance with other sectors of society merely by instituting campaign finance reform. Instead, many critics focus on ways of enhancing
the representation of those poorly represented in our interest group
system. In the 1960s, the government responded to the criticism that
the poor were not represented in policymaking by mandating their participation in the War on Poverty. This approach was incorporated in
legislation such as the Economic Opportunity Act (1964) and Model
Cities (1966), which required citizen participation in the programs' development at the local level.[23]

Since the 1960s, the solutions proposed for the ills of our democracy have often incorporated a call for *more* democracy. More people
need to participate in politics so that policies will more closely approxi-
mate the true wishes of the citizenry. *More participation inevitably
means more interest groups.*

CONCLUSION

The events of the 1960s led many Americans to question the way their
democratic system was operating. For their part, American political
scientists were more and more disillusioned with the dominant theory
in their discipline that purported to explain how that democracy
worked. Both alienation from American government and scholarly re-
jection of pluralism contributed to a powerful new idea: Increased participation was needed to balance a system of interest groups that
skewed policymaking toward organizations unrepresentative of the
American people.[24]

Although no new theory as such came along to replace pluralism,
the idea of expanded interest group participation by the chronically un-
derrepresented was at least a first step toward finding a new solution to
the dilemma of *Federalist* No. 10. Real-world events and the philo-
sophical musings of scholars that contributed to the movement toward
increased participation by interest groups could not be selective in
their influence. The new interest group politics went far beyond citizen

[23]See Jeffrey M. Berry, Kent E. Portney, and Ken Thomson, *The Rebirth of Urban
Democracy* (Washington, D.C.: Brookings Institution, 1993), pp. 21–45.
[24]See Andrew S. McFarland, *Public Interest Lobbies* (Washington, D.C.: American
Enterprise Institute, 1976).

participation programs and public interest groups for those tradition-ally unrepresented in the governmental process. Rather, extraordinary growth in all types of lobbying organizations raised anew questions about curing the mischiefs of faction.

In the remainder of this book we will look at the changing nature of interest group politics. The following chapter examines the growth in the number of interest groups and tries to explain the underlying causes of the expansion of lobbying activity. Chapter 3 analyzes the re-lationship between political parties and interest groups. Chapter 4 is devoted to the organization of lobbies with discussion emphasizing the origins, maintenance, marketing, and governing of interest groups. In Chapter 5, the focus shifts to the lobbyists who represent interest groups before government.

Chapter 6 considers how interest groups try to influence people at the grassroots and how Washington lobbies try to mobilize support among constituents as part of their advocacy campaigns. In Chapter 7, attention turns to political action committees, the most controversial actors in interest group politics. The ability of PACs to influence elec-tions and legislative decisions will be explored, as well as their contri-bution patterns and general mode of operation. Chapter 8 covers di-rect lobbying of the three branches of government. Chapter 9 extends that discussion to coalition politics among Washington lobbies. The same chapter also looks at the rise of issue networks and includes a case study of changes over time in the telecommunications issue net-work. Bias and representation in the American interest group system are the subject of Chapter 10.

Chapter
2

The Advocacy Explosion

*U*neasiness over the power and influence of interest group politics is part of the American political tradition. Yet today's widespread concern contrasts with American attitudes at other times in our history. The New Deal, for example, was known for its positive acceptance of interest groups because of the greater role trade associations came to have in the policymaking of newly established regulatory agencies. As recently as the 1960s, scholars were arguing that interest group politics contributed to democratic politics.

There is a pervasive belief in this country that interest groups are out of control. They have grown in number and influence while rank-and-file Americans have become disempowered. This view is echoed constantly in the press. *Time* tells us that "at times the halls of power are so glutted with special pleaders that government itself seems to be gagging."[1] Bemoaning the growing lobbying industry, the *New Republic* notes, "What dominates Washington is not evil and immorality, but a parasite culture. Like Rome in decline, Washington is bloated, wasteful, pretentious, myopic, decadent, and sybaritic. It is the paradise of the overpaid hangers-on."[2] Over 200 years after Madison thought he

---

[1]Evan Thomas, "Peddling Influence," *Time,* March 3, 1986.
[2]Fred Barnes, "The Parasite Culture of Washington," *New Republic,* July 28, 1986, p. 26.

and the other founders had developed a solution to the problem of self-interested factions, the respected political columnist, Albert Hunt, lamented that today "Lobbyists have unprecedented access, directly participating in writing legislation."[3]

Observers of the Washington scene produce a steady stream of books warning that democracy is in peril. Jonathan Rauch argues that interest groups are at the heart of both economic decline and governmental decay. "As [the interest group industry] grows, the steady accumulation of subsidies and benefits, each defended in perpetuity by a professional interest group, calcifies government. Government loses its capacity to experiment and so becomes more and more prone to failure."[4] In *Who Will Tell the People,* William Greider concludes that "The representative system has undergone a grotesque distortion of its original purpose." The reason for this "distortion," says Greider, is that "Instead of popular will, the government now responds more often to narrow webs of power—the interests of major economic organizations."[5] A lengthy examination of the campaign finance system by Brooks Jackson finds that "America is becoming a special-interest nation where money is displacing votes."[6]

Politicians ring the fire alarm too. President Jimmy Carter, in his farewell address to the nation, blamed interest groups for many shortcomings of his administration:

> We are increasingly drawn to single-issue groups and special interest organizations to insure that whatever else happens our own personal views and our own private interests are protected. This is a disturbing factor in American political life. It tends to distort our purpose because the national interest is not always the sum of all our single or special interests.[7]

Politicians haven't grown any kinder in the years since Carter's admonition. Freshman Republican representative Linda Smith arrived in

---

[3]Albert R. Hunt, "Special Interests Are Feasting at the Congressional Trough," *Wall Street Journal,* July 27, 1995.

[4]Jonathan Rauch, *Demosclerosis* (New York: Times Books, 1994), p. 17.

[5]William Greider, *Who Will Tell the People* (New York: Touchstone, 1993), p. 12.

[6]Brooks Jackson, *Honest Graft* (New York: Knopf, 1988), p. 295.

[7]"Prepared Text of Carter's Farewell Address on Major Issues Facing the Nation," *New York Times,* January 15, 1981.

Washington in 1995 and quickly declared, "This polluted system has to be cleaned up completely. Otherwise, everything will break down."[8]

Political scientists have been more temperate in their language, but many scholars have found the growth of interest group politics troubling. Robert Dahl, who, as noted in Chapter 1, once championed interest group democracy, decries the current system.[9] "In recent decades," he writes, "both the number and variety of interest groups with significant influence over policymaking in Washington have greatly increased." At the same time, "The increase in the number and diversity of interest groups has not been accompanied . . . by a corresponding increase in the strength of integrating institutions."[10]

Americans of all ideological stripes believe that interest groups are at the core of government's problems. In 1964, 64 percent of those polled agreed with the statement that government "is run for the benefit of all the people." Only 29 percent agreed that government is "run by a few big interests looking out for themselves." In 1995, a mere 15 percent agreed that the government was run for the benefit of all, while 79 percent agreed that government is run by a few big interests.[11]

In short, the popular perception is that interest groups are a cancer, spreading unchecked throughout the body politic, making it gradually weaker, until they eventually kill it.

THE INTEREST GROUP SPIRAL

These impassioned denunciations of interest group politics do not answer a simple question. Has there really been a significant expansion of interest group politics? Or are interest groups simply playing their familiar role as whipping boy for the ills of society?

---

[8]Hunt, "Special Interests Are Feasting."

[9]See Robert A. Dahl, *Who Governs?* (New Haven: Yale University Press, 1961).

[10]Robert A. Dahl, *The New American Political (Dis)Order* (Berkeley: Institute for Governmental Studies, 1994), p. 8.

[11]John T. Tierney, "Organized Interests and the Nation's Capitol," in Mark P. Petracca, ed., *The Politics of Interests* (Boulder, Colo.: Westview, 1992), p. 202; and R. W. Apple, "Poll Shows Disenchantment with Politicians and Politics," *New York Times,* August 12, 1995.

The answer to both questions is yes. Surely nothing is new about interest groups being seen as the bane of our political system. The muckrakers at the turn of the century voiced many of the same fears that show up today in *Time* or the *New Republic*. Yet even if the problem is familiar, it is no less troubling. The growth of interest group advocacy in recent years should not simply be dismissed as part of a chronic condition in American politics.

Before addressing the larger problems that arise from this trend, we must document the increasing number of interest groups. The evidence does suggest that the numbers of interest groups surged during the 1960s and 1970s. Jack Walker's survey of 564 lobbying organizations in Washington (Figure 2.1)[12] shows a clear pattern of growth, with approximately 30 percent of the groups originating between 1960 and 1980.[13] The figures do not, however, demonstrate precisely how many new groups have been started in different eras because we cannot calculate how many were started in earlier periods but have since ceased to exist. A second study, by Kay Schlozman and John Tierney, reveals a similar pattern. Their examination of groups listed in a 1981 lobbying directory shows that 40 percent were founded after 1960 and 25 percent after 1970.[14] Both surveys show that citizen groups were the most likely to have formed recently.

Other, more specialized surveys, support these findings that interest group activity skyrocketed in these two decades. A 1981 Boston University School of Management study of over 400 firms indicated that of those with Washington offices, roughly half started that office between 1970 and 1980.[15] Equally important, many corporations upgraded their Washington offices. The Boston University study shows that 63 percent of the corporate public affairs departments surveyed had increased their professional staffs between 1975 and 1980.[16] For example, General Motors went from a three-person office in 1968 to a

---

[12]Jack L. Walker, Jr., "The Origins and Maintenance of Interest Groups in America," *American Political Science Review* 77 (June 1983), pp. 390–406.

[13]See an earlier version of the Walker article, similarly titled, presented at the annual meeting of the American Political Science Association, New York, September, 1981, p. 14.

[14]Kay Lehman Schlozman and John T. Tierney, *Organized Interests and American Democracy* (New York: Harper & Row, 1986), pp. 75–76.

[15]*Public Affairs Offices and Their Functions* (Boston: Boston University School of Management, 1981), p. 8.

[16]*Public Affairs Offices and Their Functions*, p. 4.

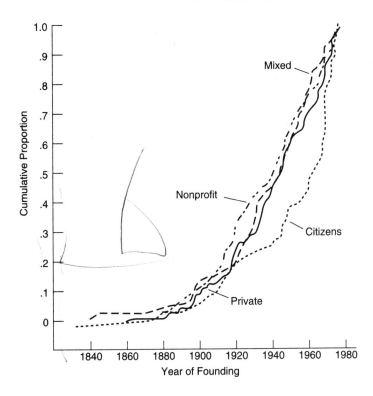

Figure 2.1   Interest Groups and Their Year of Origin

Source: Survey of voluntary associations by Jack L. Walker, "The Origins and Maintenance of Interest Groups in America." *American Political Science Review* 77 (June 1983), p. 395. The "mixed" category represents groups that have members from both the public and private sectors. Reprinted by permission.

staff of 28 in 1978.[17] In the early 1970s, I surveyed 83 "public interest groups" active in Washington. Almost half the sample (47 percent) were started in the five years between 1968 and 1972.[18] Again, as with

[17]David Vogel, "How Business Responds to Opposition: Corporate Political Strategies During the 1970s," paper delivered at the annual meeting of the American Political Science Association, Washington, D.C., September, 1979, p. 15.

[18]Jeffrey M. Berry, *Lobbying for the People* (Princeton: Princeton University Press, 1977), p. 34.

the Walker study, the amount of increase is probably overstated because the number of groups that ceased to exist before the survey was taken could not be measured.

The sharpest growth in interest group politics during this time came from political action committees. These are organizations that raise money and then make donations to candidates for office. Unlike the other manifestations of increased interest group activity, the upsurge in PACs is rooted in federal law. Throughout this century, most corporations had been forbidden to contribute funds to candidates for federal office. Although restrictions were relaxed somewhat for PACs in 1971, it was not until the passage of the Federal Election Campaign Act Amendments of 1974, and its subsequent interpretation by the Federal Election Commission, that corporations were fully free to set up committees that could solicit voluntary contributions. After these changes in the law, the number of corporate PACs shot up, and other types of PACs increased in number as well. At the end of 1974 there were 608 PACs. At the end of the decade there 2,551.[19]

The sharp rate of growth of interest groups during the 1960s and 1970s may have given way to slower expansion in the 1980s and early 1990s. Unfortunately, we do not have similar surveys of interest groups to compare with the studies discussed above that include data on the year of origin of groups. There is some data, however, that indicate a slow down. The number of PACs grew to 3,992 by the end of 1985. Roughly the same number of PACs were in operation at the end of 1994.[20]

A similar trend can be found in the number of trade associations that make their headquarters in Washington. These organizations, like the National Funeral Directors Association or the National Independent Retail Jewelers, work on behalf of a single industry. The number of trade associations in the United States has increased only modestly in recent decades, so growth in the basic population of industries has not been a factor in expansion of Washington-based business advocacy.[21] As Figure 2.2 illustrates, between 1970 and 1984 the proportion of national associations that made Washington their headquar-

---

[19]"Media Advisory," Federal Elections Commission, August 2, 1995, p. 1.
[20]"Media Advisory," p. 1.
[21]Howard Aldrich and Udo Staber, "How Business Organized Itself in the Twentieth Century," paper delivered at the annual meeting of the American Political Science Association, Washington, D.C., August, 1986.

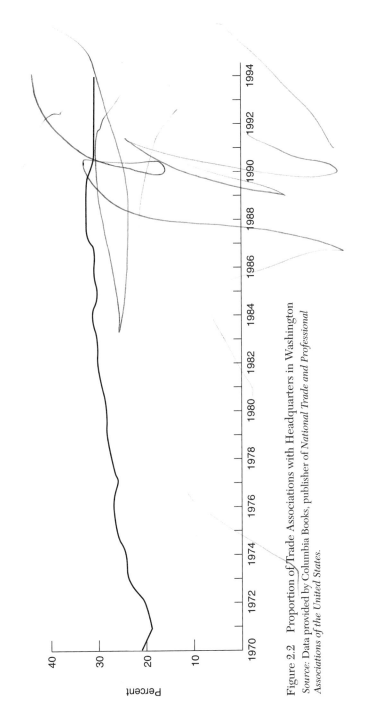

Figure 2.2 Proportion of Trade Associations with Headquarters in Washington
Source: Data provided by Columbia Books, publisher of *National Trade and Professional Associations of the United States.*

ters rose from 21 percent to 31 percent. During this time many trade associations felt it was necessary to move to Washington so that they could focus more on lobbying, and Washington replaced New York as the city with the most trade groups. Since that time, however, the proportion of trade groups in Washington has been relatively stable.

At the same time, the growth in the number of Washington lawyers has continued unabated. Between 1972 and 1994 the Washington bar went from around 11,000 to around 63,000 (see Figure 2.3). (These figures include lawyers who are not residents of the D.C. area but do some legal work there.) Washington law is lobbying law. Firms are hired by individual corporations, trade associations, foreign governments, and others to work with the government to try to solve specific problems. In the 1970s this surge was widely attributed to the rapid growth in regulatory activity by the federal government. The regulatory spiral has abated, but clearly this does not affect the amount of work for Washington lawyers. As we'll discuss later in this chapter, even if the overall amount of regulation is not growing, there has been change within existing regulatory frameworks and many industries have more competitors who vie not only for market share, but for regulatory advantages.

The evidence is mixed, but at least suggestive that there may have been a moderation in the rate of growth of Washington-based advocacy. If there has been a slowing down in interest group formation and activity, it should come as no surprise. At some point the market for different types of interest groups becomes saturated, and new entrants will find it more difficult to gain a foothold. During a period of expansion, interest group organizers identify niches in a particular policy area that they believe are underserved by existing advocacy organizations. Despite the large number of environmental organizations in existence, the National Toxics Campaign formed because founders believed that the issue was not being adequately covered by these other groups. Yet there is not an inexhaustible supply of empty niches. As a policy area becomes more thoroughly covered by new and old groups, it becomes harder for organizers to find specific issues or industry sectors not being adequately served by existing lobbies. Moreover, rapid expansion of an interest group sector reduces the amount of available resources for potential new groups.

Focusing on the overall rate of growth obscures other important factors in understanding the developmental patterns of interest groups. Even when there is a strong trend toward interest group formation per

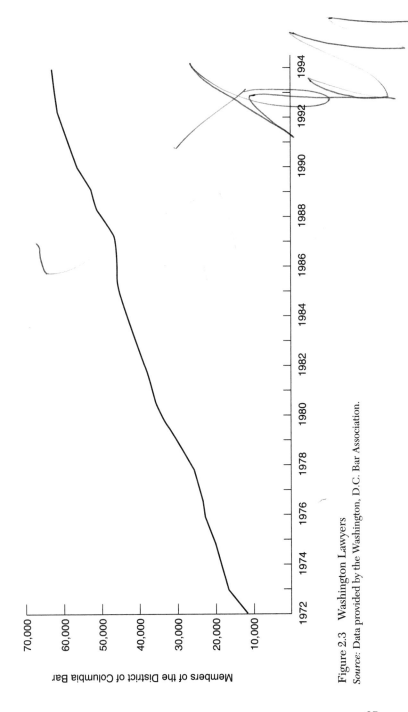

Figure 2.3 Washington Lawyers
Source: Data provided by the Washington, D.C. Bar Association.

Members of the District of Columbia Bar

se, different interest group sectors can develop at widely varying rates. Compare health care lobbies with labor unions. Measured as a percent of the labor force, union membership is down significantly. As Figure 2.4 shows, unions have gone from over 30 percent of the work force in the 1950s to about half of that in recent years. There are a number of reasons for this. One is the decline of a number of American industries like steel, rubber, and autos, leaving fewer workers to unionize in the fields of employment where unions have been traditionally strongest. Even among employees in traditional union bastions, unions have not fared well. For example, the proportion of rubber workers and petroleum refinery workers who are unionized has dropped sharply.[22] Apparently not as many workers see unions as necessary to protect them or improve their material well being. Also, employers have become more aggressive in trying to fight unionization. Unions have tried to stem their losses by organizing efforts aimed at public service employees and low-wage workers. They have had some success in this regard, and overall union membership has stabilized after dropping in the early 1980s.[23]

In contrast to unions, there's been robust growth by health care lobbies. Figure 2.5 illustrates the dramatic rise in the number of health groups represented in Washington. In the relatively short period between 1984 and 1991, health groups more than doubled in number. The primary reason for this is the increasing pressure on the federal government to rein in health care costs. When the government writes health care statutes and regulations, its decisions do not affect every part of the industry uniformly. What is good for teaching hospitals might be damaging to small community hospitals. A policy designed to help general practitioners might come at the expense of physicians who are specialists. With vast sums of money at stake every time government takes up health care reform, it is understandable that different sectors of the industry have enhanced their representation in Washington.

In analyzing the development of interest groups, scholars must look at numbers of organizations, their memberships over time, and financial resources. Although the number of PACs has been stable for a decade, the amount of money they have contributed to candidates for

[22]Richard B. Freeman and James L. Medoff, *What Do Unions Do?* (New York: Basic Books, 1984), p. 226.
[23]G. Pascal Zachery, "Some Unions Step Up Organizing Campaigns And Get New Members," *Wall Street Journal,* September 1, 1995.

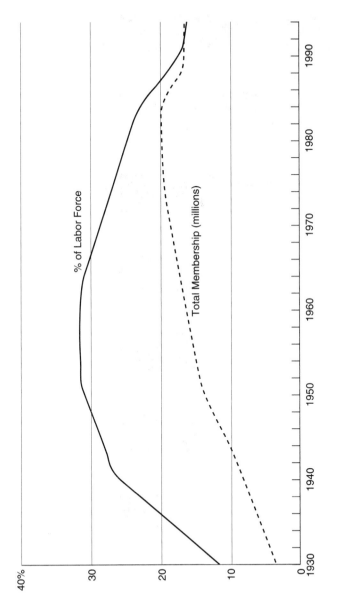

Figure 2.4   Union Membership (In millions and as a percentage of the labor force)
Source: Robert L. Rose, "AFL-CIO's Power Struggle Reflects Frustration with Labor Movement," *Wall Street Journal*, May 15, 1995. Reprinted by permission of the *Wall Street Journal*, © 1995 Dow Jones & Company, Inc. All rights reserved worldwide.

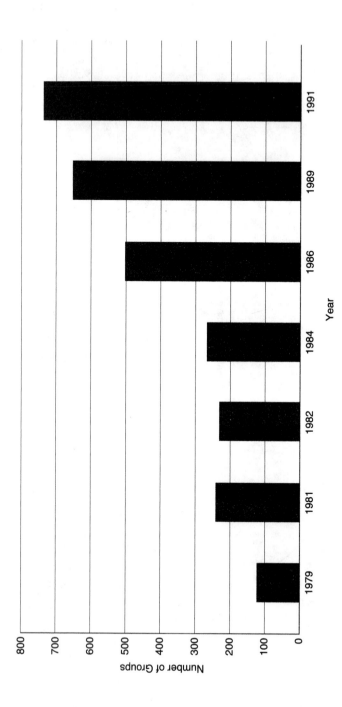

Figure 2.5   Health Groups in Washington

Source: Jonathan Rauch, *Demosclerosis* (New York: Times Books, 1994), p. 91. Copyright © 1994 by Jonathan Rauch. Reprinted by Times Books, a division of Random House, Inc.

office has continued to significantly increase. But by whatever standard we use, we can be confident that the increase in lobbying organizations since the early 1960s is real and not a function of overblown rhetoric about the dangers of contemporary interest groups. The emergence of so many groups and the expansion of those already in existence fundamentally altered American politics. Of particular importance is that this growth took place during a period of party decline. The United States was not just a country with an increasing number of active interest groups but a country whose citizens began looking more and more to interest groups to speak for them in the political process.

THE RISE OF CITIZEN GROUPS

The growth of interest group advocacy in different sectors of society comes from many of the same roots. At the same time, the sharp growth in numbers of interest groups also reflects different sectors of society responding to each other. As one segment of the interest community grew and appeared to prosper, it spurred growth in other segments eager to equalize the increasing strength of their adversaries. This spiral of interest group activity began in large part in the civil rights and antiwar movements of the 1960s.

Movement Politics

The interest group texts of the 1950s barely make mention of citizen groups.[24] Today, citizen groups seem everywhere in Washington, and they are major participants in a wide range of policy areas. What catalyzed this change is the civil rights movement. The drive of African Americans for equality began to gather steam with the 1954 Supreme Court decision banning school segregation and the 1955 Montgomery, Alabama, bus boycott. In Montgomery, blacks refused to ride the segregated system (whites in front, blacks in the back), quickly depleting the financial resources of the city's transit system. Although it took a Supreme Court order to force integration of the system a year later,

---

[24]See V. O. Key, Jr., *Politics, Parties, & Pressure Groups,* 3rd ed. (New York: Thomas Y. Crowell, 1952); and David B. Truman, *The Governmental Process* (New York: Knopf, 1951).

many other boycotts and sit-ins followed, increasing national awareness of discrimination. Public opinion was not fully galvanized, however, until the early 1960s, when blacks began holding marches and demonstrations, many of which ended in confrontation with white authorities. Some ended in violence, with marchers being attacked by police. The demonstrations, shown on network news telecasts, helped to turn the public decidedly in favor of civil rights legislation.[25] The immediate outcome was the Civil Rights Act of 1964, outlawing many basic forms of discrimination, and the Voting Rights Act of 1965, which ended exclusion of blacks from voting in many areas of the South.

Citizen group politics was also fueled by the anti–Vietnam War movement that took form in the mid-1960s. Its success was not as clear-cut as the civil rights movement's since so many American soldiers continued to fight and die during years of protest. Many Americans became hostile toward the antiwar movement because they felt it was disloyal for citizens not to support American soldiers once they were committed to a military action. Most would agree, however, that the antiwar movement hastened the end of America's role in the war in Vietnam. This unpopular war helped push President Johnson out of office and brought pressure upon President Nixon to end American participation in the fighting. The antiwar groups spearheaded opposition to the war, and their periodic demonstrations were visible evidence of growing public anger over the fighting.

A central legacy of the civil rights and anti–Vietnam War movements was that citizen groups could influence the course of public policy.[26] Ordinary citizens could organize, lobby, and influence government. This model of citizen group advocacy was soon copied by those suffering from discrimination who saw parallels between blacks and themselves. Hispanic farmworkers in California were organized for the first time by Cesar Chavez and his United Farm Workers union. Gays and lesbians would later organize into groups like the Lambda Legal Defense and Education Fund, which works for civil rights for homosexuals. Most conspicuous was the rise of the women's movement, deeply influenced by the citizen advocacy of the 1960s. Women saw the tools of these earlier groups as directly applicable to their own plight. Sara Evans describes how the National Organization for Women (NOW) was formed:

[25]David J. Garrow, *Protest at Selma* (New Haven: Yale University Press, 1978).
[26]On the influence of the civil rights and antiwar efforts, see David Vogel, *Lobbying the Corporation* (New York: Basic Books, 1978), pp. 23–68.

The lessons of the NAACP and its legal defense arm were not lost on the women who founded NOW: to adult professional women in the early 1960s the growth of civil rights insurgency provided a model of legal activism and imaginative minority group lobbying.[27]

Evans points out that many of those who became pioneers in the women's movement first gained experience working in those earlier causes.

Minorities and women were not the only ones influenced to organize by the civil rights and antiwar movements. Political activists began to look at the range of policy areas that interested them, such as consumer rights, environmental affairs, hunger and malnutrition, corporate responsibility, access to media, and so on. Although the success of civil rights and antiwar groups inspired formation of new groups in these areas, the protest orientation of these earlier organizations seemed inappropriate. Leaders of these new groups wanted to transcend "movement politics" with organizations that could survive beyond periods of intense emotion. The organizations that were needed could put the idealism of young, liberal activists in harness with financial support and policy interests of the middle class.

Public Interest Groups

Many of the new organizations in the late 1960s and 1970s became popularly known as "public interest groups." These were lobbying groups without economic self-interest, or more precisely, "a public interest group is one that seeks a collective good, the achievement of which will not selectively and materially benefit the membership or activists of the organization."[28] The most prominent of the new groups were Common Cause and the Ralph Nader organizations. Common Cause, which focuses on opening up and reforming the governmental process, was founded in 1970 by John Gardner, a liberal Republican and former cabinet secretary in the Johnson administration. Declaring that "everyone is represented but the people," Gardner used full-page newspaper ads and direct mail solicitations to build a membership of 230,000 in little more than a year, an astonishing feat for a voluntary organization.[29]

---

[27]Sara Evans, *Personal Politics* (New York: Knopf, 1979), p. 25.

[28]Berry, *Lobbying for the People,* p. 7.

[29]Berry, *Lobbying for the People,* pp. 29–30.

Ralph Nader came into the public eye in 1965 when his attack on the automobile industry, *Unsafe at Any Speed,* was published. Nader quickly became known as a consumer champion and in his first decade in Washington put together more than a dozen lobbying organizations. Many of his groups, such as the Public Citizen Litigation Group and the Health Research Group, have been major actors in Washington politics.

Many other groups, such as the Environmental Defense Fund, Zero Population Growth, and the Children's Foundation, started up as well. Older groups such as Consumers Union, the League of Women Voters, and the Sierra Club, prospered too and devoted new resources to Washington lobbying. Indeed, public interest groups have existed for years; and the most recent wave of groups is in the tradition of American reform movements.[30] Public interest groups are distinguished from earlier reform movements, though, by the breadth and durability of the lobbying organizations. Some of the liberal public interest groups have developed into huge organizations with large memberships and budgets in the millions of dollars (see Figure 2.6).[31] More importantly, these organizations have pushed their issues on to the nation's political agenda and become major influences in the formulation of public policy.

Public interest groups of this era directly benefited from the growing force of the pluralist ideal. The lack of an acceptable alternative theory of democracy and the reality of interest group politics made pluralism a compelling idea, a goal toward which America should strive. As it became accepted that pluralist democracy did not in fact exist, how was its absence to be remedied? The solution was quite simple: The influence of existing groups had to be *balanced.*[32] Madison's words

---

[30]Andrew S. McFarland, *Common Cause* (Chatham, N.J.: Chatham House, 1984), pp. 23–37.

[31]On the evolution of the environmental movement in terms of memberships and budgets, see Christopher Boerner and Jennifer Chilton Kallery, *Restructuring Environmental Big Business,* Occasional Paper #146, Center for the Study of American Business, Washington University, December, 1994; Christopher Bosso, "The Color of Money: Environmental Groups and the Pathologies of Fund Raising," in Allan J. Cigler and Burdett A. Loomis, eds., *Interest Group Politics,* 4th ed. (Washington, D.C.: Congressional Quarterly, 1995), pp. 101–130; and Mark Dowie, *Losing Ground* (Cambridge: MIT Press, 1995).

[32]Andrew S. McFarland, *Public Interest Lobbies* (Washington, D.C.: American Enterprise Institute, 1976).

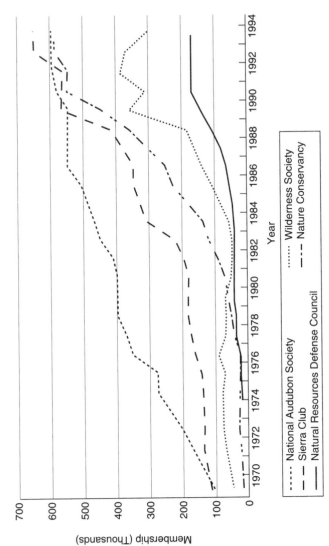

Figure 2.6 Membership in Environmental Groups
Source: Christopher Boerner and Jennifer Chilton Kallery, *Restructuring Environmental Big Business*, Occasional Paper No. 146, Center for the Study of American Business, Washington University, December 1994. Reprinted by permission.

were echoed: Democracy could be achieved not by limiting the freedom of private interests to lobby but rather by "controlling" the "effects" of the one-sidedness. The Ford Foundation articulated this simple premise in defending their sponsorship of public interest law firms during the early 1970s:

> A central assumption of our democratic society is that the general interest or the common good will emerge out of the conflict of special interests. The public interest law firm seeks to improve this process by giving better representation to certain interests.[33]

The liberal public interest movement was thus built on a vision of how democracy could work and the leaders of these groups came to a common conclusion as to how reform could be achieved.[34] Broad, sweeping reforms of the policymaking process were given only limited attention. Working through the political parties or initiating a third party wasn't given much credence as an alternative way of achieving their goals. The philosophy of the public interest movement of this period was that no matter how much government was reformed, government by itself was inherently incapable of protecting the common good. Left to its own devices, the government would always be overly influenced by private sector groups. The only solution was continuing involvement by citizen groups in policymaking to balance the influence of other organizations. Making pluralism come true was the answer.[35]

Conservative Counterattack

While liberals were trying to balance interest group politics by bringing "the people" into the political process, conservatives were coming to believe that the liberals were so successful that they had *unbalanced* the representation of interests in Washington. When the Carter administration welcomed these lobbies into the policymaking process and appointed many public interest leaders to major positions in agencies and departments, it seemed to finally incite conservatives into action.

The wellspring of the new right movement that developed in the late 1970s was a belief that the American way of life is threatened. The

---

[33]*The Public Interest Law Firm* (New York: Ford Foundation, 1973), p. 8.
[34]On the ideology of the liberal public interest movement, see Michael McCann, *Taking Reform Seriously* (Ithaca, N.Y.: Cornell University Press, 1986).
[35]Jeffrey M. Berry, "Public Interest vs. Party System," *Society* 17 (May/June 1980), pp. 42–48.

threat comes not from our enemies abroad but from the moral decay eating away at the country from within. In particular, new right groups such as Concerned Women for America and the Eagle Forum profess concern about the decline of the family. Policies seen as threatening to traditional family life, such as abortion, the Equal Rights Amendment, prohibition of school prayer, and gay rights, are associated with liberal groups that stand behind them. Alan Crawford, a historian of the new right, says this movement embodies "the politics of resentment."[36]

For conservative public interest groups, what is resented more than anything else is the women's movement. Their opposition to the liberal agenda of women's groups like the National Organization for Women focuses both on specific issues and on more generalized concerns about the American family. The preeminent issue, of course, is abortion, with the fervor of prochoice groups equally matched by the activism and commitment of prolife organizations.[37] Until it was buried, the proposed Equal Rights Amendment generated a furious conservative counterattack aimed at discrediting the need for such change in the Constitution. The underlying concern is the decline of the nuclear family. Conservative groups see feminism as one of the root causes of divorce, growing welfare caseloads, out-of-wedlock births, and many other trends they decry. Conservative advocacy in opposition to women's groups has certainly had an effect. After the Reagan administration came into power, the opportunities afforded to liberal women's groups to influence public policy decreased dramatically.[38]

Another policy area where conservative groups arose to directly counter liberal citizen groups is the environment. As the leader of a group fighting environmental organizations puts it, "The only way to defeat a social movement is with another social movement."[39] In the early 1980s the Sagebrush Rebellion advocated less federal control of land in the western states and more development. Over time it faded, but the Wise Use movement has emerged to replace it. Though not nearly as strong as the liberal environmental movement, these small conservative organizations argue against what they see as a preservationist ideology

---

[36]Alan Crawford, *Thunder on the Right* (New York: Pantheon, 1980).

[37]See Barbara Hinkson Craig and David M. O'Brien, *Abortion and American Politics* (Chatham, N.J.: Chatham House, 1993), pp. 35–71.

[38]Anne N. Costain, *Inviting Women's Rebellion* (Baltimore: Johns Hopkins University Press, 1992).

[39]Dowie, *Losing Ground,* pp. 93–94.

of environmental groups, believing resources can be used without damaging the underlying ecology of wilderness and other undeveloped areas. Unlike the groups that have worked against the liberal women's movement, many Wise Use lobbies don't really qualify as any kind of public interest group. Although they are led by citizen activists and there is some grassroots support for their work, much of their funding comes from corporations with a vested interest in resource extraction.[40]

In recent years the strongest conservative grassroots movement has been the Christian right. Religious Christians, especially those with fundamentalist beliefs, have organized to stop what they see as the moral decay of America. Instead of liberal social experimentation and welfare programs, Christian activists urge a return to strong family values and religious commitment. Although they mythologize the degree to which family life limited social problems in the past, Christian groups strike a responsive chord with their call for more individual responsibility and a smaller, less intrusive government.

A first step toward mobilizing conservative Christians came with the founding of the Moral Majority in 1979 by the Reverend Jerry Falwell, an evangelical Baptist minister from Lynchburg, Virginia. Its purpose was to bring a Christian presence into policymaking by forcing those in government to recognize fundamentalist religious values. The organization proved to be quite controversial for a number of reasons. Simply by its very name it implied that those that disagreed with it were not "moral." This enraged and energized opponents. More importantly, the Moral Majority turned out to be something of a paper tiger. Despite its lofty aims, it never developed a strong grassroots foundation. Much of the organization was directed at raising money, which in turn consumed most of the resources that were gathered. Falwell himself became part of the problem as many Americans felt uneasy with the active involvement of a preacher in the political process. Over time the organization declined and by 1987 Falwell said he was returning full-time to his duties as a minister.

The end of the Moral Majority paved the way for a new group, the Christian Coalition. Backed by the Reverend Pat Robertson, the organization has 400,000 contributors and more than 300 chapters around the country.[41] Unlike Falwell, however, Robertson, who ran unsuccess-

<hr>

[40]Dowie, *Losing Ground,* p. 96.

[41]David Broder, "Christian Coalition, Shifting Tactics, to Lobby Against Clinton Budget," *Washington Post,* July 18, 1993; and Kim A. Lawton, "The New Religious Face(s) of the Religious Right," *Christianity Today,* July 20, 1992, pp. 42–45.

fully for the Republican presidential nomination in 1988, has remained in the background. The executive director of the organization is Ralph Reed, a young, politically astute, and media savvy activist. Lacking an ecclesiastical background, Reed symbolizes a more secular, moderate approach than Pat Robertson would. The organization's success is built on its strong grassroots orientation and the committed activism of its followers. A spokesman for the organization succinctly articulated its strategy: "We think the Lord is going to give us this nation back one precinct at a time, one neighborhood at a time, and one state at a time."[42]

The Christian Coalition's close relationship with the Republican party has benefited both. More broadly, conservative citizen groups, together with conservative think tanks, have flourished in recent years as they have become the source of both activism and ideas to further the Republican cause. There is now a dense array of conservative citizen groups in Washington who have enormous access to Congress and to Republican presidents. Conservatives, however, are not only represented by citizen groups but by the traditional bulwark of American conservatism, the business corporation.

BUSINESS FIGHTS BACK

The rapid rise of liberal and conservative citizen groups in recent years can easily obscure the equally dramatic growth in business lobbying. Still, business has always been well represented in Washington, and the recent rise was aimed at meeting challenges by liberal citizen groups to the lobbying preeminence it had enjoyed. After business mobilized in the 1970s, it was ready to profit when Republican Ronald Reagan became president in 1981.

The Plague of Regulation

When business executives are asked why they've opened up a Washington office or expanded one already there, the inevitable response is government regulation. Business people feel their corporation or trade as-

---

[42]Matthew C. Moen, *The Transformation of the Christian Right* (Tuscaloosa: University of Alabama Press, 1992), p. 108.

sociation has little choice but to counter the encroachments of federal regulatory bodies. Surveys of business executives point unmistakably to the influence of regulation. A Conference Board study revealed that of those executives indicating a change in their government-relations work, 71 percent cited increased government activity as the reason.[43]

The regulatory process is particularly conducive to interest group advocacy because it deals with the most complex and esoteric aspects of public policy. As technology has complicated policy in such areas as air and water pollution, nuclear power, communications, and occupational health, the opportunity for regulatory advocacy has increased. Regulatory decisions in areas like these must be made after considering relevant technical data—data often difficult to obtain and open to competing interpretations. No one has more incentive to collect industry data than the industries themselves. At its heart, regulatory lobbying is a process of interest groups bringing their data to policymakers and trying to make these data the information base from which decisions flow.

Far from being the unfinished details of legislation, regulatory decisions are frequently critical policy determinations. Often these are needed because new regulatory legislation passed by Congress is vague, leaving key decisions to administrators. The 99 pages of the Energy Policy and Conservation Act of 1975 are described by one expert as:

> A potpourri of mandatory provisions, optional and discretionary authorizations, invocations to planning, and reporting requirements, ranging far and wide over the entire range of energy issues. But what has been gained in breadth has been lost in clarity. Indeed, if obfuscation had been the intention, the manner in which the statute is drafted could not have more successfully accomplished the purpose.[44]

The growth in business lobbying during the late 1960s and 1970s was not just a response to an increase in the number of regulations being adopted but also to the changing nature of regulation. Many of the new agencies created during this time were given jurisdiction over broad problem areas, such as pollution or occupational health, rather

---

[43]Phyllis S. McGrath, *Redefining Corporate-Federal Relations* (New York: Conference Board, 1979), p. 1. See also, "New Laws/New Jobs," Golightly & Co. International, New York, n.d., p. 1.
[44]John M. Blair, *The Control of Oil* (New York: Pantheon, 1976), p. 355.

than specific industries, such as broadcasting or securities trading. The breadth of regulatory authority for agencies like EPA or OSHA is immense, and large numbers of industries found themselves subject to their regulation. Businesses have found the new "social" regulation especially disturbing, "with its more detailed, multi-industry intrusions into areas of long-standing managerial discretion and its cost- and liability-enlarging potential."[45]

Since the late 1970s the general trend has been toward deregulatory efforts, and some areas, such as telecommunications, have been opened up to extensive competition. In other areas, such as financial services, markets have been opened to new competition but on a more gradual level. Many regulatory agencies have reduced the restrictions on companies under their jurisdictions. At first glance, this broad movement toward deregulation might seem to reduce the need for lobbyists. If an agency is easing regulations on an industry, wouldn't it stand to reason that there is less for lobbyists to do since there is less for the agency to do?

Generally speaking, deregulation has not appreciably lessened the work for lobbyists. In some areas work has been reduced, as with lawyers who fill a particular niche in preparing certain kinds of regulatory documents but have seen their relevant agencies simplify requirements. Deregulation per se, however, can just as easily increase the demand for lobbyists. Unless government removes itself completely from overseeing a market, the level of regulation is subject to change. Even if an agency does something that an entire industry likes, such as reducing pollution control requirements, that may encourage the industry to ask for other concessions. It's often the case too that regulatory standards have a differential impact on various segments of a single industry. Thus changes that may please one part of an industry may cause another to redouble its efforts.[46]

Seizing the Initiative

The expansion of regulatory activity was symptomatic of a broader problem facing business. The public had become skeptical of business

---

[45]Edward S. Herman, *Corporate Control, Corporate Power* (New York: Cambridge University Press, 1981), p. 185.
[46]Richard A. Harris, *Coal Firms Under the New Social Regulation* (Durham, N.C.: Duke University Press, 1985).

ethics, more concerned about postmaterial (quality of life) issues, and increasingly sympathetic to liberal citizen groups, which had replaced labor as business's primary political adversary.

All lobbies want to believe they have a special relationship with government, where legislators and administrators place primary importance on their interests. They want to believe that policies are made only after detailed consultation with them. They want to believe that their views carry more weight than those of other relevant interests. Finally, they want to believe that they have some control over the agenda in their policy area, where the issues they want discussed are brought to the surface and those they find distasteful can be killed or moderated by sympathetic officials. Businesses felt they had lost their special relationship with government between the late 1960s and the mid-1970s. David Vogel describes this attitude:

> For nearly a decade, most of the issues placed on the political agenda affecting business were initiated not by business, but by those who represented constituents hostile to business. Environmental protection, occupational health and safety, consumer protection, price controls on energy, affirmative action, product liability, expansion of the welfare state, prohibitions on corporate overseas payments, corporate governance, campaign reform, restrictions on corporate compliance with the Arab boycott of Israel—not a single one of those issues originated with business. To be sure, business was successful in . . . influencing many of these areas, making them less threatening than their proponents preferred. But what is critical is that for most of the decade, business was fighting its political battles on terrain set by its opponents.[47]

The resurgence of business as a force in national politics was symbolized by the creation of the Business Roundtable, a lobbying group composed of 200 or so chief executive officers (CEOs) from the nation's largest firms. Started in 1972, the Roundtable draws extensively on the resources of its member corporations and involves the CEOs themselves in lobbying. Despite the visibility of the Roundtable, the success of business mobilization came from the hundreds of trade associations that moved to Washington, the new business PACs that were started, the new corporate offices that were opened, and the expanded resources that corporations were willing to commit to government relations. The corporate mind-set fundamentally changed in the 1970s as

---

[47]Vogel, "How Business Responds to Opposition," p. 6.

business executives came to realize that they had to personally involve themselves in government relations, both in lobbying and in paying attention to the public affairs division of their corporation. The corporation became politicized as more and more people inside the corporation recognized that government relations wasn't just something a few gladhanders in public affairs did. Rather, at all levels of the corporation people were expected to donate money, become active in lobbying by trade groups, provide data and information to the government relations office, and to think more strategically about how new products and services would be affected by public policy.

In addition to the enhanced resources and commitment to lobbying government, business had another important weapon. As the economy declined in the 1970s, business became a more credible navigator to chart the nation's future. The political leadership of corporate America offered a prescription for growth in the American economy.[48] Their call for less regulation and lower taxes became increasingly attractive as Americans became increasingly nervous about their economic security.

This impressive mobilization of business interests bore a bountiful harvest when the Reagan administration came into office in 1981. A sweeping tax bill passed that year significantly reduced business taxes. Numerous regulatory changes were made that pleased major industries. The attitude of the administration was one of great concern toward the needs of business and unmistakable hostility toward the liberal public interest movement. Reagan's second term in office was not as uniformly popular with business. Again, there was a sweeping new tax bill, but this one lowered business tax rates by taking away many tax breaks for various industries. The lobbying war that erupted over the legislation badly split the business community.[49] The political mobilization of business does not, in and of itself, lead to business unity. When business was on the defensive in the 1970s, it was easier for it to unite on issues like its successful opposition to an Agency for Consumer Protection advocated by the Carter administration. After the 1981 tax cut, corporations and trade groups began to focus on lobbying the business-oriented Reagan administration for changes that would help their own

---

[48]David Plotke, "The Political Mobilization of Business," in Petracca, *The Politics of Interests,* pp. 175–198.
[49]See Jeffrey H. Birnbaum and Alan S. Murray, *Showdown at Gucci Gulch* (New York: Random House, 1987).

particular industry. What had been all for one and one for all became every industry for itself.[50]

Business continues to play a preeminent role among all Washington lobbies. Its message of growth and economic prosperity continues to resonate strongly in an era of economic uncertainty. When the liberal Clinton administration came into office in 1993, it pushed a budget reduction package that was aimed at pleasing big business. Exasperated at the need to make this program a priority and the lack of support he was getting, Clinton exploded at his staff, "I hope you're all aware we're all Eisenhower Republicans. . . . We stand for lower deficits and free trade and the bond market. Isn't that great?"[51] After the GOP swept the 1994 congressional elections, business lobbyists worked closely with the Republicans and lobbied hard on behalf of the party's Contract with America. Congressional Republicans responded not only with a wide-range of pro-business legislation, but granted unparalleled access to corporate and trade group lobbyists.[52]

CONCLUSION

By any standard, the amount of lobbying in Washington has expanded significantly. Interests previously unrepresented are now represented before the government by recently formed organizations. Interests that were already represented in Washington tend to be even better represented today.

Although the reasons for lobbying's rise in different sectors of society vary, some common threads appear in the broad movement toward interest group politics. Pluralist theory put forward the idea that interest group involvement in policymaking contributed to democratic government. Expanding governmental activity in the 1960s and 1970s, usually at the behest of interest groups, directly affected more and more constituencies and helped catalyze increased advocacy. Finally, as new interest groups form, they stimulate other constituencies to orga-

---

[50]David Vogel, *Fluctuating Fortunes* (New York: Basic Books, 1989), pp. 286–287.
[51]Bob Woodward, *The Agenda* (New York: Simon and Schuster, 1994), p. 165.
[52]Stephen Engelberg, "100 Days of Dreams Come True for Lobbyists in Congress," *New York Times,* April 14, 1995; and Jill Abramson and Timothy Noah, "In GOP-Controlled Congress, Lobbyists Remain as Powerful as Ever—And Perhaps More Visible," *Wall Street Journal,* April 20, 1995.

nize because new groups increase awareness about what various interests are doing, and, further, their formation threatens their natural adversaries.

While the advocacy explosion created new groups and expanded resources devoted to lobbying, this heightened competition between groups did not bring about a perfect balance of interests represented in Washington. Business was by far the best represented sector of American society before this upsurge in lobbying, and it remains in that position today. Business responded to the challenge of the public interest movement with ample resources and a fierce determination to maintain its advantages in Washington. It still faces potent competition from an array of liberal public interest groups, although its traditional rival, organized labor, is on the decline. The greatest restraint on business may not be its critics, but the divisions within and between industries.

The end result of the advocacy explosion is that more and more Americans have become organized into more and more groups. These lobbies pursue the interests of particular segments of society, each with its separate set of demands on the government. Many argue that as interest group advocacy grows, the greater the need for strong political parties to balance the pursuit of narrow self-interest. We turn to that subject next.

Chapter **3**

The Party Connection

Within the groves of academe, American interest groups and American political parties are very separate subfields. Distinct groups of scholars study each, and only a few hardy souls cross the boundaries to try to link these two subjects. One reason for this is that the subfields share little in terms of their theoretical perspectives. Another reason is surely the traditional incentive for scholars to specialize so that they may become a leading expert on a subject.

These reasons notwithstanding, the division between these two subfields among those studying American politics is a bit puzzling. Those studying other Western democracies have done far more to integrate the analysis of parties, interest groups, and social movements.[1] This makes enormous sense because parties, groups, and social movements do many of the same things, albeit in different ways. In terms of the roles groups play, as outlined in Chapter 1, parties also represent citizens, facilitate their participation in the political process, educate the public, push issues on to the agenda of Congress and agencies, and monitor program performance. Yet, parties and groups are linked together in our system not simply because their functions overlap, but because they need each other to accomplish their most important goals. Groups cannot enact policies or formulate regulations on their

---

[1]See, for example, the research collected in Russell Dalton and Manfred Kuechler, eds., *Challenging the Political Order* (New York: Oxford University Press, 1990).

own. Parties need the political support of interest groups, which can provide campaign donations, mobilize voters on election day, activate their membership on behalf of a bill, and influence people's attitudes.

In this chapter we look at the interrelationship between interest groups and political parties. We focus on both the ties that bind and the sources of conflict between groups and parties. A beginning point is to examine the advocacy explosion in the context of recent party history. Did interest groups prosper because parties declined?

THE ADVANTAGES OF INTEREST GROUPS

If interest groups and political parties are interrelated in many crucial ways, it stands to reason that broad-scale changes among one set of political organizations will affect the other. No one would argue that groups and parties stand in perfect balance—that as one goes up the other must go down. Yet since they compete for many of the same resources—money, identity and allegiance among political activists, and so on—it may be that the health of parties and interest groups are to some degree inversely related.

In this context, the decline of American political parties during the 1960s and 1970s may help to explain the rise of the interest group society. As people became disillusioned with parties, the number of new lobbies dramatically increased. Party decline certainly contributed to the growth of interest group politics, but as will be outlined shortly, the basic structure of the American party system is conducive to interest groups.

For political scientists, the principal indicators of party decline were the decreasing proportion of Americans who voted on the basis of party, the drop in the number of people who voted at all, the increasing cynicism toward parties and the political system, and a decline in partisan identification.[2] What followed this period of party decline is not so easy to conceptualize. Some believe that there is a rebound of sorts for American parties. They point to the significant rise in voting in the

---

[2]The literature on party decline is voluminous. See, for example, David S. Broder, *The Party's Over* (New York: Harper & Row, 1972); Everett Carll Ladd, Jr., with Charles D. Hadley, *Transformations of the American Party System,* 2nd ed. (New York: Norton, 1978); and Norman H. Nie, Sidney Verba, and John R. Petrocik, *The Changing American Voter* (Cambridge: Harvard University Press, 1976).

1992 presidential election. Increased vitality in party fundraising, particularly for the Republicans, is another sign of party revival. The Republicans' Contract with America, launched during the 1994 congressional campaign, may stimulate an increased majoritarian emphasis in elections. Still, no one is arguing that there is a full-blown party revival in America, and disillusionment with political institutions remains high.

The perception of parties as ineffective or out of touch with the concerns of average Americans surely gave those who had serious policy concerns ample reason to support a lobbying organization. The decline of parties was particularly helpful to citizen groups, which appeal to the same kind of ideological activists who are drawn to party work. Nevertheless, there are more fundamental, more enduring reasons why American interest groups have prospered at the expense of political parties. The nature of our electoral and party system facilitates interest group politics independent of the health of the parties at any one time.

Policy Maximizers

A central advantage of interest groups over political parties is that they offer individuals a direct, focused, and undiluted way of supporting advocacy on the issue they care the most about. Assume that you are politically active and are willing to spend $100 to pursue your political goals during a single year. What is the best way to spend that money so that your chances of achieving those goals will be maximized? If you care about a particular policy—saving wilderness, protecting farm subsidies, promoting workplace safety, or whatever—you may easily conclude that an interest group is the better "investment" for that $100 than a political party or one of its congressional campaign committees. Even though one cannot confidently predict the real chances that either a party or an interest group will succeed in accomplishing that one specific goal, it is clear to you as donor of the money that the interest group will work more intensively and single-mindedly toward it. A political party, on the other hand, has a constituency so broad that it will be pushed to move on hundreds of issues. But in any year, relatively few issues will be assigned priority by party leaders, and if an issue is highly controversial, the best political course for the congressional party or the president may be to act in a superficial, symbolic manner or to abstain altogether from acting on the issue.

The advantages of interest groups in the United States are accentuated by our two-party system. With plurality elections in single-member districts (and thus no proportional representation), the likelihood is that there will be two very broad parties covering a great deal of ideological ground.[3] To win an election, the parties must build a coalition of some breadth, attracting large numbers of those in the center (moderates) to go along with those who form the ideological core of the party. By their very nature, then, American political parties are *vote maximizers.* To win elections they must dilute policy stands, take purposely ambiguous positions on others, and generally ignore some, so as not to offend segments of the population that they need in their coalition.

Interest groups are just the opposite. They are *policy maximizers,* meaning that they do better in attracting members if their outlook is narrowly focused.[4] Although a few interest groups work on a broad range of policies, the typical group cares only about a few closely related issues. The appeal of the American Soybean Association, the Veterans of Foreign Wars, and the Independent Truckers Association is that each works only on the problems of soybean farmers, veterans, and independent truckers respectively. A dollar donated to these groups is a dollar spent on their narrow set of issues.

If the United States had a multiparty system, some political support that now goes to interest groups would likely be channeled to some of the additional parties that would compete with the Democrats and Republicans. For example, in a number of European countries environmental or Green parties have arisen. As environmentalism developed into an important societal value in West Germany during the 1980s, the Green party emerged to challenge the three traditional national parties. From a modest start with 1.5 percent of the vote in the 1980 election, to 5.6 percent in 1983, and then to 8.3 percent in 1987, the Greens took votes away from the existing parties. The proportional representation system in Germany meant that the 8.3 percent of the 1987 vote translated into 44 seats in the Bundestag.[5] In the United States, a party averaging 8 percent in a congressional election would likely win no seats in Congress because, as noted above, we have single-member, "first past the post" electoral districts.

---

[3]Maurice Duverger, *Political Parties* (New York: John Wiley, 1963); and Anthony Downs, *An Economic Theory of Democracy* (New York: Harper & Row, 1957).
[4]Jeffrey M. Berry, "Public Interest vs. Party System," *Society* 17 (May/June 1980), p. 47.
[5]Ferdinand Müller-Rommel, "New Political Movements and 'New Politics' Parties in Western Europe," in Dalton and Kuechler, *Challenging the Political Order,* p. 216.

The Greens in Germany and elsewhere in Europe are not vote maximizer parties. Instead, they champion a particular interest with great intensity, much the way environmental interest groups in this country push their agenda. The European Green parties do not realistically hope to win control of the government. Rather, they want to attract the votes of those who care passionately about the environment and related issues so that they can capture enough seats to be an influential force within the legislature. If the United States had a proportional representation system, a viable Green party would likely exist. (There have been some candidates running as Greens in local elections in this country, but no significant national party has developed.[6]) And if an American Green party existed, would the Natural Resources Defense Council, the National Audubon Society, the National Wildlife Federation, the Izaak Walton League, Friends of the Earth, the Environmental Defense Fund, Environmental Action, Greenpeace, the Sierra Club, and countless other local, state, and national environmental lobbies be able to coexist with it? It's doubtful that there would be enough financial support and activism to maintain such a vast array of environmental advocacy groups as well as a Green party.

Party Systems

Clearly the opportunity for interest groups to form and prosper is affected by the number of viable political parties in an electoral system. The relationship between the type of party system and the type of interest group system may also be influenced by the internal cohesiveness of the parties in the legislature. In the language of political science, does the absence of a *responsible* party system lead to more interest group politics? A responsible or strong party system is one that promotes majoritarian policymaking. During the campaign the parties issue platforms detailing their promises on major policy issues of the day. If that party wins the election, it is committed to following through on those promises.[7].

In the United States the Democrats and Republicans fall far short of the responsible party model. Traditionally, representatives and sena-

---

[6]John C. Berg, "Prospects for More Parties in the United States," paper delivered at the Conference on Party Politics in the Year 2000," Manchester, England, January, 1995, pp. 10–11.

[7]See the report by the American Political Science Association's Committee on Political Parties, *Toward a More Responsible Two-Party System* (New York: Rinehart, 1950).

tors have not felt committed to voting with their party when the party's preference conflicted with their own conscience or with the interests of their constituents. There are certainly incentives for legislators to go along with their party leadership as loyalists will be favored in committee assignments and in other ways.[8] Despite such incentives, however, members of Congress are not creatures of their national parties. Legislators are dependent on their own abilities to gain nomination, build coalitions of support in their districts or states, and collect campaign contributions. The contrast with British political parties is instructive. Those who wish to run for Parliament on the Conservative or Labour ticket must subject themselves to a gauntlet of interviews at different levels of the party before the party organization chooses who will be their nominee for available seats.[9] Once they get to Parliament, Conservative and Labour members need to vote with their party on major issues; otherwise the government could fall and new elections would have to be scheduled.

In the United States, a responsible party system is not only inhibited by the way the party system has evolved but by the divided powers of our government. A responsible party system is compatible with a parliamentary form of government, where the legislative and executive branches are intertwined, and the prime minister is the legislative leader of the party in the majority. In the United States, the president can be of one party while the other party controls one or both houses of Congress. Divided control is actually quite common in the postwar era.[10] In such cases, regardless of what one party pledges to do if elected, substantial compromise is usually going to be required before legislation promised in the campaign can be enacted by Congress into law, if it can be passed at all.

The independence of American legislators from their party is aided and abetted by interest groups. As we will discuss later in this chapter and in the chapter on political action committees, legislators are highly dependent on the contributions of interest groups to finance their campaigns. Interest groups also actively lobby candidates and ask them to detail their positions on those issues of critical concern to the

---

[8]Gary W. Cox and Mathew D. McCubbins, *Legislative Leviathan* (Berkeley: University of California Press, 1993), pp. 163–187.

[9]Pippa Norris and Joni Lovenduski, *Political Recruitment: Gender, Race, and Class in the British Parliament* (Cambridge, England: Cambridge University Press, 1995).

[10]David Mayhew, *Divided We Govern* (New Haven: Yale University Press, 1991), pp. 4–5.

group's members. Many people who are active in interest groups are also active in party affairs and in election campaigns, and their work on behalf of candidates forges a tie between their groups and legislators.[11]

Although it seems evident that a weak party system works to strengthen the role of interest groups in a political system, we cannot assume the opposite: that a strong party system works to weaken interest groups. In the British system, labor unions have enormous influence over the Labour party. British unions provide 90 percent of the Labour party's funds and cast 80 percent of the votes at the Labour Party Conference.[12] Although not as formally tied to the Conservatives, business trade associations are highly influential as well. Interest group influence can take many forms, and lobbying organizations are highly adaptable to the requirements of any democratic political system.

In parliamentary systems there is a tendency for more centralization of interest group advocacy than in the United States. In the United States, a small number of influential groups ostensibly speak for large sectors of society (such as the Business Roundtable and the AFL-CIO), but no lobbying groups enjoy a dominant position in government policymaking. In some parliamentary democracies, however, large, powerful groups are the unquestioned representative of a broad sector of society and enjoy access to government that other interest groups in that country can only dream about. Where governments recognize such groups as the formal representatives of some sector of the economy, and consult with the leadership of those organizations as a matter of course before making policy decisions, such relationships are described as *corporatist* or *neocorporatist*. In Austria, for example, the government recognizes the Federation of Industrialists and the Federation of Business as the representatives of business interests, and the organizations play a integral, formalized role in the policymaking process.[13]

---

[11]Denise L. Baer and Julie A. Dolan, "Intimate Connections: Political Interests and Group Activity in State and Local Parties," *American Review of Politics* 15 (Summer 1994), pp. 257–289.

[12]Graham K. Wilson, *Interest Groups* (Oxford, England: Basil Blackwell, 1990), p. 87.

[13]Graham K. Wilson, *Business and Politics* (Chatham, N.J.: Chatham House, 1985), p. 106. See also, Robert H. Salisbury, "Why No Corporatism in America?", in Philippe C. Schmitter and Gerhard Lehmbruch, eds., *Trends Toward Corporatist Intermediation* (Beverly Hills: Sage, 1979), pp. 219–236.

The variety in electoral and party systems among the Western democracies makes it difficult to determine how those structures influence the exact nature of interest group systems. Clearly multiparty systems provide competition to interest groups since some of the narrower, more ideological parties (like the Greens) will attract financial support and activism from people who might otherwise be more supportive of lobbies with similar policy goals. Beyond this, however, considerable uncertainty exists about how the differences in parliamentary party systems and other institutional factors affect the number, size, and role of interest groups.[14] But in the United States, with its federal structure, separation of powers, and an electoral system that lends itself to two broad, centrist parties, there is every reason to expect that interest groups are going to flourish.

WORKING TOGETHER

Most American interest groups are torn between partisanship and non-partisanship. Since control of the government is often divided between the two parties, and since policymaking in Congress is typically bipartisan in nature even when one party controls both branches, it makes obvious sense for a lobby to maintain a bipartisan demeanor. Lobbyists need access to both parties, and thus interest groups will often hire some lobbyists who have worked for Republicans on the Hill or in an agency and some who have worked for Democrats.

Although the need for access to both parties is paramount, the leaders of interest groups usually have a preference between the parties. Most business leaders prefer the Republican party because of its greater sympathy for low taxes, smaller government, and antipathy to organized labor. Business groups walk a delicate line, trying to help the Republicans gain election while being friendly enough with Democrats through their campaign donations and Democratic lobbyists so as not to alienate the party.

For some interest groups, there is such a close identification with liberal or conservative issues that there is no pretense that they are

---

[14]See Robert A. Dahl, *Dilemmas of Pluralist Democracy* (New Haven: Yale University Press, 1982), pp. 55–80.

nonpartisan organizations. The most obvious example is organized labor. The Democratic party has championed the right of unions to organize, worked for health and safety standards at the workplace, and consistently advocated raises in the minimum wage. The Republicans have been just as steadfast in their opposition to labor. Consequently, the AFL-CIO and its member unions have no reason to pretend they are not politically affiliated with the Democratic party.

While labor's alliance with the Democrats has been ongoing, most cooperative efforts between interest groups and parties are ad hoc in nature. Lobbyists are always working with committee chairs and party leaders to help build support for cherished legislation. Sometimes groups work more broadly with the legislative party and the Democratic or Republican national committees. The Republicans' effort to pass the Contract with America involved a number of alliances with interest groups. The Contract with America was a pledge of most Republicans running for the House of Representatives in 1994 to back a ten-point program of conservative policies if they were elected. This effort by the House Republicans emulated a responsible party system where candidates for the legislature stand on a common platform. (Despite the initial success of the contract in the House in 1995, the United States is still a long way from a responsible party system. Most voters, for example, weren't even aware of the contract during the 1994 campaign.)

For one of the contract's provisions, a promise to ease the regulatory burden on business, the House Republicans worked closely with trade associations and corporations to push the bill through. Indeed, the point man for the series of bills, Representative Tom DeLay of Texas, assembled the interest group coalition supporting the legislation. The coalition, Project Relief, took out newspaper ads to highlight the problems with government regulation by agencies such as the Occupational Safety and Health Administration.[15]

Cooperation between parties and interest groups extends to campaigns and elections as well. Although only a relatively minor percentage of all interest groups participate in elections beyond donating campaign funds, their activity is by no means insignificant. Since few groups are willing to make election endorsements—it's overtly partisan and thus contrary to the need to have access to both parties—those

---

[15]Timothy Noah, "GOP's Rep. DeLay Is Working in Every Corner to Exterminate Regulations That Bug Business," *Wall Street Journal,* March 6, 1995.

groups who make endorsements can offer a welcome shot of free publicity for the chosen candidate and, possibly, the votes of some members who might otherwise vote for the opposition. Groups often try to leverage their endorsement to obtain support for one of their priorities. When the National Education Association gave its first presidential endorsement to Jimmy Carter in 1976, "association officials made it clear to Mr. Carter that they wanted [a Department of Education] created to give education more visibility in the Cabinet."[16] After he became president, Carter pushed strongly for the new Cabinet department, and Congress acceded to his wish. Yet endorsements bring no assurances. When the air traffic controllers endorsed Ronald Reagan in 1980, they received a vague expression of support from the candidate to work for an improvement in the controllers' working conditions. When they illegally struck in 1981, Reagan fired them and crushed the union. What a party or a president is willing to do for an interest group is subject to the constraints of public opinion and other political considerations.

More welcome than interest group endorsements are interest group members who volunteer to work on a campaign. Even in this era of electronic campaigns fought through television commercials, volunteers are a prized commodity. When campaign workers are plentiful, it's possible to conduct voter registration drives, do literature drops in the precincts, identify supporters through phone banks, and run get-out-the-vote efforts on election day.

Since the New Deal, organized labor has provided critical volunteer support for countless Democratic candidates running for office at different levels of government.[17] More recently, the Christian Coalition has become the most important source of volunteers for many Republican candidates. In one Oklahoma congressional district in 1994, the Republican candidate, Steve Largent, had 800 to 900 volunteers during the campaign. Most of them came from Largent's fundamentalist church and Oral Roberts University, a local Christian college. Largent actually had more volunteers than he could use and some were sent to work for Senate candidate James Inhofe, who was also backed by the Christian Coalition. Both Republicans won easily, as did many other

---

[16]Gene I. Maeroff, "Teachers' Unions Are Courted and Castigated," *New York Times,* June 26, 1983.
[17]Paul S. Herrnson, *Party Campaigning in the 1980s* (Cambridge, Mass.: Harvard University Press, 1988), pp. 103–119.

Oklahoma Republicans backed by the religious right. The Oklahoma Christian Coalition, which distributed over 600,000 voter guides through sympathetic churches, was clearly a significant influence in the campaign.[18] Nationwide the Christian Coalition distributed 33 million voter guides.[19]

The Christian Coalition has not been content to merely work on behalf of the conservative Republicans who they happen to agree with. The organization has been active in recruiting candidates as well. It wants to put its own people in office, legislators whose loyalty to the organization's goals will be unwavering no matter which way the political winds are blowing. In a number of states the Christian Coalition has taken control of the Republican party organization. In Texas, for example, the group mobilized its members to go to precinct meetings so that they could begin the process of getting elected as delegates to the statewide GOP convention. The Coalition's efforts were successful as delegates sympathetic to the organization dominated the 1994 state convention. When one candidate for statewide party chair addressed the audience, she expressed the concern of Republicans who are more moderate in their political views by telling the delegates, "The Republican party is not a church." This elicited boos and catcalls and she lost the election to the Christian Coalition's candidate.[20]

It is unusual in American politics for an interest group to play such an active role within a political party. There has not been a series of groups who have played a similar role to that of the Christian Coalition within the GOP. The Republicans' most influential interest group constituency, business, largely limits its campaign endeavors to contributing money (much of which has gone to the Democrats over the years). For the Christian Coalition and organized labor, freed from the imperative of bipartisanship because of their complete antagonism to the opposition party, there is the opportunity to earn the gratitude of those elected to office. Legislators and presidents remember who their foot soldiers were the last time they were in battle.

---

[18]Nancy L. Bednar and Allen D. Hertzke, "The Christian Right and Republican Realignment in Oklahoma," *PS* 28 (March 1995), p. 13.

[19]Matthew C. Moen, "The Devolutionary Era: A New Phase of Activism Linking Religious and Secular Conservatives in the 104th Congress," paper delivered at the annual conference of the New England Political Science Association, Portland, Maine, May, 1995, p. 10.

[20]Richard L. Berke, "Wielding Fiery Words, Right Conquers Texas G.O.P.," *New York Times,* June 12, 1994.

PARTIES AND PACS

The most intimate connection between political parties and interest groups is campaign finance. Interest groups provide a large share of the cost of congressional campaigns, but along with interest group money comes the taint of taking donations from those who have a self-serving motive. Yet parties and their candidates have little choice but to pursue interest group donations. As Larry Sabato puts it, "Like Willie Sutton who robbed banks 'because that's where they keep the money,'" parties look to PACs because they hold vast sums of money to contribute.[21] And unlike robbing banks, soliciting PACs happens to be legal.

The organization and operation of PACs and their patterns of donations to individual candidates will be detailed in Chapter 7. Here we focus on the direct involvement of PACs in party politics. Although the thousands of PACs that contribute money to candidates for Congress have their own independent agendas, a significant amount of coordination occurs between the two national parties and PAC decision makers. A handful of PACs provide crucial leadership in coordinating PAC gifts along partisan lines. As we'll discuss in Chapter 7, these lead PACs gather and disseminate information to other like-minded PACs on candidates and their prospects for election.

Each of the parties has a campaign committee for each house of Congress. The four campaign arms—the Democratic Congressional Campaign Committee, the Democratic Senatorial Campaign Committee, the National Republican Congressional Committee, and the National Republican Senatorial Committee—are linked to both the congressional parties and the national committees. Each is led by a member of Congress who works with officials of their national party to coordinate fundraising and disbursement. These party committees play an important role in soliciting funds from PACs and directing PAC donations to where the money is most needed. A Republican party official who works as a PAC liaison notes, "You have to understand that most PAC operations are one- and two-person shops. . . . In many cases it's just the one person and a clerical person. Most of the person's time is spent doing things that are lobby related—lobbying on the Hill, keeping up with legislation, and that sort of thing." Hence, the party has an opportunity to provide information and guide some funding decisions.

---

[21]Larry J. Sabato, *The Rise of Political Consultants* (New York: Basic Books, 1981), p. 273.

Since PACs are often preoccupied with access to incumbents, much of their money is given to committee chairs who have safe seats and don't actually need the funds. Each congressional campaign committee works to remind PACs that the congressional *party* has a deep and abiding interest in where they send their money. They try to impress upon PAC directors that the PACs need to think about which party can do them the most good rather than which individual representatives and senators are most important.

The art of raising party money from PACs was elevated to new heights by former Democratic representative Tony Coelho. Under his leadership the Democratic Congressional Campaign Committee increased the money it raised from $1.2 million in the 1980 election cycle to $15 million in the 1986 cycle.[22] Coelho was relentless in soliciting money, and he was none too subtle in letting PACs know that he was keeping track of who was being naughty and who was being nice. Dissatisfied with the Realtors' PAC because it hadn't donated to some Democrats Coelho was trying to raise money for, he went to the group's office in Washington. Recalls one who was present at the meeting, "He berated [the PAC officials] rather lustily for failing to support some of his guys." The participant added, "Even I, with all my years in politics, was surprised by the ferocity of the attack." The Realtors complied with Coelho's requests.[23] Unfortunately, this kind of in-your-face extortion can be found in both parties. The month before the 1994 congressional elections, Newt Gingrich met with PAC directors and told them to give to GOP candidates or they could expect "the two coldest years in Washington."[24]

Another source of interest group support for the two parties comes in the form of *soft money.* "A term of epic imprecision," soft money refers to contributions that interest groups can make for party-building efforts.[25] This would include voter registration drives, voter education, and get-out-the-vote efforts. Unlike PAC contributions, which are limited to $5,000 per candidate per election, soft money is not restricted.

---

[22]Frank J. Sorauf, *Inside Campaign Finance* (New Haven: Yale University Press, 1992), p. 117.
[23]Brooks Jackson, *Honest Graft* (New York: Knopf, 1988), p. 84.
[24]Jennifer Babson and Kelly St. John, "Momentum Helps GOP Collect Record Amounts From PACs," *Congressional Quarterly Weekly Report,* December 3, 1994, p. 3457.
[25]Sorauf, *Inside Campaign Finance,* p. 147.

Corporations are the dominant source of soft money, and give millions of dollars to the parties each election cycle.

Although party building is a laudable goal, these large gifts are controversial because critics believe that the donations lead to favored treatment by government. Agribusiness giant Archer-Daniels-Midland (ADM), for example, has relied on soft money to buy itself good will with both political parties. ADM has a strong interest in policies promoting the use of ethanol, a corn-based fuel that can be mixed with regular gasoline. ADM produces 70 percent of the nation's ethanol, and its chairman, Dwayne Andreas, has donated vast sums to the parties to promote the fuel and other ADM interests. During the 1992 campaign, ADM donated $1.1 million in soft money to the Republican party. Undaunted by the GOP's loss of the White House, Andreas began to channel more money to the Democrats and gave $200,000 to the party in the first 15 months of the Clinton administration. When the Democratic National Committee held a fundraising dinner, Andreas served as co-chair of the event and kicked in another $100,000. When the EPA subsequently issued a regulation mandating that by 1996 10 percent of gasoline sold contain ethanol, was it mere coincidence that ADM had been such a good friend of the party? It's hard to argue that EPA adopted the rule strictly on environmental grounds since most environmental groups view ethanol as having little benefit to the environment.[26]

Just as soft money can be used to buy improved access to government, it can be used to punish a party that is acting contrary to a firm's interest. The Amway Corporation gave $2.5 to the Republicans in 1994 and none to the Democrats. Amway was antagonized by the Food and Drug Administration's efforts to make diet supplement companies back up the health claims they make for the pills they market.[27]

The financial support that interest groups provide to the Democrats and Republicans works to both strengthen and weaken parties. Campaign contributions allow the parties to compete more effectively in more congressional races across the country. Soft money

---

[26]Peter H. Stone, "The Big Harvest," *National Journal,* July 30, 1994, pp. 1790–1793; and Michael Parrish, "EPA Rule on Ethanol Overturned," *Boston Globe,* April 29, 1995.
[27]Jill Abramson and David Rogers, "As GOP Tries to Shrink Government, Coffers Swell with New Money," *Wall Street Journal,* February 9, 1995.

raised by the parties from corporations can be used to help build the party at the grassroots. At the same time, the more that parties depend on interest groups for their financing, the more beholden they are to them.

KEEPING PARTIES STRAIGHT AND TRUE

One of the most interesting developments in contemporary party politics is the increasingly important role of citizen groups in campaigns and elections. As we have already seen, the Christian Coalition has become an integral part of the Republican party. The activity of citizen groups in the electoral process extends far beyond this one highly visible group. Citizen groups differ from vocationally related interest groups because they are organized around members' ideological beliefs about the political system. They tend to be more passionate, more self-righteous, more abrasive, and more partisan than other interest groups. They speak for broad sectors of the American population and cannot be ignored by the parties. The two parties, though, often wish they would go away.

Parties find it frustrating to deal with citizen groups because these organizations work against the parties' vote maximization strategy. Rational parties want to place themselves squarely in the center of the American electorate, maximizing their appeal to the those with moderate political outlooks. Since most Americans are not highly ideological, most of the votes in elections come from those who are moderates rather than from hardened liberals or conservatives. Citizen groups, on the other hand, want the parties to emphasize their issues, even though those issue stances may be highly controversial and push moderates away from the party. Citizen groups assume that even if a majority of Americans don't currently share their views, an election campaign that enlightens them about the organization's issues will eventually produce a majority backing those positions.

The Republicans' primary citizen group constituencies are the Christian Coalition, antiabortion groups, other organizations emphasizing a conservative view of family values, and the National Rifle Association. The Democrats embrace women's groups, black and Hispanic civil rights organizations, environmentalists, gay and lesbian organizations, and the senior citizens' lobby. These citizen groups are involved in different ways in the two parties, but all aggressively push their issues, which are often the most controversial and emotional issues before the country.

These groups' influence in party politics is enhanced by the weakness of our political parties. Since parties do not control nominations, and many candidates can compete in primaries for those nominations, candidates must build personal coalitions of supporters to put them over the top. Candidates seek out those interest groups they have sympathized with over the years and ask for the votes of those who identify with those organizations. For example, in a Democratic presidential primary with six or seven candidates competing, it might be more useful to be known as an ardent environmentalist and advocate of women's rights than being known as a hard-working Democrat who has always been loyal to the party. If the party organization controlled the nomination, the latter might be the most important quality.[28]

As elections near, candidates will often sharpen and emphasize a particular issue stance so as to attract an interest group's followers or at least neutralize their potential opposition. Before Robert Dole, the majority leader in the Senate, announced his candidacy for the Republican nomination for president, he attracted a great deal of attention by sending a letter to the National Rifle Association promising to work for repeal of the recently enacted ban on assault rifles. The general public overwhelmingly backs a ban on assault weapons, but the NRA considers the willingness of a candidate to back any restrictions on guns as a litmus test. Even though he had not previously been a critic of the ban, Dole didn't want to lose the votes of this constituency in the Republican primaries.[29]

Citizen groups lobby the candidates as well. During the 1992 presidential campaign, gay and lesbian groups pushed Bill Clinton to take an unequivocal stand on lifting the ban on gays in the military. Clinton told the groups that if elected he would instruct the Pentagon to allow homosexuals to serve openly in the armed services. No sooner had Clinton taken office than the press and his opponents began to ask when he was going to lift the ban. Public opinion was not supportive, and Clinton quickly beat a retreat with a hastily cobbled compromise of "don't ask, don't tell." (The military wouldn't ask, and gay soldiers

---

[28]See Nelson W. Polsby, *Consequences of Party Reform* (New York: Oxford University Press, 1983).
[29]"Mr. Dole's Transparent Tactics," *New York Times,* March 2, 1995.

would not voluntarily tell people that they're homosexual.) The consequence was that this handful of small citizen lobbies caused Clinton to lose valuable momentum at the beginning of his term and shortened his honeymoon with the Congress.

Interest groups have always pushed the parties to back their issues. What is significant about the efforts of citizen groups is, as pointed out earlier, that the impact of their lobbying may push their targeted party away from the center of the electorate. A business group pushing the Republican party to adopt a plank in their platform calling for a lower depreciation allowance in the tax code is not going to drive moderates from the party. In contrast, consider the issue of abortion at the 1992 Republican convention. President Bush and his advisers knew that his antiabortion stance could hurt him in the general election. Bush had already flip-flopped on the issue years earlier, and it was difficult for him to change his position again in 1992. It would have been ideal if the platform writers moderated the staunch antiabortion language of previous platforms, thus enabling Bush to appear to be moving toward the center without publicly repudiating his current stance. Antiabortion groups, amply represented among delegates, would not hear of it. The party did not move on the issue and Bush ended up losing votes among Republicans who were prochoice.[30] To the antiabortion groups, principle was more important than victory in November.

This kind of behavior by citizen groups is hardly uncommon. In recent years citizen groups have provoked most of the platform fights at national conventions.[31] Usually these are hot-button, "wedge" issues that are highly controversial, like affirmative action, abortion, and the Equal Rights Amendment. The motivation of the groups is to draw out the differences between the two parties on the issue. For example, at the 1980, 1984, and 1988 Democratic conventions, civil rights groups initiated platform fights on affirmative action. The party was already committed to affirmative action, but these organizations intended to make sure there was no backsliding. They wanted the party's stand to be singularly unequivocal and the issue out front, in bright lights, for all to see. In Table 3.1, all the platform fights between 1980 and 1992 for

---

[30]Alan I. Abramowitz, "It's Abortion, Stupid: Policy Voting in the 1992 Presidential Election," *Journal of Politics* 57 (February 1995), pp. 176–186.

[31]Jeffrey M. Berry and Deborah Schildkraut, "Citizen Groups, Political Parties, and the Decline of the Democrats," paper delivered at the annual meeting of the American Political Science Association, Chicago, September, 1995.

TABLE 3.1   OUTCOMES OF PLATFORM LOBBYING

ISSUES WHERE CITIZEN GROUPS INITATED A PLATFORM FIGHT

		Target Party	Other Party
1980			
Republican	ERA	−	+
	Abortion Rights	−	+
	Affirmative Action	−	+
Democrat	Affirmative Action	+	−
	ERA	+	−
	Abortion Rights	+	−
1984			
Republican	ERA	−	+
	Nuclear Freeze	−	+
	Abortion Rights	−	+
	Affirmative Action	−	+
Democrat	Affirmative Action	+	−
	Nuclear Freeze/No First Use	+	−
	Simpson-Mazzoli Immigration Bill	+	−
	Nonintervention in Central America	−	−
1988			
Republican	Affirmative Action	−	+
	Abortion Rights	−	+
	ERA	−	+
	Expanding Child Care	−	+
Democrat	Affirmative Action	+	−
1992			
Republican	Abortion Ban	+	−
	Family Values	+	−
	AIDS (Liberal Approach)	−	+
Democrat	Abortion Rights	+	−
	Race Relations	+	−

NOTES: With the exception of two issues before the 1992 Republican convention (a ban on abortions and a commitment to "family values") all these conflicts were generated by liberal citizen groups. Conservative citizen groups generated the other two.

For each convention, the issues are listed in order of their salience at the time, based on press coverage of the pre-convention period and the week of the convention itself.

A minus sign means that the party stood against the citizen group's position; a plus sign means it sided with the group.

Source: Jeffrey M. Berry and Deborah Schildkraut, "Citizen Groups, Political Parties, and the Decline of the Democrats," paper delivered at the annual meeting of the American Political Science Association, Chicago, September, 1995, p. 21a. Reprinted by permission.

both parties are listed. In 23 of 24 cases, where there was a fight at one of the conventions, the parties took opposite stands. (A negative sign means that the party stood firmly against the citizen group's position; a plus sign means it sided with the group.) In short, citizen groups appear to be quite successful at using conventions to pull the party they are lobbying away from the center of the electorate on at least a few key issues. If pressuring the party they favor to move further to the left or the right costs its candidate votes in November, so be it.

Although both parties must contend with these internal conflicts, the Democrats face a broader and more diverse set of interest group constituencies, citizen and otherwise. There is tension within the party between labor and environmentalists, as well as between white conservatives from the South and the many citizen groups working to expand the rights of blacks, Hispanics, women, and gays and lesbians. The success of citizen groups in focusing the party's agenda toward their issues may have worked against the Democrats by making the party appear to be more concerned with the issues of the poor, minorities, and wealthy liberals than with the issue of how middle-class people make ends meet.[32] For the Republicans, there is the danger of becoming too closely identified with the Christian Coalition.

CONCLUSION

When Dwight Eisenhower gave his acceptance speech at the 1952 Republican convention, he spoke of the national interest and the challenges that lay before the country. He singled out not a single interest group constituency. When George Bush made his acceptance speech at the 1992 Republican convention, he appealed to interest group constituencies a total of 15 times, including four separate references affirming his support of policies backed by the Christian right.[33] These two speeches are symbolic of the growing role of interest groups in party politics. Since interest group politics has grown generally, perhaps this should come as no surprise. Interest groups want to influence public policy; political parties can help them achieve their goals. Yet

---

[32]Berry and Schildkraut, "Citizen Groups, Political Parties, and the Decline of the Democrats."

[33]Berry and Schildkraut, "Citizen Groups, Political Parties, and the Decline of the Democrats," p. 16

the marriage of interest groups to political parties is not a match made in heaven. There are reasons to be concerned about interest group involvement in party affairs.

What is probably most disturbing about the relationship between interest groups and parties is the importance of interest group money in the electoral process. In plain terms, a campaign finance system that relies heavily on PAC money is a system that favors the wealthiest interest group sectors. A further advantage for some interest groups is the soft money that can be contributed to Democratic and Republican organizations for party-building efforts. This is a great advantage to corporations, who can afford to give extravagant gifts to the parties to build good will and buy access. Critics have called soft money sewer money. It's an apt description; soft money smells and it makes the parties dirty.

Interest group influence comes not only from money, but also from the fervor of citizens who band together in lobbies to push for ideological goals. These organizations care less about working with their party to build a strong, united coalition than they are in promoting their own interests and in making the party toe the line on their issues.

What is generally worrisome about the increasing involvement of interest groups in party politics is that one of the great values of parties is that they can serve as a counterweight to the narrowly focused demands of lobbying organizations. Parties can try to balance the efforts that interest groups make by articulating broader, national interests. Walter Dean Burnham writes,

> To state the matter with utmost simplicity: political parties, with all their well-known human and structural shortcomings, are the only devices thus far invented by the wit of Western man which with some effectiveness can generate countervailing collective power on behalf of the many individually powerless against the relatively few who are individually—or organizationally—powerful.[34]

As parties become closer to groups, their majoritarian instincts can be constrained as they must search for ways to reward the groups that are providing their funding or volunteers. Parties, of course, cannot be insensitive to groups demands—they cannot win elections unless they build coalitions of many parts. More than anything else, though, parties should speak for the broad classes of people whose interests are not well represented by lobbying groups.

---

[34]Walter Dean Burnham, *Critical Elections and the Mainsprings of American Politics* (New York: Norton, 1970), p. 133.

Chapter
4

Mobilization and Organization

*T*he impressive growth of interest groups may obscure a simple fact. Even in a bull market for interest groups, not all succeed. Some may be stillborn, not attracting enough money to go beyond initial fundraising efforts. Others may enjoy initial success, then find themselves in gradual decline, slowly losing members and income. Some groups around for a long time will even fold. All this points to a significant question about interest groups: Why is it that people join such organizations?

Political scientists approach this question by asking what people expect to receive in return for dues or contributions and what leaders can do to make their organizations more attractive to potential members. Determining which marketing approaches work best for which constituencies is not the only issue. The problem of who joins and why is, at heart, a matter of representation. The better an organization is at finding and retaining members, the better it will be able to represent its constituents' interests.

The resources collected by an interest group must be allocated among competing demands within the organization. Leaders must decide which issues are of greatest importance to their constituencies and how to apportion staff time and funds to those issues. These questions, too, affect the way an interest group is able to represent its members before government.

COMPETING THEORIES

Ideally, political scientists would like to be able to predict when and under what circumstances new interest groups will form. A theory of interest group formation should specify the factors important in this formation and should further specify which of these factors are crucial to a new group's success or failure. By examining successful groups and groups that have died, scholars have tried to isolate the critical determinants in their formation.

Disturbances

A starting point for serious discussion of interest group origins is David Truman's classic work, *The Governmental Process,* which presents a pluralist vision of how interest groups come to form.[1] For Truman, interest groups are the product of two related forces. The first is society's growing complexity. As the economy and society change, new interests are formed, while others lose importance. The Brotherhood of Sleeping Car Porters was formed after the railroads developed. Although railroads transformed the American economy, they eventually declined, and the porters' union shrank along with them. Contemporary technology, however, has given us cable television and, as we might expect, a new lobby, the National Cable Television Association.

Evolving industry and society give rise to many new interests. Not all new interest groups, however, are directly linked to a new technology or profession. The second part of Truman's explanation, dealing with changing political and economic conditions, is more controversial. Truman states that people who share an interest but are as yet unorganized are brought together when they are adversely affected by a "disturbance"—some identifiable event or series of events that alter the "equilibrium" in some sector of society. The economic downturn in the 1870s disturbed the equilibrium of farmers, and that instability spurred development of the Grange. Truman writes, "Between 1873 and late 1874 the number of local Granges increased in number from about three thousand to over twenty thousand, paralleling an increase in mortgage foreclosures."[2]

---

[1]David B. Truman, *The Governmental Process* (New York: Knopf, 1951).
[2]Truman, *The Governmental Process,* p. 88.

The disturbance theory has an appealing logic: A cause-and-effect relationship between events and organizing. If people find that their political or economic interests are being adversely affected, they will organize to rectify the situation. This is the essence of pluralism: People organize when they have a stake in the outcome of controversies over issues.

Like pluralist theory itself, Truman's disturbance explanation of interest group origins is deeply flawed. It is based on optimistic and unjustified assumptions about all people's ability to organize. Those who are poor are repeatedly "disturbed" by adverse events, such as congressional budget cuts, but remain persistently unorganized. Equally damning to Truman's theory is that many groups have formed without a distinct, identifiable disturbance. Throughout the twentieth century migrant farm workers in California have been poorly treated by farmers. Low wages, discrimination, and terrible working conditions gave farm workers more than enough reason to join unions during periodic organizing efforts. But even the mighty AFL-CIO failed to organize them. In the late 1960s, though, a poor farm worker named Cesar Chavez succeeded in unionizing much of the California grape industry. The objective condition of the grape pickers was no worse than it had always been. The critical difference in the success of the United Farm Workers was unquestionably not some outside event but the inspired leadership of Chavez.

Entrepreneurs

It may be that disturbance theory could be refined to take greater account of leadership's influence in starting new groups. Political scientist Robert Salisbury argues convincingly, however, that Truman is fundamentally wrong, and that leadership is the main reason any group succeeds or dies.[3] Salisbury looked at farm groups during the same hard times in the nineteenth century that Truman did but came up with a different conclusion. Salisbury points out that farm organizations began to decline before they had achieved their goals of high, stable commodity prices. If people join groups to overcome some disadvantage, why do they sometimes quit before equilibrium is restored?

---

[3]Robert H. Salisbury, "An Exchange Theory of Interest Groups," *Midwest Journal of Political Science* 13 (February 1969), pp. 1–32.

Salisbury reasons that individuals do not join interest groups strictly because of a disturbance but because they see that benefits will accrue to them from membership. If after joining they feel they are getting their money's worth, they will continue to pay dues. If not, they quit.

In analyzing membership surge and decline, Salisbury emphasizes the role played by each interest group's organizer, or "entrepreneur." He uses this term for the organizer because he likens the founder of a new interest group to the business investor who is willing to risk capital to start a new firm. In the interest group "marketplace," entrepreneurs will succeed if they provide attractive benefits or incentives to potential members. These benefits may be of three kinds.[4]

Material benefits have concrete value. The goal of the Teamsters Union is to improve the economic lot of truck drivers and other Union members. *Purposive* benefits are associated with pursuit of ideological or issue-oriented goals that offer no tangible rewards to members. Those who join the Defenders of Wildlife do so because they have deep ideological convictions about the environment, not because they have anything to gain or lose by changes in the laws affecting preservation of wild animals. Finally, individuals may join a group because of the *solidary*, or social, rewards. Those who join the League of Women Voters rather than other good-government groups may do so because of the network of local chapters where members work together directly participating in politics. A benefit comes from being part of the group's struggle to achieve policy goals.

There is much to Salisbury's theory, for the quality of leadership and the type of benefits offered unquestionably matter in a group's development.[5] Unfortunately, since Salisbury's work appeared, political scientists have not formed more explicit propositions about successful leadership traits and benefit structures for lobbying organizations. Still, Salisbury makes a convincing point: Interest groups operate in a competitive marketplace, and those that do a poor job of providing satisfactory benefits to members will lose to more skillful entrepreneurs.

---

[4]Salisbury uses the typology from Peter B. Clark and James Q. Wilson's "Incentive Systems: A Theory of Organizations," *Administrative Science Quarterly* 6 (September 1961), pp. 129–166, in describing interest group incentive systems. We will also use the Clark and Wilson typology.

[5]Jeffrey M. Berry, "On the Origins of Public Interest Groups: A Test of Two Theories," *Polity* 10 (Spring 1978), pp. 379–397.

Selective Incentives

Another attack on the pluralist idea that people join interest groups because they are being adversely affected by public policy is in economist Mancur Olson's *The Logic of Collective Action.*[6] Like Salisbury, Olson says that people contribute money to interest groups because they receive some benefit in return. He goes beyond this, however, claiming that it generally makes sense for individuals to contribute to a group only if they get a selective benefit in return. This benefit goes only to group members, unlike a collective good, which can be shared by members and nonmembers alike.

Does it make sense for someone in business to contribute to the Chamber of Commerce to support its lobbying? If the Chamber succeeds in getting a tax bill favorable to business through Congress, people in business will profit whether they are members of the organization or not. A general change in the tax law is thus a collective rather than a selective good. Olson feels, then, that it is irrational for people in business to support the Chamber solely for its political advocacy, because they can be "free riders" and still enjoy benefits from its lobbying. He says a major reason people join is that the local Chambers of Commerce "are good places for businessmen to make 'contacts' and exchange information."[7] Only Chamber members can take advantage of the selective benefit of going to meetings, making contacts, and gaining valuable business information.

Olson makes some allowances in this general theory for cases where selective incentives do not form the basis for a group's success. Individuals in labor unions are exempted because they commonly work in closed shops, wherein membership is mandatory. Groups with small constituencies, such as an industry with only a handful of companies, do not need a selective incentive because they can exert peer pressure on nonmembers. Visibly absent nonmembers can be singled out for not doing their part.

Olson's important contribution is in drawing attention to the importance of selective incentives. They can be powerful inducements for membership in large economic interest groups. For other types of organizations, the theory is considerably weaker. Few national citizen groups offer their members any real benefits other than ideological sat-

---

[6]Mancur Olson, Jr., *The Logic of Collective Action* (New York: Schocken, 1968).
[7]Olson, *The Logic of Collective Action,* p. 146.

isfaction. No selective benefit leads people to contribute to the Natural Resources Defense Council or the American Center for Law and Justice. Olson acknowledges that his theory works poorly for these "philanthropic" lobbies.[8] Yet there are simply too many citizen groups, attracting too many members and millions of dollars, to be dismissed as anomalous or products of "irrational" behavior.

The pervasiveness of ideological lobbying also throws some doubt on the theory's adequacy when applied to business, farm, and professional organizations. Membership surveys show that an economic group's lobbying can be a significant incentive for those who join.[9] Even Olson's own example of the Chamber of Commerce is not wholly persuasive. When the Chamber became more active and visible in its political work, it saw its membership skyrocket. There may have been other causes for this, but its political vigor is surely one reason for that rise.[10] Do business people who join the Chamber of Commerce care less about the free-enterprise system than members of the Sierra Club care about the environment? It is difficult to answer with certainty, but business associations do offer members the opportunity to *mix* politics with business.

Olson claims that the lobbying activity of large economic interest groups is a by-product of other organizational activities that draw and hold members. Groups "obtain their strength and support" by offering selective incentives.[11] Viewing lobbying as a by-product may, however, underestimate how important political activities are in attracting and maintaining members.[12] The directors of Washington lobbies make a concerted effort to keep members informed of the political issues facing their organizations and of the lobbying work being carried out. Although many members of economic organizations would not join but for the selective benefits, those who run these groups clearly regard lobbying as an essential part of the organizations' appeal to members.

---

[8]Olson, *The Logic of Collective Action,* pp. 159–165.
[9]See Terry M. Moe, *The Organization of Interests* (Chicago: University of Chicago Press, 1980); and David Marsh, "On Joining Interest Groups," *British Journal of Political Science* 6 (July 1976), pp. 257–272.
[10]Ann Crittenden, "A Stubborn Chamber of Commerce," *New York Times,* June 27, 1982; and William J. Lanouette, "Chamber's Ponderous Decision Making Leaves It Sitting on the Sidelines," *National Journal,* July 24, 1982, pp. 1298–1301.
[11]Olson, *The Logic of Collective Action,* p. 132.
[12]John Mark Hansen, "The Political Economy of Group Membership," *American Political Science Review* 79 (March 1985), pp. 79–96.

What can we say in summary about these three theories of interest group formation? In looking at all three together and assessing their arguments, what do social scientists know and not know about the origins of interest groups?

1. New interest groups do evolve naturally out of changes in technology and the ever-increasing complexity of society. This evolution does not, however, explain why all groups form. Nor does it explain why one organization successfully comes to represent a new interest while another fails.

2. Disturbances (wars, turns in the business cycle, and so on) can help new interest groups form by making potential members aware of the need for political action. Disturbances are not necessary for interest group formation, though, because many groups originate without one.

3. Interest group constituencies vary widely; some are much more difficult to organize than others. Business executives may respond readily to an organization that allows them to mix their concern for free-market politics with social interaction with other business people. On the other hand, people who are desperately poor will be hard to organize under any circumstances.

4. Because interest groups operate in a competitive environment, leaders must make their organizations as appealing as possible to current and potential members. Selective incentives add to the attractiveness of membership.

SUPPLY OF BENEFITS

The work of Salisbury and Olson suggests that an organizer's chance of successfully forming an interest group is determined by the benefits offered to potential members. We will now go beyond the abstract notions of collective goods, selective benefits, and entrepreneurs to discuss more concretely the benefits leaders actually offer to their members.

Material Benefits

Any individuals or corporations who give their money to an interest group do so because they feel something worthwhile will result from the organization's activities. Consciously or subconsciously, potential contributors ask themselves one or both of these questions: (1) "If I donate this money, what will I get in return?" and (2) "If I donate this money, what will society get in return?" Material benefits are the tangible rewards that individuals or companies get in return for their donations.

The most common material reward one can get from contributing to an interest group is information. Nearly every group sends members some type of publication with articles directed at their interests. The larger, well-endowed groups will often publish magazines. The purpose is to give individuals an attractive, polished publication with articles covering the readers' broad interests rather than focusing exclusively on political issues. Only as a secondary focus does the American Bankers Association's glossy and sophisticated *Banking Journal* cover Washington politics. Another ABA publication, *Bankers News,* comes out biweekly in an inexpensive newspaper format and places greater emphasis on regulatory activity in Washington. It is sent to 26,000 members, whereas all 40,000 members receive *Banking Journal.* Once a week a third publication, *ABA Insider,* is sent out to a select group of members who have a more immediate need to know what's going on in Washington. *ABA Insider* is a fax running one to three pages in length and it focuses on current regulatory and legislative actions.

The information in interest group publications is useful to members because it can educate them on developments in their industry or profession and advise them of government actions that may affect their lives. It is difficult to generalize with any precision on just how important publications are to members and how the publications influence the decision to join or contribute. Yet in reading through samples of different organizations' publications, one is led to the inescapable conclusion that most interest groups provide their rank-and-file members with far more information than they can ever want to read. A lobbyist for a food-industry trade association said, "We bore them with information."

Information overkill by interest groups is not a bad membership strategy—far from it. Washington lobbies devote substantial resources to publications because these reinforce members' appreciation of what the national organization is doing. Publications are periodic proof that members' money is well spent. For the circle of activists in any organization, publications provide useful information to help in their political work. For the larger segment of rank-and-file members of the group, publications provide reassurance that someone is speaking on their behalf in Washington.

Another possible material reward that groups offer to members is some form of direct service. The U.S. Conference of Mayors assists individual mayors when they are in Washington to lobby the government on some matter. Its staff is at the mayors' disposal to work on individual projects. Says one lobbyist, "There is constant contact. . . . I'd say that I personally speak to five or six mayors each day." Some organizations like the National Federation of Independent Business have "caseworkers" on their staff to handle individual problems brought to them by member businesses.

Most membership services, however, are those provided without much personalized attention by staffers outside of the government relations section of the organization. The American Association of Retired Persons (AARP) offers a variety of services to its 33 million members, including a mail discount pharmacy, a motor club, a money market fund, and health insurance. This organization's lobbying is a by-product of other activities that bring members into the group. When the organization surveyed its members, only 17 percent said they joined because the group was concerned about the elderly. Twenty-two percent cited the group's publications as a reason, while 8 percent mentioned the health and drug benefits, 7 percent the health insurance, 5 percent the motor club, and 3 percent the money market fund.[13] Unlike most citizens groups, the AARP does not depend on the ideological fervor of its constituents to sustain itself.

The most important material reward is, of course, a change in public policy that directly benefits members. All groups make vague promises to deliver, but it is risky to promise specific policy rewards on any immediate schedule. If a group offers quick results rather than steady representation in Washington, the lack of success can easily disillusion members. The American Agriculture Movement, a protest-oriented group born late in the 1970s, worked for quick relief from inadequate market prices. After some initial government help no other visible successes followed, and lacking other attractive material benefits, the group began to lose membership. Arguments over strategy to be used to reinvigorate the organization badly factionalized it, and a splinter group of dissidents formed.[14]

Lobbying may be born out of specific policy conflicts ("disturbances"), but it is best for an organization to convince members that the material policy benefits will accrue gradually. In an organization's

---

[13]Paul Light, *Artful Work,* 2nd ed. (New York: McGraw-Hill, 1995), p. 73.
[14]Allan J. Cigler, "From Protest Group to Interest Group: The Making of the American Agriculture Movement, Inc.," in Allan J. Cigler and Burdett A. Loomis, eds., *Interest Group Politics,* 2nd ed. (Washington, D.C.: Congressional Quarterly, 1986), pp. 46–69.

early years, the professional staff may find themselves trying to broaden the scope of the lobbying beyond the initial issue that brought members in so that their success will not be seen as tied to that one issue.

Purposive Benefits

When people join organizations pursuing policy objectives that are of no direct, material benefit to them, they are said to be attracted by purposive incentives. Thousands of organizations across the country offer members only one thing: satisfaction that they have done their part to make the world a better place. Whether the group's goal is ending the arms race, putting prayer back in public schools, protecting endangered species, keeping the United States out of another country's civil war, or fighting pornography, people join to further a cause, not their own material self-interest.

Why do people voluntarily join a group that relies on purposive incentives? Research on political socialization reveals that parents strongly influence their children's political views—not only their partisan identification but also their general ideological attitudes. Political participation is also related to socioeconomic status: the more highly educated and wealthy an individual, the more likely he or she will participate in all forms of political activity. Schools socialize children toward believing that participation in politics is vital and that all citizens must take some responsibility for the well-being of their community. As adults, people may acquire skills on the job that are transferrable to political organizations.[15] Joining civic organizations is part of the "American way," and adults who belong to any type of political organization believe they are fulfilling part of their civic responsibilities as well as advancing their own political views. Finally, the propensity for becoming involved with political organizations can be influenced by critical events in one's life. A study of early activists in the fight to legalize abortion found that the women "shared personal experiences with the problems of abortion. Indeed, illegal abortion [for themselves or friends] had been a stark fact of their reproductive lives."[16]

---

[15]See Sidney Verba, Kay Lehman Schlozman, and Henry E. Brady, *Voice and Equality* (Cambridge, Mass.: Harvard University Press, 1995), pp. 313–320.

[16]Kristin Luker, *Abortion and the Politics of Motherhood* (Berkeley: University of California Press, 1984), p. 101.

The correlations between variables such as education and political participation reflect tendencies rather than deterministic laws of behavior. We cannot accurately predict why any person will care enough about politics to donate money or time to an ideological organization. For whatever reasons—family, opportunities, experiences, and individual personality—those who join share the feeling that they must do something beyond just voting.

The benefit you get in return for committing resources to a group primarily offering purposive incentives is that you have made at least a small contribution to the betterment of society. Although this reward is vague and abstract, these groups pursue visible, substantive issues. Contributions to Amnesty International will be used to fight torture, human rights violations, and political imprisonments by authoritarian regimes. Donating to the group is a very direct way to link one's concern for the oppressed with political advocacy on their behalf. The degree to which an individual's contribution works to accomplish such a goal as stopping abuses of human and political rights is obviously rather negligible. Donors adopt the attitude, however, that even though their own contributions cannot possibly be critical to the organization's continuing existence or success, the organization could not exist if everyone took that view.

Solidary Benefits

One advantage of ideological groups is that they are a "cheap" way to participate in politics. For the busy individual who worries about the problem of campaign finance, but has neither the time nor true commitment to work personally on the issue, mailing a $30 check to Common Cause can fulfill a need to do something. For many Americans, though, mailing a check off to Washington is not enough—they want to be involved.

When people volunteer their time to a political organization, they are powerfully motivated by their ideology. Yet they are also motivated by the desire to work and associate with others. Stuffing a check into an envelope is a political act, but it lacks the drama and excitement and enjoyment of politics. The solidary incentive is the inducement to be part of a collective struggle with like-minded colleagues.

The activists in a political organization can form a community for the individuals who come to devote their time to it. In an organization like Operation Rescue, which has engaged in actions such as blocking abortion clinics, solidary incentives play a crucial role. The small number of activists who form a chapter of the organization give strength to each other by reaffirming the value of their protests. The support activists give each other contributes to their own sense of well-being, their belief that they are doing something important. While those outside the organization may regard Operation Rescue as rather obnoxious, those inside it find the joint struggle with their comrades to be personally fulfilling.

Social incentives are not usually as significant as they are in Operation Rescue, but it is common for them to have at least some role in an interest group. In the National Association of Broadcasters (NAB), busy corporate executives who run the member television and radio stations can gain social benefits from NAB activities. Like so many other national associations, it has a circle of activists in each state whose responsibility is being grassroots lobbyists. These broadcasters will work to influence their own legislators in Washington. They will do such work at the request of NAB staffers and derive the satisfaction of taking part in a coordinated advocacy effort to help the industry. Some status too can be gained by dealing with members of Congress and their staffs, who are receptive to talking with such important constituents. The NAB's annual convention offers further social (as well as material) inducements that give members a chance to socialize, do business, meet with Federal Communications Commission officials and members of Congress who appear there, and enjoy camaraderie in the collective fight for sensible government policy toward broadcasting.

The role of solidary incentives varies among interest groups. These may be at the core of the decision to join Operation Rescue but have nothing to do with the decision to donate money to the National Committee for an Effective Congress. When social incentives do play a role, they must still be combined with other incentives. Solidary benefits can only complement the avowed purposive or material goals of a lobbying organization.

The Mix of Benefits

Each organization has its own benefit structure that affects its ultimate success in attracting and maintaining members. If entrepreneurs cannot offer appealing benefits to their constituency, the group will cease to exist. Can it be said that the organizers' choice of benefits to offer is an overriding factor in organizational development? Although significant, it is difficult to explain the rise or fall of many interest groups in terms of specific benefit choices made by leaders. One reason is that choices are fairly limited. The variety of benefits to choose from is not endless, and the ones that can be used may already be widely available. Nothing is novel about a new interest group publishing a topnotch newsletter, giving members a chance to work at the grassroots, or offering members the satisfaction of belonging and doing their part. Services not readily available elsewhere can sometimes be developed, of course, but cost and administrative feasibility are serious constraints on what may ultimately be offered, especially for modest-sized organizations.

Newly forming interest groups often find themselves in a highly competitive market with existing groups and must be quite adept at targeting their potential membership. Finding a particular niche to target may be far more important than the exact nature of the benefits themselves.[17] A new general business organization is going to be a tough sell given the substantial competition that already exists. The American Business Conference was able to attract a membership by its focus on rapidly growing firms. No group had previously seen that constituency as a niche in the business interest groups marketplace.

In the final analysis, it is often hard for organizers (or political scientists) to know exactly which benefits or combination of benefits bring people into different organizations. In many groups, members receive a package, and it is not easy to distinguish which part of the package is most essential to their participation. A single group can offer social, material, and ideological incentives to join. Asking members their most important reason for joining provides some clues as to the comparative value of benefits, but it may be the overall package that makes the group so attractive.[18] In time, the information an individual receives may turn out to be the most valued part of the membership, but he or she might never have joined if there had not been the promise of aggressive lobbying in Washington. In the real world, the

---

[17]William P. Browne, "Organized Interests and Their Issue Niches," *Journal of Politics* 52 (May 1990), pp. 477–509.

[18]Groups that use direct mail do pretest their appeals to see what kind of material inducements produce the largest return. See Paul E. Johnson, "How Environmental Groups Recruit Members: Does the Logic Still Hold Up?," paper delivered at the annual meeting of the American Political Science Association, Chicago, September, 1995, pp. 17–18.

benefits blend in a member's mind, and it is difficult for entrepreneurs to determine which parts of their package are critical to making the sum so attractive.

MARKETING INTEREST GROUPS: DIRECT MAIL

If an organization operates in a competitive environment and offers benefits similar to those of other groups, how aggressively it markets itself may make the critical difference in its ultimate success. The segment of the interest group community in which competition is probably fiercest is that of citizen groups. For almost every conceivable constituency, there are overlapping groups. Conservatives have a choice between literally dozens of national citizen groups who promise to lobby vigorously for conservative policies. The same is true for liberals who face a seemingly endless variety of groups asking for their support.

Citizen groups frequently depend on direct mail to solicit members or donations from people around the country. Direct mail campaigns often involve mailings of hundreds of thousands of individual letters. They are popular with advocacy groups because they are a means of communicating individually with prospective members, bringing to their attention the good work of the organization. Many people will toss direct mail solicitations into the waste basket unopened, considering it junk mail. (One study found that 87 percent of the direct mail appeals by nonprofit organizations are thrown away unopened.)[19] Still, some people do open, read, and ponder the letters. When direct mail works, it can transform an organization. The Center for Science in the Public Interest grew from approximately 32,000 to 80,000 members in a three-year period, an increase the organization attributes to its direct mail operation.

A lobby wanting to engage in a direct mail campaign begins by hiring consultants and renting mailing lists. Consultants are hired because direct mail involves a number of steps requiring expertise as well as expensive computer and printing equipment that few groups have reason to own. Consultants help groups select a mailing list or sets of lists. The larger consulting firms have their own lists of donors to various causes that they rent to clients; other consultants will rent them from brokers.

---

[19]Gregg Easterbrook, "Junk-Mail Politics," *New Republic,* April 25, 1988, p. 21.

Picking a list is critical, because if the mailing turns out poorly, the lobby will lose money, hardly a desirable outcome. Typically, a one-time use of a list rents for about $8,000 for 100,000 names.[20] The usual types of lists give names of people who are members of other interest groups, donors to political campaigns, or subscribers to magazines with a distinctly liberal or conservative point of view. Direct mail has become so popular that lists get used to the point of saturation, inundating the same people with growing numbers of solicitations. A lobbyist for an environmental group complained that "more and more [groups] are using direct mail, which means that each of us gets less money."

Most direct mail solicitations have three important parts. The first is the envelope. What's on the outside is significant because it may determine whether or not the individual will open it and read what's inside. Direct mail designers try to think of ways to spark the reader's curiosity. The conservative Alexis de Tocqueville Institution sent out an envelope designed to look like an official government communication that said only, "NOTICE ENCLOSED: Regarding Public Condemnation of Private Property." When recipients opened up the envelope they were surely relieved to learn that it wasn't their property that was condemned, but if they read the enclosed letter they were told government seizes land because it doesn't care about property rights. The liberal People for the American Way used a large, bold-faced tease that simply said "Two-Faced." Those who opened the envelope could learn about how the Christian Coalition's political director Ralph Reed's moderate statements on the separation of church and state contrast with founder Pat Robertson's far more radical views. Other groups will try to get recipients to open and read the letter by declaring that a poll is enclosed. Some groups use reverse psychology, printing nothing on the envelope but an unidentified return address in Washington or New York, forcing the recipient to open the letter to find out what it contains and who sent it.

Inside is the most important ingredient, the appeal letter. The best letters contain a good amount of detail along with passages that will provoke the reader's emotions. Typically, the letters are four single-spaced pages with significant passages underlined or indented to break up the long blocks of text. The key to direct mail is to make the reader

---

[20]Erik Eckholm, "Alarmed by Fund Raiser, The Elderly Give Millions," *New York Times,* November 12, 1992.

angry or scared. To do so, groups will try to provoke the emotions of recipients by dwelling on a villain, someone the reader likely hates. No sooner had the Republicans taken over the Congress in 1994 than Ralph Nader was out with a direct mail piece that began "There's Newt Gingrich, grinning over the rubble of the Congress he's gleefully tearing apart." In terms of fundraising, Nader told the *Wall Street Journal,* "Oh, is Gingrich going to be wonderful!"[21]

Letters do not simply request money, they demand action by the severity of the situation they describe. After he got through raising the specter of Gingrich unbound, Nader lectured his readers:

> There can be no daily democracy without daily citizenship. If we do not exercise our civic rights, who will? If we do not perform our civic duties, who can? The fiber of a just society in pursuit of happiness is a thinking, active citizenry. That means you.

A common third part of the direct mail package is one or more pieces of literature not written in letter format. Often included is a document offering persuasive evidence that the crisis outlined in the letter is as real as the organization says it is. Alternatively, a document might provide evidence that the organization is worthy of the public's support. The Cato Institute includes a brochure with accolades from leading publications like *Newsweek,* the *New York Times,* and the *Wall Street Journal.* A return envelope and a contributor's card round out the typical direct mail package.

Direct mail is likely to be more successful when it is tied to highly visible current events. During the fight over the ratification of the Panama Canal treaties, conservative groups enjoyed an unusually prosperous period. A torrent of direct mail was sent out by groups like the American Conservative Union, the National Conservative Political Action Committee, the Conservative Caucus, and the Council on Inter-American Security. In the end, somewhere between seven and nine million letters were churned out by conservative groups fighting the treaties, which in turn generated over $3 million in contributions and added over 400,000 names to the mailing lists of the organizations.[22]

---

[21]Timothy Noah, "Liberal Victories May Become Harder to Come By in Wake of Republican Win," *Wall Street Journal,* November 11, 1994.

[22]George D. Moffett III, *The Limits of Victory* (Ithaca: Cornell University Press, 1985), pp. 166–180.

For all the success many groups have had with direct mail, it is still a risky enterprise because of its substantial costs. When a group prospects with a rented list, it's likely to get a response rate of between 1 and 2 percent, usually not enough to cover the costs of the mailing. A group is willing to risk losing money on such prospecting because those who do contribute can be put on the "house list." This list of those who have already contributed to the organization usually generates a response rate of over 10 percent.[23] For that reason a group's members are continually solicited for special contributions. Environmental organizations, for example, send each member an average of around nine mailings a year asking for money.[24]

There are some groups that are best described as direct mail mills, accomplishing little more than providing income to the direct mail consultants and a few entrepreneurs who started the organization. Senior citizen groups have been able to form by sending direct mail to older Americans warning of catastrophic consequences of changes in Social Security or Medicare being considered by the Congress. One group, 60/Plus, raised $1.3 million through direct mail in the space of a year, but the whole organization consists of just two staff members. The United Seniors Association raises $5 million annually, but only a small portion of that is spent on its modest lobbying office of eight employees.[25] When it comes to direct mail from interest groups, let the consumer beware.

MAINTAINING THE ORGANIZATION

Direct mail is but one tool by which interest groups market their "product" and retain their members once they enlist them. Whatever the means, all organizations must maintain themselves by raising money on an ongoing basis so that they may continue to operate. It is not simply a matter of raise money or die. Although organizations can go under if fundraising drops dramatically, the more common problem is keeping funding up to avert project or staff cutbacks. Ideally, of course, interest groups expand their base of support so that they can take on more advocacy, research, membership outreach, and other ac-

[23]R. Kenneth Godwin, *One Billion Dollars of Influence* (Chatham, N.J.: Chatham House, 1988), p. 12.

[24]Johnson, "How Environmental Groups Recruit Members," p. 15.

[25]Marilyn Webber Sarafini, "Senior Schism," *National Journal,* May 6, 1995, p. 1093.

tivities. Fundraising is difficult and competitive, though, and most groups will usually do well to keep up with the annual rate of inflation.

Still, as I emphasized earlier, the number of interest groups has grown significantly, and many interest groups that have been in business for many years have expanded their operations. Use of direct mail indicates a larger trend: Interest groups have been able to market themselves better. There are two parts to this advance. First, entrepreneurs have successfully identified new or undersubscribed markets where members could be found for their organizations. Second, interest group leaders have been able to expand their funding beyond membership dues.

Interest group funds come from a variety of sources. Research by Mark Peterson and Jack Walker demonstrates that different types of groups vary substantially in their dependence on dues. Groups in the "profit-sector" category (mostly trade associations) draw almost two-thirds (63 percent) of their funds from membership dues. Other types of organizations in their survey sample (citizen groups, nonprofits, and profit and nonprofit mixed memberships) receive only about one-third to one-half of their funds from membership dues.[26]

Where does the rest of the money come from? The following sources of money supplement dues as interest group income.

Foundations   Citizen groups, which receive the smallest part of their money from members, are the biggest beneficiaries of foundation grants among all types of lobbies.[27] Liberal public interest groups received extraordinary support from foundations during the 1970s. Between 1970 and 1980, the Ford Foundation contributed roughly $21 million to liberal groups under its public interest law program.[28] In recent years foundations with a conservative outlook have played a key role in funding advocacy organizations on the right. The Smith Richardson, Bradley, and Carthage foundations provided much of the

---

[26]Mark A. Peterson and Jack L. Walker, "Interest Group Responses to Partisan Change," in Cigler and Loomis, *Interest Group Politics,* p. 174.

[27]Peterson and Walker, "Interest Group Responses to Partisan Change," p. 174.

[28]*The Public Interest Law Firm* (New York: Ford Foundation, 1973); *Public Interest Law: Five Years Later* (New York: Ford Foundation, 1976); and "Ford Ends Public Interest Law Program," *Citizen Participation* 1 (January/February 1980), p. 9. See also, Debora Clovis and Nan Aron, "Survey of Public Interest Law Centers," Alliance for Justice, Washington, D.C., n.d.; and Michael Greve and James Keller, *Funding the Left: The Sources of Financial Support for "Public Interest" Law Firms* (Washington, D.C.: Washington Legal Foundation, 1987).

support to get the Center for Individual Rights off the ground. The Center is a public interest law firm that specializes in defending college professors and students who see themselves as the victims of "political correctness" on campus.[29]

Fees and Publications   Money derived from publications, conferences, and training institutes is a common source of interest group income. With their unusually good command of the issues, interest group employees are able to produce handbooks, booklets, and even full-size books that can be marketed to the general public. Staffers for the Health Research Group produced a bestseller, *Pills That Don't Work*, which brought roughly $1 million to the organization.[30] Sales of that magnitude are uncommon, but it is not at all unusual for a group to count on publications for a modest segment of its income. Interest groups can also use specialists on their staffs to attract individuals for conferences, including training institutes that teach participants various business, communications, or political skills.

Wealthy Patrons   Leaders of organizations know that they can substantially increase the group's activities if they can add large individual donations to the sum they raise through regular membership fees. Furthermore, for groups with little or no membership support, large donations from wealthy patrons may be their lifeblood. This was the source for the National Welfare Rights Organization during the few years that it flourished. Its dynamic leader, George Wiley, was effective in face-to-face meetings with wealthy liberals. Some of these, like Anne Farnsworth Peretz (heiress to the Singer Sewing Machine fortune) and Audrey Stern Hess (granddaughter of the founder of Sears, Roebuck), contributed large sums to keep the militant civil rights organization going for a while.[31]

---

[29]Davidson Goldin, "A Law Center Wages Fight Against Political Correctness," *New York Times,* August 13, 1995.

[30]Michael deCourcy Hinds, "Advocacy Units Seek New Funds," *New York Times,* January 9, 1982.

[31]Nick Kotz and Mary Lynn Kotz, *A Passion for Equality* (New York: Norton, 1977), pp. 241–242. See also, Anthony J. Nownes and Allan J. Cigler, "Public Interest Groups and the Road to Survival," *Polity* 27 (Spring 1995), pp. 379–404.

A group representing people on welfare certainly needs large donations, yet many other kinds of interest groups rely in part on such gifts. The National Association of Manufacturers receives a disproportionate share of its funds from a few very large firms that are members. These large gifts in the form of sliding-scale dues give the lobby tremendous financial resources while allowing it to keep dues reasonable for smaller manufacturers and thereby retain them in the organization.[32]

Government Grants   A main factor in interest groups' growth during the 1960s and 1970s was the parallel growth in domestic spending by the federal government. The categorical grant programs of this era increased the funds available to citizen groups, nonprofit professional organizations, and trade associations. These groups aggressively sought federal grant money for training, planning, economic development, and other activities and projects.

The Council of State Community Development Agencies (COSCDA) is an example. It started in 1974 with a budget for the year of $25,000. Its two staff members were supported by dues from 9 states. Within six years it had grown to a nine-person staff and an annual budget of around one-half million dollars. All 50 states had become members, but most of the budget's growth came from grants by the Economic Development Administration, the Farmers' Home Administration, the Office of Personnel Management, and the National Science Foundation.

As the federal government's budget deficit deepened and conservatives gained in power, administrative agencies have been under pressure to reduce their support of advocacy organizations. Since the Reagan administration started cutting domestic programs in 1980, COSCDA's growth has been curtailed. The group's budget in 1994 was $600,000, an increase of only $100,000 since 1980. Its staff has been reduced to as low as four. As grants from the government shrunk, dues were raised, but they have not offset the loss of those funds. Since most of the groups that have significant government support are liberal, it is no surprise that when Republicans have controlled the White House or

---

[32]Moe, *The Organization of Interests,* pp. 193–194.

Congress, they have tried to eliminate the grant programs that provide such funds.[33]

When an interest group loses income from one of these sources, it must either cut its budget or find new sources of income. Sometimes there are no new potential members to recruit. Corporate downsizing in the railroad industry meant fewer dollars for the Association of American Railroads, the trade group that represents the industry. With no new railroads to approach about joining up, the organization cut its budget by 22 percent and laid off 90 employees, half of whom worked in the Washington office.[34] Groups can be affected by changes in the political environment as well as by the economic environment. The environmental movement enjoyed spectacular expansion from the 1960s through the 1980s, but the softening economy in the early 1990s appeared to have curtailed growth.[35] When Bill Clinton captured the presidency in 1992, it was a further blow to fundraising by the environmental movement because Clinton was considered highly sympathetic to the cause, unlike his two predecessors, George Bush and Ronald Reagan. For those concerned about the environment, there was less to worry about with Clinton in office and, thus, less reason to send money off to the Sierra Club, the Wilderness Society, Friends of the Earth, or countless other environmental groups.

With all the vagaries of fundraising, interest groups must work continually to identify new sources of income. Otherwise, they risk organizational decline. If a group can weather a difficult storm, it may come out stronger in the end. During the heyday of the civil rights movement in the early 1960s, the NAACP, the Student Nonviolent Co-

---

[33]See Christopher Georges, "Republicans Take Aim at Left-Leaning Groups That Get Federal Grants for Assistance Programs," *Wall Street Journal,* May 17, 1995. More broadly, Republicans succeeded in cutting categorical grant and benefit programs supported by liberals. See Paul Peterson, "The Rise and Fall of Special Interest Politics," in Mark P. Petracca, ed., *The Politics of Interests* (Boulder, Colo.: Westview, 1992), pp. 326–342.

[34]Peter H. Stone, "From the K Street Corridor," *National Journal,* December 10, 1994, p. 2913.

[35]See Christopher Boerner and Jennifer Chilton Kallery, *Restructuring Environmental Big Business,* Occasional Paper #146, Center for the Study of American Business, Washington University, December 1994; and Christopher J. Bosso, "The Color of Money: Environmental Groups and the Pathologies of Fund Raising," in Allan J. Cigler and Burdett A. Loomis, eds., *Interest Group Politics,* 4th ed. (Washington, D.C.: Congressional Quarterly, 1995), pp. 101–130.

ordinating Committee (SNCC), the Congress of Racial Equality (CORE), and the Southern Christian Leadership Conference (SCLC) all enjoyed growing support among liberals. As the mood of the country changed and financial support began to diminish, SNCC, CORE, and SCLC did not adapt and devise new ways to appeal to donors or expand their base of funding. Increasingly, they were seen as militant, and the more moderate NAACP prospered in the long run. The other three never regained their support, and all eventually lost their standing in the civil rights movement.[36] Since organizational finance is such a critical priority, groups devote considerable internal resources to such efforts and research shows that unlike the civil rights groups discussed here, lobbies have had a good deal of success in adapting to changing fundraising environments.[37]

WHO GOVERNS?

Membership dues and other funds raised by interest groups must be converted into actions representing the donors' interests. This work is critical to any lobby's overall effectiveness. Interest groups are organizations, and the way in which each organization makes decisions about its resources directly affects how well members' interests are represented before government.

Authority

Like any other type of organization, interest groups must have a means for governing themselves. Even the smallest group with no more than a handful of staff members creates roles giving some workers more authority than others. The authority structure of an interest group generally provides a framework for decision making on allocating resources, selection of issues, personnel, change in leadership, lobbying tactics, bylaws, and accountability of staff.

A common impulse among voluntary associations is to create a democratic organizational structure to govern themselves. The founding

---

[36]Doug McAdam, *Political Process and the Development of Black Insurgency, 1930–1970* (Chicago: University of Chicago Press, 1982), pp. 208–213.
[37]Jack L. Walker, *Mobilizing Interest Groups in America* (Ann Arbor: University of Michigan Press, 1991).

bylaws of an interest group almost always prescribe a procedure whereby some body representing the membership, such as a board of directors or an annual convention, has final authority over all major decisions. Even if, like some public interest groups, a lobby has no real membership, it is still likely to have an independent governing board with formal (if rarely exercised) authority over staff operations.[38] But even if the board of directors is usually a passive body willing to let the professional staff run the organization as they please, it is an important safety valve when trouble strikes. When it was revealed that the executive director of the NAACP, Reverend Benjamin Chavis, spent organizational funds to settle a personal lawsuit against him, the board stepped in and fired Chavis for this impropriety and for general financial mismanagement.[39]

Just as it is true that interest groups almost always appear on the outside to be democratic, it also seems that they are almost always oligarchic on the inside.[40] This contradiction will not surprise anyone who has belonged to a voluntary organization. A small cadre of workers invariably dominates such organizations. Relatively few of the rank and file feel they have much time to devote to the organizations they belong to. The full-time staff or officers, with their greater command over information and organizational resources, easily gain preeminent influence within the organization. This natural tendency, which sociologist Robert Michels described as the "iron law of oligarchy," is pervasive among interest groups.[41]

Although interest groups are generally oligarchic, groups differ in the amount of influence the rank and file have within the organization. In some lobbies, members do actually exert some significant and direct influence on organizational decisions, yet these differences are not easily explained by the way lobbying organizations are designed. Compare the American Hospital Association (AHA) and the U.S. Conference of Mayors. Both have conventions twice yearly at which the memberships have an opportunity to formulate policy. Both also have boards that

---

[38]Jeffrey M. Berry, *Lobbying for the People* (Princeton: Princeton University Press, 1977), pp. 195–199.

[39]John H. Cushman, Jr., "Short of Cash, N.A.A.C.P. Stops Paying Its Employees," *New York Times,* November 2, 1994.

[40]Truman, *The Governmental Process,* pp. 139–155.

[41]Robert Michels, *Political Parties* (New York: Free Press, 1958). Originally published in 1915.

meet periodically during the year to make timely decisions about questions of policy.

The similarity in the formal governing structures of these organizations tells little about the way they are actually run. Mayors have a much larger part in their organization than hospital administrators do in theirs. An AHA spokesperson said that issues are not brought "raw" to the House of Delegates' conferences. Rather, the staff "massages the issues through the system," so that by the time they hit the agenda of the House of Delegates, the positions are fairly clear. A spokesperson for the Conference of Mayors paints a different picture. The large conventions and board meetings give the mayors an opportunity to set priorities. "Lobbying is completely determined by the policies passed by the mayors," said one staffer.

Why the differences between the organizations? To the AHA lobbyist, the marginal role played by rank-and-file members makes perfect sense. "Statutory and regulatory problems are the business of AHA. The hospital administrators are too busy running their hospitals." Mayors, on the other hand, see statutory and regulatory problems as very much their business. As elected officials, they feel more comfortable and confident dealing in the political world. Also, the partisan differences between Republican and Democratic mayors places an unusual constraint on the organization. Mayors of the party controlling the White House do not want the organization staff working against the president's domestic policies unless they give them specific permission to do so.

Some organizations make a concerted effort to elicit the members' views before setting policies. Common Cause polls its members; then its board uses the responses in setting priorities. Yet the vast majority of interest groups use a governing structure like that of the AHA and the Conference of Mayors, whose board and possibly national conference are the means by which members theoretically control the staff. In most of these groups, the staff runs the organization with modest guidance and little direct interference.

In sum, then, we have two conclusions. First, the governing structures of lobbies, as laid out in their written charters, usually do little to stop the iron law of oligarchy from taking hold. Only if a group takes exceptional steps to build in polling or some other device for direct control by the members does the formal structure of a lobbying organization affect the way the group is governed. Second, if rank-and-file members of an organization want more than a passive role in making decisions, they must prove to the lobbying staff that they will be highly active and will not acquiesce to faits accomplis. Few organizations have this type of membership.

Anticipation

Dominance by staff in most interest groups may seem to be a rather undemocratic and disconcerting part of interest group politics. Still, though members generally have very little direct influence over the staff of their organization, they do have a great deal of indirect influence. Remember that most interest groups are voluntary organizations. Members can "vote with their feet" by leaving the group if they don't like what the organization is doing.[42]

That membership is generally voluntary is fundamental to the relationship between leaders and followers in these organizations. Members join groups because they agree strongly with their goals. As noted earlier, even if some service is an attractive inducement to join, political goals can remain an instrumental part of the decision. Consequently, rank-and-file members usually do not worry about how important organizational decisions are made because they observe the lobbying group pursuing the issues they feel strongly about. A trade association lobbyist said of his membership: "They care about the results, not how we get them."

Despite the trust members have in their staffs, continued support of those members is not ensured. The initial issues that bring people into a group may lose importance and be replaced by others. The staff must anticipate members' reactions to these new issues as they rise to the fore. As the organization leaders consider how to approach an issue, they ask themselves what their members want. Said one lobbyist, "I have to put myself into the heads of the members." It is not usually difficult for them to anticipate the membership's preferences, however, because limited resources largely restrict groups to their most important issues. Environmental groups do not have to stop to think about whether their members are in favor of strengthening the Clean Air Act when it comes before Congress.

---

[42]Albert O. Hirschman, *Exit, Voice, and Loyalty* (Cambridge: Harvard University Press, 1970); and Lawrence S. Rothenberg, *Linking Citizens to Government* (New York: Cambridge University Press, 1992), pp. 100–124.

Yet there are times when those governing an interest group cannot take the membership's stance on an issue for granted. A difficult problem arises when an issue affects some members of a group differently than others. The American Petroleum Institute (API) is an example. Many proposals pertaining to the oil industry affect companies quite differently because they vary in size, ranging from giants like Exxon and Mobil to the small independent wildcatter. Smaller companies often want to be treated separately by Congress when it is writing tax laws for the industry, knowing that there is more sympathy for the "little guy" than for huge corporations. As a result, says one API lobbyist, consensus on many issues is a "long time coming." On broad issues cutting across the membership, API's stand is sometimes "no stand" due to lack of consensus.

Occasionally interest groups are subjected to outright rebellion by dissidents in the organization. Labor unions seem most susceptible to open conflict within the ranks. A primary reason is that labor union members cannot really vote with their feet and leave the organization if they are dissatisfied. Workers who begin employment at a plant or office where union membership is required are not given a choice as to which union to join. Thus, it is not rare for a union presidency to be contested by differing factions. The whole AFL-CIO was split in 1995 when 73-year-old President Lane Kirkland announced he was running for another term. The decline in the position of organized labor bothered many rank-and-file members and union leaders, and dissident unions announced they would support another candidate. Under pressure, Kirkland finally bowed out, and an open election between two candidates led to John Sweeney's selection as head of the labor federation later in the year.[43]

For every lobby that has an open fight for control of the organization, however, hundreds of interest groups hear nary a discouraging word from their members. Harmony continues in most groups because of congruence between members' opinions and the avowed purposes of the organization. Also, in voluntary organizations, most internal protest consists of the relatively passive act of failing to renew one's

---

[43]Louis Uchitelle, "Battle for Presidency of A.F.L.-C.I.O. Emerges After Kirkland Withdraws from Race," *New York Times,* June 11, 1995; and Peter T. Kilborn, "Militant Is Elected Head of A.F.L.-C.I.O., Signaling Sharp Turn for Labor Movement," *New York Times,* October 26, 1995.

membership. Finally, peace usually reigns within interest groups because staff members are careful not to move the organization toward policy positions that are likely to alienate a significant portion of the membership. For almost all interest group staffers, maintaining the organization is more important than ideological purity.

MAKING DECISIONS

We have dwelt on how organizations are designed to carry out their tasks and who has the authority to decide what those tasks will be. We can now study the actual dynamics of how decisions are made.

In the minority of organizations whose members are heavily involved, the decision-making structure becomes complex because of the broader participation. Such organizations must develop a practical means of selecting issues to lobby upon. No matter how democratic an organization sincerely wants to be, it is unwieldy to involve large numbers of people in making decisions. One means of getting periodic membership input into decision making is to have an executive council of members that meets every few months. As noted earlier, when members are given this type of formal opportunity to participate, they must be aggressive in staking out their role; if not, they can quickly come to play a minor part in the organization. Another method is the task force, on which the Business Roundtable relies to draw upon the prestige and influence of chief executive officers of member firms. To successfully involve these CEOs and to get them to commit time to the organization, they must be given a real say in deciding its direction.

The Business Roundtable has task forces in international trade, regulatory reform, antitrust, taxation, energy, and many other areas, all chaired by a CEO of a member firm. By the staff's account, the chairmen of these task forces are quite active in developing the policy recommendations to be made. Yet in the Roundtable, as in so many other lobbies, deciding on issue positions is not the dilemma they face. Rather, says a top official of the group, the real question the CEOs find themselves asking is, "Why do *we* have to get in on this issue?"

Even this relatively wealthy organization, with its budget in the low millions and with access to the resources of member firms, is limited in the number of issues it can work on. For interest groups, the law of resources is that *on any given day, any given group will have more relevant issues before it than it can possibly handle.* Whether a group is staff dominated or has some direct membership influence, allocating resources between issues is the most troublesome part of making decisions.

How do organizations deal with this problem of setting priorities? There are no clear-cut decision rules, but this description by a lobbyist for the National Council of Senior Citizens (NCSC) is instructive:

> We try to [make decisions] on as rational a basis as possible. We first judge the potential impact on older people. Generally speaking, we represent all elderly people, but primarily due to our own lack of resources, we concern ourselves with the low-income elderly. We are more likely, therefore, to be more involved with an issue like a reduction in the cost of living adjustment rather than the reauthorization of the FTC—although there are issues there of concern to all elderly. We try to quantify things. We make judgments based on the [interests of the] needier. We also have to make judgments on the basis of timeliness. Things change. It's an evolving sort of process here in Washington. We have to govern our flow of work on the basis of how things come up on Capitol Hill. This tends to create some confusion. Sometimes it's not easy to decide what to let go of.

A number of important points about decision making by interest groups appear in this account. First, leaders of interest groups do try to think systematically about how to budget their resources. The National Council of Senior Citizens tries to be "rational" and to "quantify things." Yet the lobbyist also acknowledges that much of their decision making comes down to "judgment." This is the contradiction that all interest group officials must live with. They do try to think rationally about resource allocations by weighing the merits of each issue in relation to the interests of their constituency. Relative merits, though, can never be calculated by a formula or strict decision rule. Rather, human judgment must be relied upon.

Second, some issues matter so deeply to the organization that without question they must receive high priority for lobbying resources. For the NCSC, any proposed "reduction in the cost of living adjustment" is a vital issue since it determines the degree to which Social Security payments keep up with the rate of inflation. Some issues command a large commitment of an organization's resources; other decisions must be made around those issues. As the lobbyist for another group put it, "On the hot issues, we know what they are and there's little debating."

Third, the timeliness of issues makes planning extremely hard. Interest groups do not control their own destiny because they cannot control the political agenda. Social Security has always been of the utmost concern to the elderly, but it has waxed and waned as a major political issue. As a practical matter, though, just how and when issues begin to take center stage can catch even the most experienced lobbyists off guard. No matter how carefully an interest group plans allocation of its resources over the next year, it is always going to be it-all-depends planning. A lobbyist for a farm group noted, "In this town, you're dead if you're not able to react quickly."

Fourth, and finally, it is much easier for an interest group to take on a new issue than to drop a current one. Just because a new issue vital to the group arises, other issues do not become unimportant. Consequently, "it's not easy to decide what to let go of." Issues can become less pressing in a relative sense as the lobbyists rush to an emergency that needs their immediate attention. Nevertheless, interest group staffers do not operate on a zero-sum principle; for every new allocation of their time they do not consciously eliminate an equally time-consuming activity. In practice, of course, the zero-sum principle must hold because the day has only so many hours. Issues get crowded out by the demands of more urgent issues without some official articulation of a new ordering of priorities.

These generalizations describe the dynamics of resource allocation. There are, of course, variations. Some years can be stable for an interest group, with few surprise issues or relevant changes in the political environment. Eventually, though, the problems outlined here plague all types of interest groups. They have trouble planning, and their allocation of resources evolves out of incremental decisions, many of which are automatic because they involve issues at the core of the group's purpose.

CONCLUSION

The rapid expansion of interest group advocacy in recent years has focused attention on the sophisticated theorizing on origins and maintenance of lobbying organizations. The work of Truman, Salisbury, and Olson in particular provides insight into the ways in which interest groups form and attract support from constituents. Further research is needed, however, to improve our understanding of the relationship between incentives and the success of groups in attracting members. A next step for researchers is to fully explore how interest groups distinguish themselves in competitive markets and how they try to find niches that can be exploited.

Although a good deal of work has been done on how interest groups originate and how they raise their money, relatively little scholarly work has been done on how lobbies govern themselves. Like most voluntary organizations, lobbies with memberships reflect the iron law of oligarchy. Only in theory are most interest groups democratically governed. They are staff-dominated organizations not simply because rank-and-file members do not have the time to participate at a level that would allow them to be influential, but because the governmental process is highly complex. Members have every reason to defer to the expertise and experience of those on the job in Washington.

An interest group's ability to accomplish its goals is affected by its organizational strengths and weaknesses. We do know that lobbies have trouble establishing firm priorities and that they often find themselves reacting rather than planning. Selecting issues often results from emergencies crowding out older policy concerns. Yet interest groups are not organized in an irrational or even anomalous manner. Whatever their organizational structure or planning process, they have the flexibility to devote the greatest portion of their resources to the policy problems that most affect their members.

Chapter
5

Lobbyists

*T*he word *lobbyist* still conjures up a negative stereotype: a smooth-talking arm-twister. This unsavory image comes from many scandals over the years involving representatives of interest groups who offered some illegal inducement to a government official. No wonder most lobbyists bridle at the title, claiming instead that they work in "public affairs" or "government relations." They resent the name not only because of its unflattering connotations but also because it doesn't adequately describe what they do.

Little of what a contemporary lobbyist does amounts to arm-twisting or pressuring a government official with some sanction if the desired option is not followed. Very few lobbyists have done anything in their work that can be described as unethical. They work long hours under trying conditions to represent their constituents before government. No matter how professional they are on their job, though, theirs is not an occupation that is highly valued by the American people, nor one that is particularly well understood.

A DAY IN THE LIFE OF A LOBBYIST

To appreciate and understand what lobbyists do, it is best to begin by simply asking how they spend their time. In interviews, a number of legislative lobbyists were asked to describe their "typical" day. Their responses, like this from a representative for a professional association, illustrate the job.

I am one of those people who gets to work no later than 7:45. The first hour is spent reading the papers—the *Washington Post, Wall Street Journal,* and *New York Times,* trade association publications, and the *Congressional Record* from the prior day. Each of these plays into my need to plan the activities for the current day. The next activity is meeting with the staff for a brief period to check the work plans for any changes. There is then one or more hearings on the Hill in the morning. After lunch, I usually meet with committee staff or use that time to lobby specific members of Congress. I'm usually back by 4:00 to meet with the support staff to check on what's happened while I was gone and if we are on top of the work planned for the day. About 5:30 I usually leave for some reception or fundraiser to represent [our group]. These settings give me an opportunity to swap stories and positions with members and other lobbyists who are concerned with the same issues we are. I usually get home for dinner about 8:00.

The head lobbyist for a large Midwestern corporation describes her typical day:

We get the *Washington Post, New York Times, Wall Street Journal,* and the Bureau of National Affairs' *Tax Reporter,* so I read the tax-related articles in those papers. Then I go through my in-box. Then I might have meetings on the Hill. I make calls to Capitol Hill or to other lobbyists to obtain information, like current updates on legislation we're following. I might make final preparations on testimony that we're giving. . . . I might attend one or two meetings, either in-house or on the Hill or downtown with other lobbyists. This would be a coalition setup, where we share information, find out the current status of whatever we're interested in, or hand out materials or a document of some sort. . . . Then I might have a luncheon appointment with either another lobbyist or with someone from the Hill, which usually involves talking about jobs. Or someone wants to take me to lunch to give me a resumé. I might then attend a hearing on the Hill. I talk to people from Labor or Treasury on the telephone. Then I might do some correspondence. I might write a follow-up letter to someone I met with the day before or the week before. I talk to my company, which is based in Chicago. I give them updates on legislation or talk about testimony they're going to give here. Then I return phone calls and go back to my in-box. In the evening I attend fundraisers.

Finally, the lobbyist for a tiny public interest group offers this account of his routine:

I don't think I have a typical day. I usually work 8:00 until 6:00. The first half hour is spent reading the papers. . . . I spend a lot of time on the phone finding out what's happening on the Hill—gathering intelligence, I guess you might say. About 9:30 or 10:00, I take off to the Hill for hearings or a markup in committee. This usually lasts all morning. I grab a quick lunch and sometimes I stay on the Hill and do some lobbying by visiting congressional aides. Oftentimes the chairman [of our group] comes with me to visit the aides. I come back to the office in midafternoon. I return calls, find out what's happened while I was out of the office—to see if there have been any new events. Usually at this point I'll go through the *Congressional Record,* answer my mail, write memos, just get caught up.

Although these three legislative lobbyists work for dissimilar organizations, their work patterns have quite a bit in common. Most striking about the way they spend their days is the premium they place on collecting the latest information. Close attention is paid to all relevant sources of news. There is constant checking on the phone and with office colleagues to see if anything has happened since the last time the lobbyist was in the office. A good deal of the contact they initiate with government officials is of the "what's happening?" kind.

The emphasis on current information comes, in part, from the culture of Washington. One measure of status in Washington is the amount of inside information you have. Someone who is not in the know risks being thought unimportant. More fundamental to the substance of lobbying is the bearing current information has on short-term planning. To do the job well, a lobbyist must know what amendments are being drafted, if a key senator has met with the opposition, or if the administration is flexible on some provisions of the legislation. Day-old information is as valuable to a lobbyist as day-old bread is to a bakery. It simply does no good to try to influence the situation that used to be.

Another common work trait shared by these and other lobbyists is the effort to make their presence felt. Contrary to the image of lobbyists as back-room operators, much of their time is taken up in trying to be visible. They spend valuable time at congressional hearings even though nothing of great consequence is likely to happen there—it's a chance to touch base with other lobbyists and congressional staffers. They'll make repeated visits to different Capitol Hill offices, even if all they're likely to accomplish is leaving a message with a secretary that they were by to see the administrative assistant. If a PAC is making a donation to an incumbent, says one PAC director, "You just don't write out a check and drop it in the mail."[1] Rather, the lobbyist will go to the office and hand it over in person. The ubiquitous after-work receptions are a chance to exchange a word or two with members of Congress or their aides simply to remind them who the lobbyist represents. Much of what a lobbyist does then is to validate the role that the group plays in policymaking. They are constantly reminding legislators, staffers, and other lobbyists that they are around and that their views ought to be considered when policy decisions are being hammered out.

A related part of the Washington representative's job is to keep in touch with interest group allies and to do whatever can be done to spur them on. Coalition politics is characteristic of all sizes and types of interest groups. The constant interaction is a means for exchanging information, but it also affords an opportunity to develop strategy, offer and receive moral support, and politely push the other group to do more.

Lobbyists differ, of course, in the way they carry out their job. Public interest lobbyists are not as likely as their counterparts from large corporations to show up at congressional fundraisers. Some lobbyists will be able to rely on letters written by their constituents to aid their efforts; others do not have large memberships to draw on. These descriptions have dealt only with legislative lobbying. Trying to influence the content of a regulation involves considerably less time prowling the corridors than Capitol Hill work does. There are various reasons for this. To begin with, an agency usually has fewer relevant offices to visit on forthcoming regulations. More importantly, though, civil servants who do the lion's share of the work in drafting regulations can feel constricted in their relations with lobbyists. They may take the attitude that frequent meetings with industry representatives can compromise their neutrality. Ex parte rules prohibit private communications between group representatives and agency officials when a case involving the group is under way. At the same time, bureaucrats recognize that meetings with interest group representatives can help them to learn what all the facts are. At some agencies officials cannot do their jobs without data supplied to them by industry representatives.

For all lobbyists, though, the daily work is being the eyes and ears of their organizations. They must keep the members of their group

---

[1]Dan Clawson, Alan Neustadtl, and Denise Scott, *Money Talks* (New York: Basic Books, 1992), p. 80.

abreast of policy developments. They must stand ready to provide information for the organization's newsletter, answer phone calls from members, and keep their superiors supplied with a steady stream of information. Lobbyists are the nerve endings of an interest group; they spend most of each day carrying messages back and forth between their environment and their organization.

EFFECTIVE LOBBYING

Lobbying is a difficult and sometimes frustrating occupation. The hours are long and the prestige rather low in a town of senators, ambassadors, and cabinet secretaries. The pressures can be great when a critical vote in Congress or an administrative decision approaches. Regardless of how hard lobbyists work, policy outcomes will often be determined by factors out of their control.

The job is not without its satisfactions, however. It can be heady, exciting work. As with any other job, accomplishing what one sets out to do has its own inner rewards. And like any other job, lobbying has its own valued skills and professional norms. Lobbyists are convinced that effective lobbying is maximized by close adherence to the following "rules."

Credibility Comes First   When lobbyists are interviewed about a variety of subjects, no theme is repeated more frequently than their need to protect their credibility. It is the fundamental dogma of their religion. "Washington is a village," said one labor lobbyist. "You are known by your good name and integrity."

Lobbyists emphasize their reputation because in a job designed to convince others of your point of view, it is easy to stretch the truth to make one's argument seem more powerful.[2] But it is as dangerous as it is easy. Mislead a member of Congress and "you can expect a member never to listen to you seriously," commented one veteran lobbyist. For the lobbyist, then, honesty is not so much a matter of virtue as of necessity. Lobbyists simply cannot do the job if there are any doubts about their credibility. As one corporate representative put it, "All you have is your word."

---

[2]See Scott Ainsworth, "Regulating Lobbyists and Interest Group Influence," *Journal of Politics* 55 (February 1993), pp. 41–56.

Only the Facts Count   Credibility is a precondition for getting your message heard, but it is not sufficient to exert influence. What does make a lobbyist's communications persuasive? The lobbyist who represents a powerful constituency may begin with the advantage of speaking for a well-identified point of view. Individual lobbyists cannot really affect the nature of their own constituency, but they can affect the design of the message they send to policymakers. Lobbyists are unequivocal about what makes an effective message—the more factual the better. In memos, handouts, reports, formal comments on regulations, and in conversations, the only content that counts is the specific fact. "You have to know how to separate the wheat from the chaff, facts from rhetoric," said a trade association lobbyist.

It is of little value to a policymaker to hear platitudes about what's in the "public interest." They are already aware of the general pro and con arguments on an issue. If lobbyists are to do anything to influence members of Congress or administrators beyond the opinions they already hold, they must have something new to bring to their attention. A coalition of colleges and universities from 18 rural, low-income states was not making much headway on its own in persuading the federal government to expand research funding to a broader range of schools. (Most federal dollars go to the large, prestigious research universities like Berkeley and M.I.T.) The coalition hired Stewart Van Scoyoc, who has his own lobbying firm, to help. Van Scoyoc's primary lobbying strategy was to interview school administrators and scholars to identify research specialties in each state. The firm then helped the schools develop material that could be used by college administrators and Van Scoyoc in meetings with the most pertinent federal agencies who could fund work in those areas.[3]

Lobbyists increase their effectiveness as they increase their knowledge of their policy area. Amid the deepening complexity of public policy problems, the lobbyist must become a determined and continuing student of these issues. Although the increasing technical complexity of issues makes lobbying a more difficult challenge, therein lies the opportunity. Lobbyists who have mastered the complexities of their policy area enter a select group of experts who talk the same language. Washington representatives with a high level of policy expertise are

---

[3]Michael Wines, "New Lobbyists: Knowledge, Not Connections," *New York Times,* November 3, 1993.

more valuable to those in government because policymakers can draw upon their knowledge in efforts to solve difficult issues.

Never Burn Your Bridges   Alliances can shift rapidly, or, as one trade association lobbyist put it, "You may be friends on one issue and enemies on the next." Lobbyists cannot afford the luxury of venting their anger toward policymakers who act contrary to their wishes. When President Clinton and many congressional Democrats began to push for the North American Free Trade Agreement (NAFTA), organized labor considered it nothing short of treason. Although the long alliance between labor and the Democratic Party was strained, it didn't break. Labor lobbyists knew they would need the Democrats who deserted them for other issues down the road, and, despite some bluster at the time, the unions forgave the sinners.

To keep from burning bridges while pushing hard to get the group's policies adopted, a lobbyist, says one trade association representative, should be "responsible, firm, and nonemotional." Yet some public interest lobbyists dissent from this rule. Common Cause has made it a practice to single out members of Congress for criticism when they feel they have acted in a particularly offensive way. Ralph Nader, who provides leadership for a number of groups started under his sponsorship, has a similar philosophy toward those who act in a manner he regards as egregiously out of line with the public interest. He derided the then head of the Atomic Energy Commission, Dixy Lee Ray, by publicly declaring that she had a "distorted . . . capacity for reason."[4] This is not exactly the kind of language that builds friendships.

When public interest lobbyists fail to follow the don't-burn-your-bridges rule, it is not always because they place an exalted premium on principle. It is true that some of them approach their work with a degree of moralism that makes it difficult for them to tolerate those who are unfaithful to the cause. Yet it is more than a pious attitude that leads some public interest lobbyists to go out of their way to personalize issues. Frequently they see it as a tactical advantage to identify a villain. The idea is to portray the issue at hand as a fight between good and evil; ridicule and vilification are useful for putting their opponents on the defensive. Nader and other citizen group lobbyists who use this tactic

---

[4]Jeffrey M. Berry, "Lessons from Chairman Ralph," *Citizen Participation* 1 (November/ December 1979), p. 4.

sacrifice whatever future cooperation they might get from their targets in the expectation that other policymakers will be more fearful of such denunciation and thus be more helpful. For most lobbyists, though, this remains a high-risk strategy. For those representing corporations and trade associations, such a moralistic approach has no credibility.

Success = Compromise   It is often said that "politics is the art of compromise." If so, lobbyists must be fine artists. No interest group ever achieves all it wants, and so the difference between success and failure is achieving an acceptable compromise. An integral part of the lobbyist's job is to aggressively seek out workable compromises that can satisfy all necessary parties. The task each day, says one business lobbyist, is to "go solution searching." Lobbyists must see themselves as a catalyst for compromise, finding and promoting policy changes that are going to get a bill or regulation through in acceptable form.

Lobbyists attempt to give up that which is least valuable to their group while persuading policymakers and other interest groups to agree to the higher priorities their group is pushing for. The skill that is involved is knowing how much to give up and just when to make those concessions. For the Congress, that skill consists of determining which trade-offs or policy changes will attract votes from legislators who have strong reservations about the bill at hand. Lobbyists and their congressional allies look for sweeteners that will make the bill more attractive by adding or subtracting particular provisions. Sometimes compromises cannot be reached because one or more factions must give up too much to keep the result palatable for them. But the good lobbyist keeps searching and keeps trying to find the middle ground.

Create a Dependency   The optimal role for a lobbyist to play is that of a trusted source of information whom policymakers can call on when they need hard-to-find data.[5] A reputation for credibility and high-quality factual information are prerequisites for becoming a lobbyist from whom government officials request help. The final ingredient is developing the relationship gradually, with the lobbyist providing the right kind of information at the right time. "Maintain constant communication," says one public interest representative. "Churn out a lot of material at their request. Create a dependency."

---

[5]See John Mark Hansen, *Gaining Access* (Chicago: University of Chicago Press, 1991).

Lobbyists in particular policy areas try to develop working relationships with the agency officials and congressional committee members and staffers who have responsibility for relevant programs. This familiarity in time gives lobbyists the advantage of repeated opportunities to interact with policymakers and to display their expertise. The lobbyist for a group representing urban affairs specialists mentioned that their long work with certain agencies led to calls from those agencies when the Reagan administration was developing an urban enterprise zones proposal (a plan to give tax breaks to companies investing in poor inner-city areas). "They needed to know how many states already had enterprise zones, how they're working, what they look like, and so on. This happens all the time." The long nurturing of the relationship with agencies handling urban issues enabled this lobbyist to get in on the ground floor of the enterprise zones issue. The same lobbyist added, "That's the key to being a good lobbyist—to establish a two-way street not only with agencies, but with members of Congress, especially for technical areas. You need to have them depend on you for your area of expertise."

The best of all possible worlds for a lobbyist is to be respected by key policymakers who come to value them as a friend. This will maximize access for the lobbyist and, thus, give this person a competitive advantage over other lobbyists who are trying to bring information to the attention of the same official. With thousands of lobbyists in Washington competing for policymakers' attention, however, interest groups can hardly depend on personal relationships as the basis for influence. Still, lobbyists who can raise money for congressional campaigns or do other political favors have an advantage in building long-term relationships.[6]

These unwritten rules of effective lobbying are, of course, general. Because they are so widely accepted and quickly grasped by any aspiring Washington representative, simply following them does not ensure success. Wide differences in the skill and perseverance of lobbyists remain as they try to become issue experts or facilitators of compromise. Furthermore, no matter how skilled lobbyists are, they are severely restricted in accomplishing their goals by the political popularity of their

---

[6]See, generally, Jeffrey H. Birnbaum, *The Lobbyists* (New York: Times Books, 1992). Personal relationships between lobbyists and legislators appear to be more important on the state level. See Alan Rosenthal, *The Third House* (Washington, D.C.: Congressional Quarterly, 1993).

group's stand on issues and the strength of the group's constituency. Yet, so far as any one lobbyist can make a difference, adhering to these norms will help to maximize his or her influence.

LOBBYING AS A CAREER

Lobbying is an unusual profession, in that people do not aspire to become the representative of an interest group. This attitude is tied to the low prestige of lobbying and the uncomplimentary image it has had over the years. There is no career path, then, that people consciously choose in order to prepare themselves for the lobbying profession.

Recruitment

If individuals do not set out to become lobbyists, how do they end up in such jobs? Generally, people become lobbyists because previous jobs lead them to it. Specific skills or areas of background are acquired, and soon opportunities present themselves or may even be pursued. A common route into lobbying is government work. Legislative aides frequently leave their positions to take lobbying jobs at significant increases in their salaries. James C. Healey, who worked for a House Ways and Means Committee chair, was a valuable catch for Black, Manafort, Stone & Kelly, a leading public relations and lobbying firm. His ties to the tax-writing committee bolstered the firm's credibility with potential corporate clients. Some former members of Congress even take up lobbying after they retire or lose an election. Liberal New York Democrat Tom Downey turned to lobbying after he lost his House seat in 1992. His firm, Thomas Downey & Associates, quickly lined up lucrative clients like Time Warner, Joseph A. Seagram's, and DuPont. These companies knew that Downey was not only highly knowledgeable about tax law, but that he had close contacts with the Clinton White House.[7]

There are other routes to lobbying besides government work. A lobbyist for a computer manufacturer describes his career ladder:

---

[7]Jackie Calmes, "Revolving Door Between Congress and Lobbyists Spins on Despite Yearlong Cooling-Off Period," *Wall Street Journal,* January 24, 1994.

My background is as a lawyer. I practiced in private firms in Washington for 16 years. Before I came [here] I was a partner in a large Washington firm. I started out as a lawyer [with this company] and I worked on intellectual property, copyright, and trade issues. When the government relations office moved I went with it and last year I became head of government affairs.

Whatever the route taken, the common denominators are *experience* and *expertise*. Qualification by experience does not mean having to wait until one becomes a graybeard before lobbying organizations become interested. Generally, once one reaches a position of responsibility, interest groups and lobbying firms will begin to take notice. Expertise is usually acquired through the task specialization that comes from working in any organization, though academic training can provide the necessary background as well.

Some aggressively seek out lobbying positions instead of being recruited or falling into them. Most commonly, those who search for and avidly pursue such jobs are citizen activists. They are looking not so much for a job as a lobbyist as for a job that will allow them to work for a cause. The satisfaction derived by pursuing ideological goals makes jobs with citizen groups highly attractive. As an environmental lobbyist put it, "It doesn't give you a hell of a lot of money and it may not give you much prestige, but when you come home at the end of the day you feel good about your work." For the private sector lobbyist, the issues they will be lobbying on may not be the main attraction to the job.[8] It's not necessary to have a "moral commitment to that which you are lobbying for," said one oil company representative.

Despite the divergent career paths that lead into lobbying positions, the jobs themselves usually are filled in the same manner: By word of mouth. Although some jobs may be advertised, organizations looking for an outside candidate will rely heavily on personal recommendations from those they consult. "In D.C. in the job market, what's open is really off the record," noted a business lobbyist. In any issue network, most participants are already well known to other actors. If a farm group loses one of its lobbyists, the director of the organization will naturally consider respected staffers on the agriculture committees in Congress and officials in the Department of Agriculture, whether those people are looking for new jobs or not. Intermediaries may put

[8]Lester Milbrath, *The Washington Lobbyists* (Chicago: Rand McNally, 1963), pp. 109–114.

the director in touch with others who might fill the group's needs. One lobbyist described his recruitment as "one of those typical Washington stories. You know, where you know someone who knows someone."

Background

Although no precise route opens into the lobbying profession, three spawning grounds nurture most Washington representatives: law, government, and business. Because expertise and experience are the most important qualities in a lobbyist, it is easy to understand why these three backgrounds predominate. Service in government not only gives prospective lobbyists experience in the workings of Congress and agencies, it also gives expertise on policy and contacts that may help to open doors. Lawyers easily metamorphose into lobbyists because their education and experience make them familiar with the way statutes and regulations are written. A few years of work as an associate in a Washington law firm or in an agency's legal counsel office gives them added preparation. Business is also a common background because the majority of lobbyists represent either trade associations or individual corporations. The technical complexity of most public policy issues makes experience in one's industry a helpful credential.

One of the most serious ethical dilemmas involving interest group politics is circulation of people out of government and into lobbying. The issue is this: You are working for the government at the taxpayer's expense, developing expertise and experience that make you attractive to the private sector. When you leave government and parlay that background into a lobbying job, it is usually at a much higher salary and for a position designed to exploit your contacts with those you know in government. In some cases individuals gain experience working on foreign trade issues for the government, then take jobs with foreign corporations as lobbyists. Thus, after receiving training as government employees, they then work to help companies abroad compete more effectively against American businesses.[9]

One of the most glaring examples of parlaying a government job into a lucrative lobbying career is Michael Deaver's exit from the Reagan White House. He started his own lobbying firm and immediately

---

[9]Pat Choate, *Agents of Influence* (New York: Alfred Knopf, 1990). There is a one-year ban on former executive branch employees who wish to lobby or advise a foreign government or political party.

attracted clients like TWA, Philip Morris, and the countries of Canada, Singapore, and Mexico. Before a special prosecutor began investigating him, Deaver was taking home about $400,000 a year for what he euphemistically referred to as "strategic planning" for his clients. Deaver responded with surprise to criticism that he was exploiting his contacts in government: "I wonder what people thought I was going to do when I left the White House—be a brain surgeon?"[10]

When he took office, President Clinton issued new rules for top officials so that his administration would not be tarnished by the ethical transgressions of Deaver and others who served under Reagan and Bush. Clinton said he wanted to "stop the revolving door from public service to private enrichment."[11] The Clinton rules prohibited former administration appointees from lobbying their former agencies for five years after they left their posts. A year after the guidelines were issued, however, it was business as usual. Clinton's legislative liaison chief, Howard Paster, announced he was leaving the administration to take a job as the head of the local office of Hill & Knowlton, a public relations firm whose branch in Washington specializes in government relations. Paster's salary was estimated to be close to $1 million a year. Roy Neel, the deputy chief of staff, left around the same time to become president of the United States Telephone Association, which lobbies on behalf of the seven regional Bell telephone companies. Neel's new salary was about $500,000, quadruple what he was making at the White House. Although the Clinton administration's own ethics rules forbade Paster and Neel from personally lobbying the White House for five years, the rules do nothing to stop them from directing the work of others. Clearly, Paster and Neel's new employers didn't seem to think the new rules would hamper their effectiveness.[12]

The problem of "in and outers" goes far beyond highly visible presidential aides; it is pervasive throughout the government. At the

---

[10]Marjorie Williams, "Mike Deaver's Fall from Grace," *Washington Post National Weekly Edition,* July 27, 1987; and David Rapp, "New 'Revolving Door' Restrictions Proposed," *Congressional Quarterly Weekly Report,* April 12, 1986.

[11]Richard Berke, "Many Will Escape Ethics Restriction," *New York Times,* December 9, 1992.

[12]Clifford Levy, "Hill & Knowlton Hires Former Clinton Aide," *New York Times,* December 7, 1993; Douglas Jehl, "Lobbying Rules for Ex-Officials at Issue Again," *New York Times,* December 18, 1993; and "Clinton Announces New Ethics Standards," *Congressional Quarterly Almanac, 1992* (Washington, D.C.: Congressional Quarterly, 1993), p. 62.

Department of Defense large numbers of officials leave every year to take jobs with Defense Department contractors. Others take work with consulting firms that help corporations get Defense Department contracts. The incestuous nature of former Defense aides lobbying the offices they just left finally led the Congress to prohibit top officials from taking a job for two years after leaving the Pentagon with defense firms whose procurement contracts they had substantial responsibility for.[13]

A broader effort to restrict the revolving door is the 1978 Ethics in Government Act, which forbids executive branch officials from lobbying the agency they left for a period of a year and prohibits them from lobbying it at any time on issues they worked on substantially while in government. Restrictions now also apply to former members of Congress, who may not lobby the legislative branch for a year after they leave, and congressional staffers, who may not lobby the member, office, or committee for whom they worked for a year. Nevertheless, the ethics laws, like the Clinton guidelines (formulated for his administration only), have not stopped the revolving door. As we have seen, the rules are easy to get around as the former government officials merely have to refrain from directly contacting certain offices for a period of time. The *Wall Street Journal* observed that the temporary lobbying ban for former government employees is "a nuisance at best."[14]

There are frequent calls to establish more restrictive rules on former government employees. The counterweight to such arguments is the freedom of individuals to pursue the kinds of jobs they want and the fear that tightening such restrictions will deter good people from joining government in the first place.[15] Over 50 percent of lobbyists have some form of government experience, so it's clear that interest groups depend heavily on government as a source of qualified labor and that lobbying jobs are quite popular with government workers.[16] The Congress did pass some reforms in 1995 aimed at policing those who do

---

[13]See "DOD Revolving Door," Government Accounting Office, Briefing Report, GAO/NSIAD-86-180BR, July, 1986; *Top Gun* (Washington, D.C.: Common Cause, 1987), pp. 21–24; and *Federal Register,* April 16, 1987, pp. 12,383–12,387.

[14]Calmes, "Revolving Door Between Congress and Lobbyists."

[15]G. Calvin MacKenzie, "If You Want to Play, You've Got to Pay," in G. Calvin MacKenzie, ed., *The In-and-Outers* (Baltimore: Johns Hopkins University Press, 1987), pp, 77–99.

[16]Robert H. Salisbury, "Washington Lobbyists: A Collective Portrait," in Allan J. Cigler and Burdett Loomis, eds., *Interest Group Politics,* 2nd ed. (Washington, D.C.: Congressional Quarterly, 1986), p. 153.

lobby. It banned any gifts from lobbyists to legislators, except those which are of trivial value. A new law also requires that lobbyists register with the Congress and file reports listing their clients, the expenses they incur in lobbying, and their compensation. (A previous registration law passed in 1946 was toothless and ineffective.) The law applies not only to congressional lobbying, but to executive branch advocacy as well.

Lobbyists are impressive in their educational backgrounds, commonly holding advanced degrees beyond the bachelor's. The most popular advanced degree is in law, but assorted masters' degrees in fields such as economics, business, and political science are often found too.[17] The relatively high educational level that characterizes the lobbying profession has to do with the requirements of the jobs that frequently precede work as an interest group representative. Beyond the earlier need to advance in business, law, government, or other fields, lobbyists find their advanced educations useful, if not essential, to their interest group work.[18] Again, the technical nature of many public policy areas and the need to understand administrative law and other arcane legal matters make academic credentials highly valuable to a lobbyist.[19]

Traditionally, lobbying has been a "man's world." A survey conducted in the early 1980s found that only 22 percent of all lobbyists were women.[20] One of the reasons that it was so difficult for women to break into lobbying is that the people in government who made decisions were likely to be men, and the quiet, off-the-record negotiations that are part of policymaking easily turned a woman into an outsider. As more women have moved into all offices and institutions of government, this barrier to equal employment seems to be eroding. Impressionistic evidence suggests that women are making progress in the lob-

---

[17]"The Washington Executive" (Washington, D.C.: Boyden Associates, 1980), p. 2; and Jeffrey M. Berry, *Lobbying for the People* (Princeton: Princeton University Press, 1977), pp. 88–90.

[18]John P. Heinz, Edward O. Laumann, Robert L. Nelson, and Robert H. Salisbury, *The Hollow Core* (Cambridge, Mass.: Harvard University Press, 1993), p. 147.

[19]The ability and credentials of contemporary lobbyists contrast with the opposite pattern found in one major study of the 1950s. See Raymond A. Bauer, Ithiel de Sola Pool, and Lewis Anthony Dexter, *American Business and Public Policy* (New York: Atherton, 1963), p. 345.

[20]Kay Lehman Schlozman, "Representing Women in Washington: Sisterhood and Pressure Politics," in Louise A. Tilly and Patricia Gurin, *Women, Politics, and Change* (New York: Russell Sage, 1990), pp. 339–382.

bying field, and many prominent corporations like Coca-Cola, Ford, and Motorola have lobbying offices headed by females.[21]

Lobbyists are not an underprivileged lot. A survey of over 800 Washington representatives revealed that they had an average income of around $90,000 a year. Attorneys in private practice were the highest paid, with annual incomes averaging around $167,000. Trade association executives earn just over $100,000 a year, while officers in citizen groups average $48,000. Ordinary citizen group lobbyists are at the bottom of the pay scale with salaries of about $37,000.[22]

LOBBYISTS FOR HIRE

In addition to lobbyists who are employed full time by interest groups, there are also many lobbyists for temporary hire. Lobbyists hire out on a retainer or fee for services for two reasons. First, many corporations and trade associations do not have an office in Washington. Most such organizations need a lobbyist infrequently, and it is less expensive to hire one as the need arises. Second, most interest group offices are small and may not have the resources for a major lobbying campaign that the parent organization wants (and is willing to pay for). Again, it is more economical to hire outsiders to do tasks that are highly specialized or require an extensive staff for a limited time than it is to carry such people on the payroll all year. In Washington, the pool of labor for lobbying work is deep. Lobbyists for hire come from the many lobbying shops, law firms, and public relations firms that eagerly court government relations work.

Lobbying Firms

Most lobbying shops are small to medium-sized firms started by people with some expertise or experience that make them of value as advocates before government. Some of the most notable lobbying firms are built around former presidential aides whose visibility and experience

---

[21]Jill Abramson, "Women Are Now Key Players in Lobbying Game, for Big Companies or Heading Their Own Lobbying Firms," *Wall Street Journal,* August 2, 1995.
[22]Salisbury, "Washington Lobbyists," p. 155.

easily attract clients who need help with the executive branch. The Duberstein Group, for example, was started by Kenneth Duberstein, a former legislative assistant to President Reagan.

Although some firms have a general lobbying practice, many others specialize in a particular niche, using their high level of expertise in a policy area as their primary marketing tool to attract clients. Capitol Associates, with 14 lobbyists on its payroll, is known for its work on health issues.[23] Liz Robbins Associates has labored for many years in the area of social services and is often employed by state and local governments who are looking for more money from Washington.

Sometimes the small boutique firms develop such good reputations that they are able to grow into much larger firms with diversified interests. Cassidy & Associates was begun by two former staffers for the Senate Select Committee on Nutrition and Human Needs. They worked initially on nutrition issues and with universities seeking government grants. The firms expanded over the years, and, in a relatively new twist in lobbying, Cassidy & Associates has taken an equity interest in some of the firms it is working to promote. The lobbying firm is a partner in Galway Capital, which tries to attract investors to high-tech start-ups. If Cassidy & Associates helps any of Galway's clients win contracts with the federal government, it not only collects its lobbying fee, but benefits by its partial ownership in the companies through Galway.[24]

Law Firms

The Washington law firm is no ordinary law firm. These firms are largely in the business of representing clients before government. Lawyer-lobbyists in Washington can earn lucrative salaries by developing expertise in an area of regulatory policy. Senior partners in successful firms can easily make $250,000 a year or more.

Corporations are by far the largest group of customers for Washington law firms. The complex administrative process is intimidating to

---

[23]Wines, "New Lobbyists."
[24]Jill Abramson and David Rogers, "Some of Washington's Influence Peddlers Reap Added Benefit of Stake in Firms They Promote," *Wall Street Journal,* October 12, 1994.

corporate executives who have little Washington experience. Even Washington representatives of a corporation can find themselves unable to understand adequately the technical jargon and legalese of administrative regulations. The stakes can be very high, and a company will search for the lawyer who can do the most for it in a particular area. As one corporate lobbyist put it, "We decide who to use based on the issues, the firms' specialty, track records, contacts, and reputation. If you have a brain tumor, you go to a brain surgeon. The issues are very important." When Japanese machine tool companies became concerned about protectionist sentiment in the United States, they went to Stanton Anderson, an attorney who specializes in international trade. They wanted to make sure that their representative before the Commerce Department and other agencies had an excellent understanding of both American trade policy and Japanese business practices.[25]

Individuals who join Washington law firms are aware of the special nature of this type of law practice. They know a good part of their time will be spent pleading some corporation's cause before government. They choose Washington law over, say, Wall Street law (arranging stock offerings and mergers) because they find it more challenging or find the politics of lawmaking and rulemaking more intriguing. Frequently Washington lawyers enter private practice after gaining valuable experience working for a congressional committee or an administrative agency. Thus they become part of the in-and-out pattern of using a government job to later command handsome fees from those who have a problem with the government.

As pointed out in Chapter 2, the number of lawyer-lobbyists has climbed steadily. This growth has made Washington law more competitive and firms are aggressive in marketing what they offer. In the fall of 1992 when it seemed like Bill Clinton had a good chance to win the presidency, the Washington office of Manatt, Phelps, Phillips & Kantor, invited clients and prospective clients to a meeting promising an inside look at the Clinton campaign. The meeting was conducted by Charles Manatt, former chair of the Democratic National Committee. One of the speakers at the meeting was Mickey Kantor, a partner in the firm and a top Clinton campaign aide, who talked about the priorities

---

[25]Clyde Farnsworth, "Japan's Top U.S. Lobbyist," *New York Times,* June 2, 1985.

of a prospective Clinton administration. The message was unmistakable: the Manatt firm could do a lot for its clients.[26] (Kantor later became the Special Trade Representative in the Clinton White House, offering even more reason for corporations and trade associations with international interests to hire the firm.)

The best-known law firm in Washington, renowned for its lobbying prowess, is Patton, Boggs & Blow. The 180-lawyer firm is, in the words of the *National Journal,* "the icon of Washington's mercenary culture."[27] It has 1,500 active clients, a large proportion of whom come to the firm because they want something from the federal government. Although viewed as particularly close to the Democrats because of the identity of some of its current and former partners (like the late Ron Brown, also a head of the Democratic National Committee, who became President Clinton's Secretary of Commerce), it actually thrived during the Reagan and Bush years. Of all Patton, Boggs & Blow's partners, none is more respected and sought after by clients than Tommy Boggs. Politics is in Boggs' blood. His father, Hale, was Majority Leader in the House, and his mother, Lindy, replaced her husband in Congress when he died in a plane crash. Connections, however, are only a minor part of Boggs' success. He is a brilliant legislative strategist and a dogged advocate for his clients. His labors are rewarded with an annual salary of more than $1 million, but for his firm and his clients he's worth every penny.[28]

Public Relations Firms

Organizations or industries in need of Washington representation make use of public relations firms when they feel they need to change public opinion. The government of India, for example, hired Edelman Public Relations Worldwide because it wanted it to improve India's image. More specifically, it wanted American policymakers to understand that India was a good place for foreign investment, and that it wasn't consumed by sectarian violence. The Kashmiri American Foundation, which supports independence from India, pays Black, Manafort, Stone

---

[26]Jill Abramson, "Influence of Lobbyist Groups Likely Won't Diminish," *Wall Street Journal,* November 5, 1992.

[27]W. John Moore, "The Gravy Train," *National Journal,* October 10, 1992, p. 2295.

[28]Moore, "The Gravy Train," p. 2296.

& Kelly Public Affairs $15,000 a month to burnish Kashmir's image and to promote independence for the Indian state.[29]

The stock in trade for Washington-based public relations firms is gaining favorable publicity from the print and television reporters who cover national politics. To that end they pitch stories to reporters they know, set up interviews for clients, and create events worthy of media coverage. As noted in Chapter 6, these firms also design campaigns to sway mass opinion, a difficult process at best.

The advantage public relations firms have over law firms is that they offer more services to clients. A large public relations firm will have specialists in lobbying, advertising, and media work. Some firms will even teach a corporate executive how to be effective in a television interview. The largest firms are trying to expand their services to offer "one-stop shopping" to potential clients in need of a wide range of services (see Table 5.1). Seeing the trend, one large law firm, Arnold & Porter, created a subsidiary lobbying and public relations firm, Apco Associates, so that they could "really service a client."[30]

CONCLUSION

As American politics has changed since the 1960s and interest groups have proliferated in Washington, the job of the lobbyist has changed as well. Veteran business lobbyist Charls Walker describes how the job of a lobbyist evolved since the 1950s:

> In those days, I would have a fifty-minute meeting with [Speaker of the House] Sam Rayburn. For forty-eight minutes we would talk about Texas, family, and friends. In the remaining two, we would settle what I had come to talk about. He always knew what I was there for, and would say, "It's taken care of, Charlie," or "I just can't do that for you." Now that kind of thing just doesn't happen any more. With the decline of parties, the decline of leadership in the Congress, business lobbying groups have to cover the field. Many more bodies and much more time are needed to accomplish what we did then.[31]

---

[29]W. John Moore, "A Firm That's Making Rupee," *National Journal,* February 19, 1994, pp. 428–430.

[30]Burt Solomon, "Clout Merchants," *National Journal,* March 21, 1987, p. 663.

[31]Anne Colamosca, "The Trade Association Hustle," *New Republic,* November 3, 1979, p. 16.

TABLE 5.1   ONE-STOP SHOPPING

	Law	Washington lobbying	Grass-roots lobbying	Coalition building	Public relations	Media strategies	Advertising	Art/media production	Direct mail	Economic consulting	Management consulting	Political consulting	Political fund-raising	Opinion polling	Issues monitoring	Event planning
Arnold & Porter, law: Apco Associates, lobbying and consulting subsidiary; the Secura Group, financial consulting affiliate	•	•	•	•	•	•					•	•		•		•	•
Black Manafort Stone & Kelly Public Affairs Co., lobbying: Campaign Consultants Inc. (formerly Black, Manafort, Stone & Atwater), political consultants; National Media Inc., media production and placement		•	•	•	•	•	•	•	•		•	•	•	•		•	•
Burson-Marsteller, public relations (parent company—Young & Rubicam Inc., advertising agency): Rogers Merchandising, direct-marketing subsidiary; Cohn & Wolfe Inc., PR subsidiary		•	•	•	•	•	•	•	•	•				•	•	•
Hill & Knowlton Inc., public relations (parent company—JWT Group, advertising): Strategic Information Research Corp., opinion polling subsidiary		•	•	•	•	•		•	•			•	•	•	•	•
The Kamber Group, communications		•	•	•	•	•	•	•	•			•	•		•	•
Ogilvy & Mather Public Affairs (parent company—the Ogilvy Group, advertising): Targeted Communications, direct-mail affiliate; Charls E. Walker Associates Inc., partly owned lobbying affiliate		•	•	•	•	•	•	•	•	•	•			•	•	•

Source: Burt Solomon, "Clout Merchants," *National Journal,* March 21, 1987, p. 664. All rights reserved. Reprinted by permission.

Walker surely exaggerates the ease with which most lobbyists could solve their problems in the 1950s. Yet the job of a lobbyist was simpler then. The business lobbyist had much less competition from public interest adversaries. This too was the heyday of the so-called iron triangles, in which policymaking was carried out in a consensual manner by a small number of lobbyists, agency administrators, and congressional committee chairmen. Industries were less regulated; a lobbyist had fewer agencies to deal with and fewer sets of complex regulations to monitor. The job of lobbyists today is more demanding. Not only do they have more groups to compete with, but the policies that lobbyists deal with are increasingly complex. The norms or rules of lobbying have not greatly changed, but how much expertise on issues a Washington representative brings to the job seems increasingly important.

The growth of Washington lobbying in recent years has created a large, highly competitive industry. Law firms, public relations firms, and other lobbying outfits need a steady flow of clients to keep profits growing. Consequently, lobbyists are hardly shy about tooting their own horns. To drum up business and make their high hourly fees and retainers appear reasonable, lobbyists for hire are prone to exaggerate their prowess with government. They also must hide what Paul Taylor of the *Washington Post* calls the "dirty little secret about high-priced Washington lobbyists. . . . They lose a lot."[32] Nevertheless, clients keep coming because public policy stakes are high, and there are enough lobbying successes—some of them spectacular—to give the advocacy industry credibility.

---

[32]Paul Taylor, "Gladiators for Hire—Part I," *Washington Post,* July 31, 1983.

Chapter
6

Public Opinion and Grassroots Lobbying

*M*uch of what interest groups do is directed outside of Washington to those outside of government. Interest groups have strong reasons to convince people at the grassroots of the righteousness of their arguments, believing that changed public opinion will eventually lead to changed elite opinion in Washington. Interest groups also know how valuable it is to have the people back home communicate their opinions to those in Washington. Thus lobbies try to mobilize those who share their views to participate in some way so their own voices will be heard by policymakers. Interest groups try to build support for their efforts by appealing to different audiences. On the broadest issues, lobbying organizations may try to reach the mass public. Although it seems mere common sense for all interest groups to want to reach as many people as possible, it is usually impractical for lobbies to try to influence mass public opinion. By narrowing their efforts, they may direct them instead at an "attentive public"—groups in the population concerned about particular issues who follow their development in Washington. An organization may also confine its efforts to its own members or activists.[1] Whatever route lobbies take in trying to inform citizens and policymakers, a constant is their relentless hunt for media coverage.

---

[1] Francis E. Rourke, *Bureaucracy, Politics, and Public Policy,* 3rd ed., (Boston: Little, Brown, 1984), pp. 50–53.

This chapter begins by asking how interest groups try to shape the public's basic values. Changing people's values may make it more likely that the public will define some social phenomenon as a *political* problem. Next, how do interest groups try to educate people about a particular issue? Lobbies want to do whatever they can to ensure that their set of facts, not those of their adversaries, defines the issue at hand. One type of advocacy organization, think tanks, specialize in research and try to influence policymaking through the new knowledge they generate. We will also examine how citizens can become directly involved in lobbying government officials. Finally, we will ask if new high-tech tactics for informing and mobilizing the public have changed the way interest groups use their members to influence government.

LOBBYING FOR VALUES

Although most interest groups focus on issues affecting a single profession, industry, or company, many lobbying groups are primarily concerned about the general direction of American life and culture. Political decisions of all kinds are affected by societal values, those deep-seated collective attitudes of Americans on such matters as family life, economic principles, and the purpose of government. Sometimes, lobbying to change or reinforce values is connected to a policy decision. Often, however, interest groups advocating closer adherance to a set of values are targeting general attitudes rather than a specific policy conflict before decision makers. As pointed out in Chapter 1, such activity can contribute to *agenda building.* As the attitudes change, the public may come to believe that more attention should be paid to problems that government has minimized or overlooked altogether.

Since the 1960s there has been a sharp and continuing struggle to define "the American way." Interest groups have fought bitterly over their competing visions of what basic American values are. The antiwar movement of the 1960s, for example, evolved into a frontal assault on the materialist values of American society. The movement found the American intervention in Vietnam to be symptomatic of a society that mindlessly followed the interests of corporate America. The target of the antiwar movement was not simply policymakers in Washington, but the culture of the 1950s that enshrined the man in the gray flannel suit. He was a loyal servant of a faceless corporation and was the sole breadwinner for a homemaker wife and children who lived in a split-level house in suburbia. This stereotypical family was, allegedly, depoliticized by a focus on the acquisition of material goods. The counterculture attacked these values with a vengence, and many Americans were emancipated by the greater freedom in lifestyles that came out of the 1960s.

Most of the continuing struggle over social values has centered on the American family: the role of women, abortion rights, the primacy of parental values over those introduced by the schools or television, and the perceived moral decay of America that undermines religion and the traditional nuclear family. The conflict over the defeated Equal Rights Amendment (ERA) to the Constitution during the 1970s illustrates this debate. The bitter struggle over the ERA involved a large number of people working for or against the proposed amendment. As one scholar notes, "The irony in all this is that the ERA would have had much less substantive effect than either proponents or opponents claimed."[2] For both sides, the importance of the fight over the ERA was largely symbolic. Those against the ERA cited many serious issues, such as women and the draft and divorce laws. But underlying these policy arguments was antagonism toward the women's movement. For the homemakers who fueled the opposition to the ERA, the women's movement represented a different conception of what an American woman's life should be.[3] For proponents, the ERA symbolized full equality of the sexes and public validation of women's rise from second-class citizenship.

In recent years the Christian right has gained considerable support from both the public and conservative politicians for its effort to promote traditional family values. These Christian fundamentalists see a weakening of the moral fiber of this country, which they attribute directly to the declining importance of Biblical precepts. The rising divorce rate, abortion on demand, rampant crime, and use of drugs by young people are all viewed as the result of corrupted values. Conflict comes from efforts of the Christian right to prescribe remedies that would inhibit these trends.

A number of interest groups are pushing for a Christian social agenda, such as Concerned Women for America, Focus on the Family,

---

[2]Jane J. Mansbridge, *Why We Lost the ERA* (Chicago: University of Chicago Press, 1986), p. 2.

[3]Alan Crawford, *Thunder on the Right* (New York: Pantheon, 1980), pp. 144–164.

the Family Research Council, and the Christian Coalition, the clear leader of the Christian right. Ironically, but probably not coincidentally, the increasing success of the Christian right accompanies the Christian Coalition's increasing focus on secular issues.[4] Although the rhetoric of the organization emphasizes moralistic themes, its political agenda has been characterized by pragmatism and a rather expansive view of what constitutes "Christian issues." After the Republican sweep of the 1994 congressional elections, the Christian Coalition said its top priority was a $500-a-child tax credit.[5] The group regards a tax credit as pro-family because it would provide a little extra financial support to those who choose to have children. Nevertheless, most Americans would be hard-pressed to see the religious connotations of a change in the federal tax code.

The strategy of the Christian Coalition is not to overplay its hand by reaching for policies that are morally just but unwinnable. A few weeks after the 1994 election, the new Speaker of the House, Newt Gingrich, moved to reward the Christian right's efforts on behalf of GOP candidates by publicly offering to put a constitutional amendment allowing prayer in schools at the top of the House's agenda. Christian Coalition leader Ralph Reed rejected the offer and said, "I, for one, don't think we'll turn this country around by having public acts of piety."[6] Reed didn't want to be bought off on something that was never likely to get the necessary support to be put into the Constitution. More significantly, though, he wanted the Christian Coalition to be perceived as mainstream and to not provoke any additional opposition to the group's more immediate goals. Consequently, he has directed the organization's lobbying toward those issues where there is strong conservative support per se and where the Christian Coalition finds plenty of common ground with GOP lawmakers.

Although it is a relatively new organization, the Christian Coalition has been remarkably successful in terms of gaining attention for the values that its members cherish. Over the long-term its influence may not be accurately reflected by its lobbying victories on votes where the

---

[4]Matthew C. Moen, *The Transformation of the Christian Right* (Tuscaloosa, Ala.: University of Alabama Press, 1992).
[5]Jackie Calmes, "Tax-Cut Battle Is Gearing Up in Senate Following House Approval of Its Package," *Wall Street Journal,* April 7, 1995.
[6]Catherine S. Manegold, "Some on Right See a Tactical Misstep on School Prayer," *New York Times,* November 19, 1995.

Christian Coalition is the dominant force on one side and liberals are on the other. Rather, the Christian right's greatest impact is that it has been moving the country toward taking its set of issues more seriously. Its influence is especially significant in comparison to the contemporary liberal religious groups, like Bread for the World, which advocate a considerably different set of values.[7]

Lobbying for values may seem to be most suited for ideological citizen groups and religious organizations, but corporate America has not shied away from fighting for its values as well. Business plays such a prominent and critical role in society that it is hard to believe that corporate leaders feel that the values underlying our economic system are in jeopardy. Yet people in the business world worry about the future of free-market economics. A legacy of the rise of the public interest movement during the 1960s and 1970s and its anti-corporate ideology is that business was put on the defensive. Referring to the free-enterprise system, a corporate public affairs official said, "There are popular misconceptions which we must correct." A broad perception is that many people don't understand the position of business on major issues or even understand the role business plays in American society. In the words of one corporate official, "Most people have no idea what free enterprise is all about."

Business has taken a number of steps aimed at enhancing the public's appreciation of free-market principles. Large corporations have used advocacy ads in newspapers and magazines to promote the virtues of capitalism rather than any product or service they sell. Corporations and business leaders have also donated money to colleges and universities to create programs, endow professorships, and sponsor lecture series designed to increase students' understanding of the benefits of capitalism. Likewise, corporations have donated educational materials on business to school systems across the country. Donations have also been made to conservative think tanks to support research on solutions to our major social problems.

Large corporations, which have the resources to fund such endeavors, understand that it is beneficial to lobby for the long-term interests of business as well as on more immediate policy problems. Like

[7]See James L. Guth, John C. Green, Lyman A. Kellstedt, and Corwin E. Smidt, "Onward Christian Soldiers: Religious Activist Groups in American Politics," in Allan J. Cigler and Burdett A. Loomis, eds., *Interest Group Politics*, 4th ed. (Washington, D.C.: Congressional Quarterly, 1995), pp. 55–76.

other interest groups, corporations recognize the simple truth that ideas are powerful. As one corporate public affairs official put it, "In a democratic society, people vote on ideas." Despite the large sums of money spent by corporations toward these kinds of activities, it is hard to know what impact they have had. One poll showed that only 6 percent of those interviewed considered corporate issue ads to be "generally credible," and 53 percent found them "not credible."[8] Nevertheless, corporate leaders can point to the strong pro-business climate that helped elect Ronald Reagan and shape his agenda. Although the disappointing American economy during the 1970s was surely the primary reason business enjoyed a political resurgence during the 1980s, it seems likely that the cumulative effect of business's lobbying for values has played at least a small role in influencing the way Americans think. Policies are inextricably tied to prevailing values; when those values are changed, mountains can be moved.

EDUCATING THE PUBLIC

At one time or another, almost all interest groups find themselves trying to educate the public about an issue. Usually the effort takes the form of the Washington office of a lobby attempting to get attention in the media for the facts that support its side of an issue controversy. When the media ignore the research that interest groups bring forward, wealthier lobbies will sometimes turn to paid advertising to get their point across.

Disseminating Research

Leaders of interest groups believe that part of the problem they face is that the public does not understand the issues the lobby is involved with. This is not condescension—a belief that people are basically ignorant—but a realistic assumption that most people care only marginally about most political issues. Moreover, the complexity of public policy problems makes it difficult for nonspecialists to acquire more than a

---

[8]Herbert Waltzer, "Advocacy Advertising and Political Influence," paper delivered at the annual meeting of the American Political Science Association," Washington, D.C., August 1986, pp. 23–24.

superficial knowledge of issues unless they conscientiously seek information. Interest group officials believe that if they can bring their facts to people's attention, they will win them over because of the "truth" in their case.

To get their facts out to the public, interest groups frequently engage in research to uncover data on their own or try to make people aware of largely ignored studies by academics and others. An interest group with one or more staffers who have a strong research background may go as far as to undertake a book-length study. But, because the demand on resources is great, and time is often of the essence in lobbying, this is not usually feasible. More modest research reports are common, though, and practically every day in Washington one group or another releases a short study of some type.

The National Solid Waste Management Association invests significantly in publications that can be used to educate the public, journalists, and policymakers. It issues reports of 8 to 12 pages on such subjects as "The Cost to Recycle at a Materials Recovery Facility," "Interstate Movement of Municipal Solid Waste," and "Privatizing Municipal Waste Services," which are full of tables and graphs presented in an eye-catching format. The reports clearly strike the right balance between scholarship and readability.

One of the most successful studies ever published by an interest group was conducted by Citizens for Tax Justice, which is supported by organized labor. The group's director, Robert McIntyre, used his background as a tax lawyer to calculate the actual taxes paid by the 250 largest corporations during the period between 1981 and 1983. He found that 17 companies paid no taxes at all for the three years under study, 48 did not have to pay taxes during two of the years, and another 128 firms paid zero taxes in at least one of the years. When the report was sent out to the press, it produced a gusher of publicity. The study was repeatedly cited as evidence that corporate America was not paying its fair share of the tax load.[9] It certainly helped to build support for the corporate tax increases that were part of the 1986 tax overhaul passed by Congress.

The success of group-sponsored research is heavily dependent on the quantity and quality of press coverage. The coverage a group re-

---

[9]Alan Murray, "Trained by Nader, This Populist Tax Lobbyist Takes Aim at Big Business That Avoids Taxes," *Wall Street Journal,* May 2, 1985.

ceives is based on subjective editorial judgments as to what is "news." Still, an interest group can improve its chances of gaining news coverage by producing high-quality research—research that is orginal, draws upon respected sources, is thoroughly documented, and is sophisticated in its approach. When the National Education Association recognized that educational quality was becoming a public issue, it saw a window of opportunity in which teacher salaries could benefit from the increased concern. To give validity to its point of view, it hired the highly respected Gallup Poll to ask a random sample of Americans a series of questions about education. The poll showed that Americans were willing to pay significantly more to teachers than they were currently being paid. The Gallup organization's prestige and its independence from the NEA helped the teachers' group gain publicity for the study.[10]

An individual lobbyist's goal is to become known for expertise in a policy area so that those in government will solicit his or her views and data. Lobbyists want to be known and trusted by the press in the same way. To achieve this recognition, they must be able to offer information not easily available elsewhere. They must also make sure that their own bias does not so color their findings that it will damage their credibility. The Union of Concerned Scientists, an antinuclear public interest group, has achieved the goal of being seen as a credible expert by the news media. One study showed that it was "the most widely quoted 'independent expert' source on nuclear energy on television newscasts."[11] Given time, lobbyists who are useful sources of information may be able to develop mutually beneficial relationships with reporters. Ideally, a lobbyist wants to be able to take the group's report to a syndicated columnist or to a reporter from the *New York Times* or the *Washington Post* and have that journalist feel confident enough about the source that he or she writes a story using that information.

An individual report by an interest group or the effort of a single lobbyist can play a crucial role in the policymaking process, but more often than not it is the cumulative effect of media coverage that is more important in influencing a policy decision. From its inception until the late 1950s, the pesticide industry enjoyed overwhelmingly positive

---

[10]Gene Maeroff, "Poll Backs Raises in Teachers' Pay," *New York Times,* July 2, 1985.
[11]Stanley Rothman and S. Robert Lichter, "Elite Ideology and Risk Perception in Nuclear Energy Policy," *American Political Science Review* 81 (June 1987), p. 393.

treatment from the nation's press. The vast majority of articles dealt with the economic benefits of pesticides. As one study put it, "Pesticides meant agricultural bounty, an end to hunger, and possibly . . . an end to human diseases borne by insects."[12] Over time the focus shifted, and by the 1970s the vast majority of stories on pesticides concerned health risks. Scientific discoveries and the independent work of journalists is responsible for some of this negative coverage, but so too is the relentless criticism of pesticides by the environmental movement.[13] Those groups that did advocacy on pesticides used their resources to bring the scholarly research to the attention of policymakers and to do what they could to make the general public anxious about the chemicals in their food.

Public Relations

When an interest group feels the press is not giving sufficient coverage to an issue or is unsympathetic to its point of view, it may decide to initiate a public relations campaign. By controlling its own copy, a group can bring home to the reader or viewer the terrible consequences it sees if the action it is advocating is not taken.

A particularly controversial public relations campaign was the "Harry and Louise" television advertisements. After President Clinton unveiled his ambitious proposal to reform the nation's health care system, the Health Insurance Association of America (HIAA) swung into action. HIAA represents small to medium-sized insurance companies, firms which believed they would be hurt by the Clinton plan. Using the same two actors, HIAA spent $14 million to run a series of ads where a husband (Harry) and wife (Louise) discussed the Clinton proposal and expressed exasperation with the plan's shortcomings. The ads generated considerable publicity about the ads themselves, and many newspaper and TV news stories contemplated the impact that the ads might be having. Yet for all the money spent by HIAA and the controversy engendered by the TV campaign, a survey failed to find any significant impact of the ads on public opinion.[14]

---

[12]Frank R. Baumgartner and Bryan D. Jones, *Agendas and Instability in American Politics* (Chicago: University of Chicago Press, 1993), p. 110.

[13]Baumgartner and Jones, *Agendas and Instability,* pp. 113, 184–192.

[14]Darrell M. West, Diane J. Heith, and Chris Goodwin, "Harry and Louise Go to Washington: Political Advertising and Health Care Reform," *Journal of Health Policy, Politics and Law,* 21 (spring 1996), pp. 35-68.

It is more common for interest groups to pay for print ads than TV commercials. The American Civil Liberties Union, for example, ran four separate full-page ads in the same issue of the *New Republic,* each of which contained some public opinion data that the group regarded as counterintuitive. The four topics were the Christian Coalition, gay rights, marijuana, and abortion. Each page ended with the tag line promoting tolerance, "American Civil Liberties Union, Live and Let Live."[15]

Unlike the Harry and Louise ads, few public relations campaigns by interest groups are formally evaluated. Most campaigns are too episodic to realistically expect that their impact could be measured. Executives of interest groups must face this problem when contemplating whether to expend their resources on public relations. A lobbyist for the chemical industry put the problem this way: "No one knows what the bottom line is or how to measure it." Since the impact of ads is so uncertain, the enormous costs of public relations loom even larger. A campaign that puts ads in major papers across the country reaches six figures very quickly. A full-page ad in the Sunday *New York Times* alone can run as high as $70,000.

Beyond cost and uncertainty are further problems. TV or print ads must be brief, catchy, and simple. Most policy problems are anything but, and it's often difficult to write ads on complex issues that stand a chance of influencing opinion. An insurance industry lobbyist said that his trade group concluded that "our issues are too technical to get them down to a simple, relevant, understandable message." But even if ads have an understandable message, those ads will be seen as just that—ads. Americans face a barrage of advertisements each day and are, understandably, a bit jaded by what Madison Avenue throws at them. Advertisements by interest groups calling for specific policies that will benefit them are going to be interpreted by many people as self-serving political statements. Groups can only hope that the power of their argument makes their case persuasive in spite of this transparency. Finally, by themselves, advertisements won't make things happen. Policymakers are not so easily moved that they will change their minds or charge into action because an ad powerfully articulates some group's proposal or grievance. Ads make the most sense when they are part of a larger campaign that involves other tactics as well. Otherwise, they are likely to amount to little more than an expensive means of raising public consciousness.

---

[15]*New Republic,* July 17 and 24, 1995, pp. 15, 17, 19, 21.

THINK TANKS

Until recently think tanks were not considered to be advocacy organizations. Instead they were thought of as little universities without students. Serious scholars pursued research on public policy questions and hoped that those in government would notice their publications. Their organizations, however, did not generally have a particular political agenda that they wanted to push government to adopt. Typical of the old-style think tank was the sober Brookings Institution, known for its high quality analyses of the federal budget and economic policymaking. Although Brookings was known as being closer to the Democratic Party's philosophy than the Republicans', the organization itself did little more than advertise its books as a way of promoting the work it produced. If someone on Capitol Hill asked a scholar at Brookings to testify or advise them on legislation, so much the better.

Though some think tanks (including Brookings) still follow the universities-without-students model, a large number of the newer research organizations in Washington are oriented toward advocacy.[16] Advocacy think tanks take a more direct route to trying to influence public policy. These think tanks design more of their projects to cover issues where congressional or administrative action is imminent, fashion more of their work into shorter, more accessible formats, devote more of their resources to public relations and media outreach, and are more inclined to hire professional staffers who are comfortable with actively trying to influence those in office.

Prototypical of the new advocacy think tanks is the Heritage Foundation, a conservative organization that aggressively seeks a role in the policymaking process. Heritage is a large think tank with an annual budget of over $25 million. It is less involved in doing research on its own than in drawing on existing research and repackaging the ideas into short position papers. Heritage staffers prepare close to 300 "backgrounders" a year, which rarely exceed 20 pages and synthesize extant research findings that support Heritage's positions.[17] A Heritage executive describes the organization's philosophy this way: "We state up front

---

[16]See Kent R. Weaver, "The Changing World of Think Tanks," *PS* 22 (September 1989), pp. 563–578.

[17]Christopher Georges, "Conservative Heritage Foundation Finds Recipe for Influence: Ideas + Marketing = Clout," *Wall Street Journal,* August 10, 1995.

what our beliefs are and admit that we are combatants in the battle of ideas. We are on one side and we make that clear. We are not just for better government and efficiency, we are for particular ideas."[18]

Advocacy think tanks like Heritage play an "inside-outside game," focusing intensely on disseminating their material directly to policymakers as well as to the broader public or attentive public who follow a particular issue. Heritage's resident expert on welfare, Robert Rector, illustrates both sides of the think tank's efforts to influence policy. Rector works closely with conservative Republican members of Congress, actually laboring with staffers drafting legislation. He feels he plays a critical role, bringing proposals to the table to encourage Congress to consider new ways of solving old problems. "I'm basically an entrepreneur of ideas," says Rector. His expertise also brings the press to him for analysis of the ongoing debate on welfare. When a *Wall Street Journal* reporter met Rector at Heritage on a Wednesday afternoon, Rector had already done 20 interviews that week.[19]

Yet the press attention to Rector or other think tank experts does not come about simply because they are knowledgeable—Washington is full of brainy people. Virtually all think tanks employ media specialists (as do many other types of lobbies) whose job is to put journalists in touch with the research staff and to gain publicity for studies when they are published. The media staffers pitch stories to journalists much the same way public relations specialists do, but think tanks have considerably more credibility than public relations firms because their *raison d'etre* is policy expertise. This credibility along with aggresive marketing has given think tanks considerable success in gaining media attention. The Worldwatch Institute's clipping service found 8,000 articles mentioning the think tank during a recent year. Says a spokesperson for the organization, "We spend a lot of money getting the word out about our work. We don't mess around."

One of the reasons think tanks are so successful in getting their research noticed is that they leave few stones unturned in finding ways to communicate the central findings of their research to people who are unlikely to read the original work. Beyond distributing their actual research reports, said one think tank spokesperson, "We also send out

[18]James A. Smith, *The Idea Brokers* (New York: Free Press, 1991), p. 205.
[19]Hilary Stout, "GOP's Welfare Stance Owes a Lot to Prodding from Robert Rector," *Wall Street Journal,* January 23, 1995.

press releases, use talk radio, write op-ed pieces, send mailings to everyone on the Hill or just select committee members." Yet in a town full of organizations and people desperately seeking media attention, think tanks cannot succeed on media savvy alone. As an official at one think tank put it, "Sometimes it doesn't matter how aggressive your marketing is. The way to make your work stand out is simply to make your work stand out."

As the think tank population in Washington has grown, specialization has become more evident as each new organization tries to establish itself in a particular niche. The Center for Equal Opportunity offers a conservative viewpoint on issues of race, ethnicity, and immigration. The Institute for Policy Studies has a decidedly leftist point of view, while the Progressive Policy Institute is emphatic in pursuing what it sees as centrist solutions to policy problems. The Institute for International Economics was started because its founders saw all the economics oriented think tanks focusing on the domestic American economy. The Washington Institute for Near East Policy publishes a dozen or more monographs a year in the hope that it can influence policy toward Israel and its Arab neighbors.

Think tanks are the embodiment of the old Washington saw that information is power. They sell expertise to the public and policymakers, and today's market seems receptive to their product. An interesting trend in Washington is the convergence of think tanks and regular lobbies. The new advocacy-style think tanks, which combine lobbying with their information strategies, are not much different from regular interest groups that try to educate the public at the same time they're lobbying policymakers. For their part, regular interest groups seem to be placing greater emphasis on gathering and disseminating information, which brings them closer to the role played by think tanks.

DEMONSTRATIONS AND HISTRIONICS

The popularity of political demonstrations is directly rooted in the civil rights movement of the 1960s. Before blacks took to the streets to march, civil rights groups working for legislative remedies to segregation and discrimination made negligible progress. The first and foremost goal of all political protests is the same: to gain coverage by the media. Like a tree falling in the forest, a protest without media coverage goes unappreciated no matter how much noise it makes. As the late

E. E. Schattschneider pointed out, when an interest group sees itself at some disadvantage, it is natural for it to want to expand the conflict: "The outcome of every conflict is determined by the *extent* to which the audience becomes involved in it."[20]

In short, interest groups protest because they feel no one will listen to them otherwise. They also reason that once the injustice about which they are protesting is brought to the attention of a larger audience, enough of the public will side with them to force policymakers into action. Yet attracting attention from the media for a protest is still only one step in a lobbying campaign. Few protests are convincing enough in themselves not to require other tactics as a follow-up. Usually then, they are part of a larger strategy in which the protest is designed to bolster direct lobbying efforts.

The civil rights demonstrations were particularly compelling stories for the media because of the violence that some produced. Evidence from the historical record shows that some of the marches were undertaken with full knowledge that they would provoke outbursts of violence against blacks by antagonistic white policemen. David Garrow writes that Martin Luther King, Jr.'s Southern Christian Leadership Conference (SCLC) consciously decided to "evoke public nastiness and physical violence" from the lawmen who were to confront them at Selma, Alabama.[21] The result was a horrified nation that saw network news coverage of defenseless blacks beaten with nightsticks and chased by mounted policemen. The marches quickly became a symbol of struggle between good and evil, justice and injustice, and Americanism and racism.

Few interest groups that have relied on protest have had anywhere near the success of the SCLC and other civil rights groups. It is not only a matter of authorities learning that their violence can increase sympathy for protesters, but also that few protests are directed toward a point of view that could crumble so easily in the court of public opinion as did racial segregation. Only in the South was there any measurable public support for it, and when the marches forced the issue to the top of the political agenda, congressional action became inevitable.

---

[20]E. E. Schattschneider, *The Semisovereign People* (Hindsdale, Ill.: Dryden Press, 1975), p. 2.
[21]David J. Garrow, *Protest at Selma* (New Haven: Yale University Press, 1978), p. 54.

The legacy of the civil rights movement (and less so the anti–Vietnam War movement) is that protests can work. For citizen groups the lesson seemed to be that organizations like themselves could have an effect with such aggressive, even abrasive behavior. Because citizen groups often feel that they lack the entree to policymakers that groups in the private sector have, demonstrations are a way of forcing people to pay attention to their demands. Yet protests are a two-edged sword. Even though they may succeed in attracting attention, they may end up doing more to alienate the public than to garner sympathy. People may see protests as unruly exercises or as reflecting a narrow, selfish view.[22] The widespread use of protests by citizen groups, though, has encouraged many other types of interest groups to use them. Labor unions too have felt they weren't getting a hearing in Washington and have resorted to protests to attract attention to their grievances. Protests have become so popular that their sheer frequency has made them less effective in attracting coverage by the media. Only a very large protest at the Capitol has a chance of making the network news.

Since few groups can attract thousands of people to a protest, they sometimes resort to histrionics instead. To capture the attention of the media when a conventional demonstration seems unlikely to generate much publicity or when too few protesters are available to put on a credible march, groups may decide on some highly imaginative and unusual protest. No tactic has seemed too extreme for Operation Rescue, which believes that abortion is so great a sin that the organization must do whatever it can to attract attention to the issue. In one protest outside an abortion clinic, an Operation Rescue leader stunned those around him by holding up an aborted fetus. Tim Bailey, dying of AIDS, told his friends in Act Up, an AIDS protest group, to do something political with his body when the end came. After he died, Act Up put his body in a van, drove to Washington, and tried to carry Bailey's open coffin into the Capitol. Capitol police forced the activists to put the coffin back in the van, but photographers and camermen recorded the scene first.[23] Still, no matter how eye-catching a demonstration is, it will amount to little more than a public venting of anger unless it is coupled with other tactics in a sustained lobbying drive.

---

[22]Benjamin I. Page, Robert Y. Shapiro, and Glenn R. Dempsey, "What Moves Public Opinion?," *American Political Science Review* 81 (March 1987), p. 37.

[23]Kenneth Janda, Jeffrey M. Berry, and Jerry Goldman, *The Challenge of Democracy,* 4th ed. (Boston: Houghton Mifflin, 1995), p. 331.

DIRECT CITIZEN LOBBYING

Even though the tactics described so far are widely used, few interest groups feel they can rely on them exclusively. When a bill is being debated in Congress or an agency is about to write a new regulation, interest groups will usually want to build on any lobbying of public opinion they have done and proceed to activate direct constituency contact with policymakers. From this perspective, those in government must be reminded how strongly constituents feel and about the implicit risks of going against a group's followers. Groups also feel they must match lobbying by adversary groups, who in turn will be trying to prove how strongly their members feel about the issue at hand.

Organizations typically use their memberships for direct lobbying by asking them to write letters or by asking those members seen as particularly influential to phone or see a policymaker in person. Washington lobbyists are nearly unanimous on how valuable this kind of support is to their own work. In interviews, they made these kinds of comments about their members:

They're essential.

That's where the leverage is.

The strength of our organization is our grassroots.

We depend on our constituents heavily—they are the salvation of our power.

For lobbyists, members' letters and phone calls legitimize their activities. One business lobbyist stated simply, "My entree comes because I represent the people back home." When letters and phone calls come into the congressman's office, the role of the lobbyists is enhanced and their access is likely to be greater than normal. Lobbyists understand intuitively what political scientists have demonstrated empirically: Members of Congress are more influenced by their constituents than by Washington lobbies.[24] To maximize their own influence, then, lobbyists will try to couple their efforts with those of their rank-and-file members.

---

[24]William P. Browne, "Organized Interests, Grassroots Confidants, and Congress," in Cigler and Loomis, *Interest Group Politics,* p. 288; and John W. Kingdon, *Congressmen's Voting Decisions,* 2nd ed. (New York: Harper and Row, 1981).

Although spontaneous mail from constituents is given most weight by congressional offices, lobbyists usually cannot wait for their group's members to act on their own. On most issues, the organization must try to stimulate letter writing. And Americans are willing to write. During the 1993–94 session of Congress, 158 million pieces of mail were delivered to House and Senate offices.[25] When interest groups want to activate a letter-writing campaign, they will occasionally use some of the public relations tactics described above. Ads will ask people to write their member of Congress and may even include a form that can be clipped, signed, and sent on to Washington. Usually a phone number is listed for more information; the people at the group's headquarters who answer the phone will offer more details about the issue and encourage callers to phone their members of Congress. Firms like Bonner and Associates use a computerized database to identify individuals whose profile suggests sympathy with the interests of the lobby that has hired the company. Bonner employees call those people and inform them of what's in the bill that the lobby opposes or supports, and then, if the target of the call voices concern, will offer to patch the call through, free of charge, to that person's representative or senator. But there's no free lunch. Hiring Bonner and Associates to generate such a grassroots campaign is expensive, and a trade group or corporation hiring the company might be charged $3 million for a month's work.[26]

Since such efforts at mobilization are so expensive, interest groups will more frequently narrow their focus to only those who are members of their organization. One such strategy is to mobilize their membership before floor action, concentrating on an upcoming committee decision. To facilitate such advocacy, the Washington lobbying offices will have their computerized membership lists retrievable by congressional district. A simple command to the computer storing the list can produce letters to all those in the organization who live in the districts or states of legislators on a particular committee. In this manner, letters

---

[25]Kenneth M. Goldstein, "Tremors Before the Earthquake: Grass Roots Communications to Congress Before the 1994 Election," paper delivered at the annual meeting of the American Political Science Association, Chicago, September, 1995, p. 4.

[26]Stephen Engleberg, "A New Breed of Hired Hands Cultivates Grass-Roots Anger," *New York Times,* March 17, 1995; and Robert Wright, "Hyperdemocracy," *Time,* January 23, 1995, pp. 17–18.

from members can be directed to the key legislators prior to a crucial committee vote.

Another way in which interest groups break down their memberships for lobbying is to develop a list of organizational activists. This type of list will be composed of people who hold positions with state and local affiliates, who have done lobbying work for the group in the past, or who are otherwise active in the organization. The National Restaurant Association has an "Action Network" of food-service executives who do government relations work in their own firms. Groups rely heavily on their activists for letter writing or phone calling because they feel they can make requests many times in a year and still get a high response rate. The more general membership is seen as equally valuable and willing to write letters but not with the same frequency or reliability. Therefore, requests to the broader membership are usually done through the newsletter, while activists will get faxes or special mailings.

The critical assumption in activating letters to members of Congress is that legislators can be moved by such efforts. This assumption seems well grounded in fact. Members of Congress do keep a close eye on how the mail and faxes are running. Part of every legislator's day is spent going through correspondence, and although he or she can't read every letter that comes in, the staff will summarize and even tabulate the sentiments expressed. Congressmen watch the mail closely because their responsiveness to their constituencies affects their chances for reelection and, even more simply, because it is part of their job and they take their job seriously. Letters do not usually make those with well-established positions switch sides, but they can be helpful in swaying opinion among fence sitters. Equally important, the mail can help to influence members of Congress at an early stage, before an issue has fully crystallized into legislation before a committee.

One of the most impressive letter-writing campaigns ever conducted was prompted by a law that would have instituted tax withholding on interest and dividend income earned by individuals. An effort against the law was spearheaded by bank lobbies such as the American Bankers Association and the U.S. League of Savings Institutions. These groups and many banks prompted letters with ads in newspapers, posters in bank windows, and inserts in monthly bank statements. (Putting a flier into bank statements was virtually free since the postage was already paid.) The outpouring of mail was so great—22 million people wrote—that Congress turned around and repealed the with-holding law, which it had passed only the year before. One reporter called the letter-writing campaign "the Hydrogen Bomb of modern-day lobbying, an effort whose firepower was awesome, whose carnage was staggering."[27]

Less is known about the effectiveness of letters from interest groups on administrative policymaking. When an agency goes through rule making, the Administrative Procedure Act generally requires that the public be given the opportunity to comment on proposed regula-tions. Many of those who write to agencies are representatives of inter-est groups since the technical jargon in regulations makes them incom-prehensible to anyone not expert on the subject. Agencies do not usually change the direction of policy in response to critical letters, but overwhelming political opposition can sometimes force withdrawal or extensive revision of proposed rules. Regulations on narrow issues are more commonly modified because comments may suggest more palat-able or efficient ways of achieving the goals.

When the stakes are particularly high, as just prior to a close vote in Congress, lobbyists will often prevail on important people in their organization to come to Washington. Organizations that are composed of elites tend to depend heavily on their membership to contact policy-makers directly. A staffer for the U.S. Conference of Mayors said of the member mayors, "They are the best lobbyists on most issues because they have the impact in the districts." When the National Endowment for the Arts and the National Endowment for the Humanities came under attack from budget-cutting Republicans in Congress in 1995, the American Council for the Arts tried to sway opinion by bringing leading actors and artists to Washington for a day of lobbying. Tony Randall, Kenny G, and Garth Brooks prowled the halls of Congress looking for legislators and photo ops.[28] To help bolster the rights of ho-mosexuals, the Human Rights Campaign Fund brought Candace Gin-grich to Washington to lobby on behalf of gays and lesbians. Ms. Gin-grich, who is openly homosexual, got an enormous amount of media attention and eventually had a photo op with her half brother, the

---

[27]Paul Taylor, "The Death of Withholding, or How the Bankers Won a Big One," *Wash-ington Post,* July 31, 1983.
[28]Michael Wines, "Celebrities Take Art's Case to Congress," *New York Times,* March 15, 1995.

Speaker of the House.[29] As pointed out in Chapter 10, however, the constituents who consistently have the best access to legislators are the heads of large corporations.

Bringing group members to Washington is not always practical, and not everyone is important enough to warrant a member of Congress returning a call. Legislators, though, do not limit themselves to meeting with elites; they spend most of their time during their frequent trips home meeting with a broad range of constituents. Interest groups can arrange meetings during such visits home, and local activists can buttonhole members of Congress at political events and social gatherings. The National Education Association goes as far as printing a form (in triplicate) that local members are expected to fill out after meeting with one of their members of Congress. They're specifically asked to briefly analyze the "member's feelings about the issue discussed." The NEA's Washington representatives apparently find this useful in the lobbying that follows.

HIGH-TECH LOBBYING

Like the rest of American society, the lobbying world has been altered by the telecommunications revolution. Interest groups have embraced the new technology for the same general reasons that other businesses have: these new tools offer them the opportunity to increase their productivity by introducing efficiencies in the way they conduct everyday tasks.

When people speak of high-tech politics, they are referring to a whole range of activities, some of which are not particularly new or technologically sophisticated. Talk radio, one of the most heavily critized media, uses decidely old technology (radio and telephones). Disdain at the role of radio in politics isn't any newer than the technology. In the 1930s Father Charles Coughlin used the radio to not only moblize the support of his group, the National Union for Social Justice, but to spew forth his venemous anti-Semitism as well.[30] Other high-tech tactics, such as e-mail, overnight polling, direct mail, the World

---

[29]Katherine Q. Seeyle, "Gingrich's Sister Lobbying on AIDS," *New York Times,* March 6, 1995.
[30]Alan Brinkley, *Huey Long, Father Coughlin, and the Great Depression* (New York: Vintage, 1983).

Wide Web, fax machines, and cable TV, are of varying vintage and are used in diverse ways by groups intent on improving their ability to influence government.

The impact of this technology on the governmental process is far from clear. We know that direct mail, which has been around awhile and been subjected to scholarly research, has had a profound impact on the way new interest groups are organized.[31] We don't yet know what differences some of the newer technologies have had. Many groups now have home pages on the World Wide Web and use their Web site to make documents available to the public as well as to market membership, publications, and services. These Internet resources surely make it easier for the computer literate to interact with lobbies, but considerable research has to be done before we fully understand how the policymaking process might be affected by this.

What does seem to be clear is that high-tech lobbying has quickened the pace of politics. An insurance lobbyist emphasized that "Response time is critical. If you rely on sending out letters and having a response mailed back you are way behind the curve." A bank lobbyist said, "We use faxes and telephone conferences to get out instantaneous information for a response from our members." High-tech tactics certainly give lobbies greater opportunity to mobilize the grassroots when events are rapidly changing and votes are quickly scheduled. On October 4, 1994, the House passed a lobbying reform bill that some interest groups felt would have inhibited certain types of grassroots advocacy. The groups faxed their activists, conservative talk radio hosts like Rush Limbaugh called their listeners to arms, and warnings were posted on computer bulletin boards. The bill went down to defeat in the Senate, and many credit the flood of faxes that deluged that body in the 48 hours between the House and Senate votes. There's no conclusive evidence that this is the reason, but considering that a similar measure passed the Senate with 92 votes the year before, this new opposition seems to have played a part.[32]

Impressive as this is, it's important to remember that such lobbying is a variation on a theme, not a whole new symphony. In the last analysis, faxes and e-mail are simply letters that constituents send to

---

[31]R. Kenneth Godwin, *One Billion Dollars of Influence* (Chatham, N.J.: Chatham House, 1988).

[32]Graeme Browning, "Zapping the Capitol," *National Journal,* October 22, 1994, pp. 2446–2447.

their members of Congress—they just get there faster. When firms like Bonner and Associates whip up a constituency out of thin air and a congressional office receives 100 communications a day on an issue that was previously receiving 1 or 2, the manufactured nature of such campaigns is all too obvious. This is not to say that manufactured calls or faxes are ignored, but they are easier to discount. Ironically, the capabilities of high-tech tactics for mobilizing public opinion may have actually raised the threshold that mail, calls, and faxes must cross before someone in a congressional office begins to pay attention.

High-tech enthusiasts claim that the Internet and other advanced technologies are beneficial to our political system because they empower citizens. House Speaker Newt Gingrich says putting congressional documents online shifts power "toward the citizens out[side] of the Beltway."[33] It does no such thing. It does allow people to obtain documents quicker than if they had to wait until they go into print and get sent through the mail, but the "citizens" who will make most use of this technology will be lobbyists and not rank-and-file Americans. Nothing about the Internet makes lawmaking any less arcane and public policy any less complicated. In short, no lobbyist will lose his or her job because of electronic access to government databases. Lobbyists will still be the ones who monitor government, read the documents, and mobilize the troops. High-tech tactics empower the same people who have always been empowered by interest group politics: those who are educated and have the necessary financial resources.

CONCLUSION

Lobbying is a multifaceted process and ideally involves the communication of valuable information from the interest group to the policymaker as well as political pressure applied from the grassroots. In a world of complex policy problems and in a city with thousands of interest groups, lobbies must do more than call on their friends in government. To make a persuasive case they need some sort of factual base that demonstrates why a particular policy is required and why a chosen alternative will work. To accomplish this interest groups must devote

---

[33]Wright, "Hyperdemocracy," p. 15.

resources to researching, synthesizing, packaging, disseminating, and promoting information.

The explosion in the numbers of interest groups has heightened competition among them. This has pushed Washington offices to search further for means of augmenting the work of their lobbyists; one consequence of this is the growing utilization of members and other followers in advocacy campaigns. Although breakthroughs in communications have facilitated grassroots lobbying, it has always been considered an important part of interest group politics.[34] Washington lobbyists know that their own efforts are aided by a strong show of support from those back home. Activism by rank-and-file citizens adds to the effectiveness of a lobbying campaign by demonstrating to policymakers that people are truly concerned about an issue and that they are waiting to see what policy decisions are going to be made.

High-tech tactics have offered interest groups new ways of involving their members in directly trying to influence their legislators. For interest groups a key virtue of high-tech politics is that lobbying campaigns can be put in place in a couple of days. Speed is of the essence, and the telecommunications revolution gives lobbies greater opportunities to utilize their members as players in the process. Yet additional tools for speeding the policymaking process are worrisome. The Framers of the Constitution envisioned a legislative process built around deliberation in a system that inhibits quick action. Contemporary America is surely a society in need of more reflection and fewer faxes.

All the various means of grassroots lobbying that are available give citizens a chance to participate in politics. Clearly, many people welcome these opportunities and take advantage of them to make their voices heard in the political process. For those able to participate in interest group politics, activism through their lobbies is a way of trying to right the wrongs of government and to fight a personal sense of powerlessness.

---

[34]Kay Lehman Schlozman and John T. Tierney, *Organized Interests and American Democracy* (New York: Harper & Row, 1986), p. 157.

Chapter 7

Political Action Committees

*F*rom grade school on, Americans are encouraged to participate in political life lest government become unresponsive to the will of the people. Such activities as writing one's congressman, joining an interest group, or signing a petition are presented as virtues. One form of political participation—donating money for election campaigns—comes with a mixed message: Contributing is good—up to a point. Too much money coming from any one source is widely seen as a danger. The concern, of course, is that those who give a lot may get back a lot. Maintaining the integrity of government means that we must somehow balance the need to fund campaigns, the desire to have people actively involved in elections, and the obligation to keep government from being unduly influenced by those with the most money to contribute.

In practical terms, the question of balancing these needs is one of determining limits on how much individuals and interest groups can contribute to candidates for office. Although these questions were directly addressed by campaign finance legislation in the 1970s, the proliferation of political action committees (PACs) since then has sparked controversy. Their importance in the electoral process forces us to confront again the classic dilemma of interest groups in a democratic society: How can the freedom of people to pursue their own interests be preserved while prohibiting any faction from abusing that freedom? The difficulty of choosing an appropriate policy involves not only the abstract question of conflicting rights but also the problem of assessing the effect of campaign contributions. What exactly are the effects of interest group money on both election results and legislative decisions? Would-be reformers must not only try to determine the answers to these questions, but must also try to assess the future consequences of their actions—consequences that are not always easy to foresee.

MOVEMENT FOR REFORM

The greatest worry today is that PACs are donating so much money to candidates for office that constituencies without PACs are put in an inferior position in the governmental process. Much of this attention is focused on business-related PACs. The fear of corporate wealth is familiar in American politics, and as far back as 1907 corporate gifts to candidates for federal office were prohibited by law. Subsequent reform legislation tried to limit the influence of wealthy individuals by placing a ceiling on the contributions they could make to candidates. Until the reforms of the 1970s, though, the wealthy had little trouble donating what they wanted by making small gifts to different campaign committees that supported the same candidate.

The most recent period of reform began with the sharp increase in the cost of campaigning stimulated by the use of television advertising. To pay for ever more costly campaigns, candidates turned more and more to wealthy contributors who could provide large donations. The extreme was insurance magnate W. Clement Stone, who gave approximately $2.8 million to Richard Nixon's campaign for the presidency in 1968.[1]

Congress took a major step toward reforming the nation's campaign financing system by passing the Federal Election Campaign Act (FECA) of 1971. Among its major requirements was that candidates disclose an itemized accounting of all expenditures and donations of more than $100. Each contributor was to be listed by name, address, and occupation. A separate bill, the Revenue Act of 1971, provided a basis for public financing of presidential elections by allowing taxpayers to donate a dollar from their tax payment to a federal presidential campaign fund by checking a box on their tax return. (The checkoff is now $3.)

---

[1]Herbert E. Alexander, *Financing Politics*, 3d ed. (Washington, D.C.: Congressional Quarterly, 1984), p. 59.

Just after these reforms came the Watergate scandal. Because money raised for reelecting President Nixon bankrolled the break-in at the headquarters of the Democratic National Committee and other illegal activities, pressure built for further reform in campaign financing. The result was the Federal Election Campaign Act Amendments of 1974, a major intent of which was to institute a system for broader public financing of presidential elections. Matching funds for small donations were made available to presidential candidates during the race for their party's nomination. Full public financing of the general election for president was set for 1976. Spending limits were also set for congressional races, although the Supreme Court subsequently struck them down.[2] In the same case, *Buckley* v. *Valeo,* the Court ruled that the 1974 amendment to the FECA limiting individual and group contributions to a candidate was valid. The limits are $1,000 for individuals and $5,000 for groups per election. (Primaries, runoffs, and general elections all count as separate elections.) An individual is further limited to contributing $25,000 overall in any calendar year, but no limit is set on the aggregate donations made by a PAC.[3]

Another part of the 1974 FECA amendments covered the prohibition against government contractors forming political action committees. This provision had prevented most businesses from operating PACs because few major corporations do not sell some service or product to the federal government. Labor unions, which like businesses were forbidden by law to make direct contributions to campaigns, used PACs to collect voluntary membership contributions and pass them on to candidates in the name of their shadow organization. For many years, the AFL-CIO Committee on Political Education (or COPE) was the best-known PAC for its widespread contributions to supporters of labor.

Concerned that litigation in the federal courts could ultimately put an end to labor PACs, the AFL-CIO sought changes in the law. Some modifications were made in 1971 at labor's request, and the ban against government contractors was lifted in the 1974 act. In going to Congress, the AFL-CIO knew it was taking a risk because the legislation would have to treat business and labor equally if it was to stand a

---

[2]*Buckley v. Valeo,* 424 U.S. 1 (1976). The Court permitted limits on spending by presidential candidates when those candidates accept public funding for their campaigns.
[3]See Alexander, *Financing Politics,* pp. 37–52, on the evolution of the FECA.

chance of passage. Labor leaders believed, however, that businesses would not form large numbers of PACs.[4] They were wrong. As Figure 7.1 demonstrates, the most significant growth in the number of PACs came from individual corporations. One observer notes that "If the labor movement has suffered a worse self-inflicted political wound, it does not come readily to mind."[5] After the FECA amendments of 1974 were passed, the Sun Oil Company went to the Federal Election Commission, which administers the FECA, and asked for a ruling concerning the administration of its PAC. The Federal Election Commission further broadened the opportunity for active corporate participation in the electoral process by declaring that corporate PACs could solicit money from both stockholders and employees and that general corporate funds could be used to administer and solicit donations.[6] With the amended act and the commission's liberal interpretation, the floodgates were opened.

PACS AND POLITICAL FINANCE

PACs today are a major, but not dominant, source of campaign funds. Of the $741 million contributed to the general election campaigns of House and Senate candidates during 1993–1994, PACs donated about $179 million (or 24 percent).[7] In comparison, PACs provided 17 percent of all contributions in the 1978 election. In recent elections, however, the proportion of donations from PACs has not risen.[8] Just as the growth in the proportion of campaign money donated by PACs has leveled off, the number of PACs has also stabilized. As Figure 7.1 demon-

---

[4]Edward M. Epstein, "Business and Labor Under the Federal Election Campaign Act of 1971," in Michael J. Malbin, ed., *Parties, Interest Groups, and Campaign Finance* (Washington, D.C.: American Enterprise Institute, 1980), pp. 112–113.

[5]Mark Green, "Political PAC-Man," *New Republic,* December 13, 1982, p. 24.

[6]Epstein, "Business and Labor under the FECA," p. 113. Amendments to the FECA in 1976 restricted solicitations to stockholders and corporate management. Also included in the 1976 law was a nonproliferation clause. Its purpose is to prevent an organization from getting around the contribution limit by utilizing multiple committees.

[7]"1994 Congressional Fundraising Climbs to New High," Federal Election Commission, April 28, 1995, p. 4.

[8]"1994 Congressional Fundraising Climbs to New High," pp.18–19; and Frank J. Sorauf, *Money in American Elections* (Glenview, Ill.: Scott, Foresman/Little, Brown, 1988), p. 55.

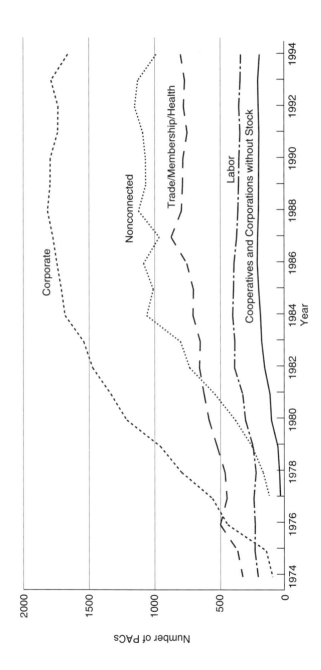

Figure 7.1   PACs, 1974–1994

Source: "FEC Releases Semi-Annual Federal PAC Count," Federal Election Commission, January 9, 1995, p. 2.

strates, the number of PACs is not growing. At the end of 1994 there were 3,954 PACs, down from a peak of 4,268 in 1988.[9] The PAC count, however, can be a misleading indicator of strength because many PACs are quite small and give only a modest amount to political candidates. Indeed, of all the PACs registered with the Federal Election Commission during the 1994 election cycle, 57.5 percent contributed a total of $5,000 or less to candidates.[10]

Aggregate funding levels vary considerably among the different categories of PACs. During 1993 to 1994, corporations gave $69.6 million to all candidates running for office; labor unions, $41.8 million; the "nonconnected" category (which includes ideological citizen groups), $18 million; and trade, membership, and health organizations, $52.8 million. This latter category includes many business trade association PACs, such as the National Association of Home Builders, as well as numerous professional association PACs, such as the American Optometric Association.[11]

At the simplest level the huge sums of money that PACs contribute reflect the desire of interest groups to gain access to policymakers. As one corporate PAC director put it, "My job is to get access so I can get my information in there." Groups also participate because they see themselves as competing with other interest groups. They are afraid of being at a disadvantage if they don't give. This striving to be heard extends beyond the natural antagonism between business and labor and between ideological groups of the left and the right. Interest groups fear being lost in the shuffle among all the thousands of groups. Contributing money is seen as an important advantage in getting policymakers to pay attention to *their* problems rather than someone else's. One businessman defended his company's PAC with this simple logic: "Talking to politicians is fine, but with a little money they hear you better."[12]

---

[9]"FEC Releases Semi-Annual Federal PAC Count," Federal Elections Commission, January 9, 1995, p. 2.
[10]*Annual Report 1994* (Washington, D.C.: Federal Election Commission, 1995), p. 74.
[11]Cooperatives gave $3 million and corporations without stock contributed $4.1 million. "PAC Activity in 1994 Elections Remains at 1992 Levels," Federal Election Commission, March 31, 1995, p. 3. The Federal Election Commission's six categories are hardly a model of clarity, and the trade, membership, and health grouping is especially troublesome. It throws together such organizations as the American Bankers Association, the National Rifle Association, and the National Association of Retired Federal Employees.
[12]Green, "Political PAC-Man," p. 20.

The emergence of PACs is not only a cause of increased campaign spending but a consequence of it as well. In today's media-oriented politics, campaigns are costly affairs. The specific need for television or other items, though, is almost secondary to the basic impulse of a campaign that drives candidates to spend whatever they can raise. Candidates push their fundraising efforts to collect the greatest possible sum because they are afraid of being outspent by their opponents.

Members of the House and Senate constantly troll for contributions—they're like fishermen who never leave the lake. It's not surprising that incumbents place a premium on raising campaign money from all sources. "Their lives and jobs depend on it," said one PAC official. But incumbents do not merely solicit contributions from PACs, they pressure them by having staffers or campaign officials communicate that the representative or senator considers their participation in the campaign as important. A survey of PAC managers revealed that 84 percent said that incumbents pressured them for a contribution at least occasionally.[13] The pressure can sometimes be extreme. When the Republicans took over Congress after the 1994 election, they immediately went after PACs that had supported incumbent Democrats who had lost. House Majority Whip Tom DeLay wrote to such PACs citing the specific amount they had contributed to a Democrat and said that he was "surprised" that the group supported the other party. DeLay offered absolution, however, by telling each PAC that it now had "the opportunity to work toward a positive future relationship."[14]

The Yield

If donating money can get a foot in the door, it follows that giving a lot of money can get a foot into a lot of doors. Some of the larger or wealthier constituencies have been contributing extremely large aggregate sums to congressional candidates. As Table 7.1 shows, the largest PACs contribute more than $2 million each to congressional candidates. Sheer size enables these PACs to go beyond the common pattern of contributing to a modest number of candidates, most of whom are incumbents sitting on committees relevant to the group's policy interests.

---

[13]Dan Clawson, Alan Neustadtl, and Denise Scott, *Money Talks* (New York: Basic Books, 1992), p. 61.
[14]Richard L. Berke, "G.O.P. Seeks Foes' Donors, and Baldly," *New York Times,* June 17, 1995.

TABLE 7.1   TOP TEN PACS, 1993–1994
CONTRIBUTIONS TO CANDIDATES FOR FEDERAL OFFICE

1. United Parcel Service Political Action Committee	$2,647,113
2. American Federation of State, County, and Municipal Employees	2,529,682
3. Democratic Republican Independent Voter Education Committee	2,487,152
4. American Medical Association Political Action Committee	2,386,947
5. National Education Association Political Action Committee	2,260,850
6. Association of Trial Lawyers of America Political Action Committee	2,164,035
7. United Auto Workers Voluntary Community Action Program	2,147,190
8. National Rifle Association Political Victory Fund	1,853,038
9. Realtors Political Action Committee	1,851,978
10. Dealers Election Action Committee of the National Automobile Dealers Association	1,832,570

Source: "PAC Activity in 1994 Elections Remains at 1992 Levels," Federal Election Commission, March 31, 1995, p. 20.

It is not only how much PACs give that is important, but how much of what they raise actually ends up in the treasuries of candidates running for office. Differences in the "yield" (percentage of money raised that is actually donated to candidates) for the major categories of PACs are interesting to note. During the 1994 campaign cycle, corporate PACs contributed 61 percent of what they raised to federal candidates, while labor (47 percent) and trade, membership, and health (55 percent) had somewhat lower yields. In contrast, groups in the nonconnected category gave as a whole only 24 percent of what they raised to candidates; when independent expenditures for or against candidates are added to direct contributions, the figure rises to just 27 percent.[15]

Why is it that nonconnected citizen PACs don't contribute more of their money to candidates? The basic reason is overhead. Although direct mail has facilitated growth of citizen PACs, it is also the underlying problem that explains why these groups give so small a percentage of their gross to candidates. It is not only that most of the money must go for mailing lists, computer resources, consultants, postage, staff, and general overhead, but part of the little that remains must be plowed back into prospecting with new lists. Solicitation costs for corporations, trade and professional associations, and labor unions are not as high as

---

[15]"PAC Activity in 1994 Elections Remains at 1992 Levels," p. 3.

those for citizen groups because they are raising money only from members of their organization, a fixed population of individuals who are already good prospects to contribute.[16] The key difference between citizen group PACs and these other kinds of PACs is the institutional base of the other organizations.[17] Corporations, trade and professional associations, and unions have solid financial bases independent of their political appeal. That financial support, in turn, allows them to subsidize the solicitation of members or employees for their PACs.

Beyond the advantages of institutional support, corporations, trade groups, and professional associations have the luxury of soliciting employees or members who tend to be relatively wealthy and well-educated. They may also have a very strong personal identification with their group and see their donations as part of their professional obligations. The American Medical Association PAC receives contributions from about 40,000 of its 300,000 member physicians. The Prudential Insurance PAC solicits contributions from only 1,500 employees (presumably executives), but 1,000 of them donate. Citizen PACs must throw their net a little wider than those in the top income strata. As noted in Chapter 4, an ideological group prospecting with a new list is fortunate if it gets 2 percent of those solicited to contribute to the organization.

Unions are different because the basis of membership is usually mandatory, though contributions to union PACs are voluntary. Yet there is a strong socialization process exerted through meetings and union leadership that encourages workers to participate in the political process through PACs and campaign work. About a third of the United Auto Workers' 1.3 million members contribute, which enabled their PAC to donate over $2.1 in the 1994 election.

Citizen PAC officials defend their groups by noting that they do not have additional funds to pay overhead costs, that direct mail is also a form of campaign advertising, and that their PACs play a broader role than just donating money, especially in influencing the debate over issues. Nevertheless, citizen PACs raise money in an extremely competitive environment, and costs of soliciting funds remain stubbornly

---

[16]Some citizen groups are "connected" PACs. They have parent organizations that lobby the government, and the PAC can restrict its solicitations to the group's membership.
[17]See Robert H. Salisbury, "Interest Representation: The Dominance of Institutions," *American Political Science Review* 78 (March 1984), pp. 64–76; and Jack L. Walker, *Mobilizing Interest Groups in America* (Ann Arbor: University of Michigan Press, 1991).

high.[18] Beyond the costs that consume most of the money given to ideological PACs is a further problem: accountability. The individuals who give money to an ideological PAC assume that a good part of it will end up in political campaigns. They are not told in the solicitation letters they receive what percentage of money donated actually reaches candidates. Donors to the National Right to Life Political Action Committee believe their money will be channeled to candidates who share their passionate commitment to stopping abortions. How many of them would give if they knew that in the last election only $200,000 of the $1.4 million raised by the group (just 14 percent of the total) was actually contributed to congressional candidates?[19]

Other Assistance

For the vast majority of PACs, campaign efforts are limited to donating funds to candidates for office. There are some PACs, however, that work to benefit candidates in other ways.

Independent Expenditures   For PACs the appeal of spending money on their own in favor of or against a candidate is that PACs can spend as much as they want rather than being restricted by the $5,000-per-election limit. They must truly work independently, refraining from any kind of consultation with candidates or their campaign officials. The National Conservative Political Action Committee's seeming success with independent ads harshly attacking liberal Democrats in the 1980 election led many to believe that independent spending would be the wave of the future. It has not turned out that way. During the 1993–1994 election cycle, PACs made independent expenditures totalling only $4.7 million. This is 2.5 percent of all the money that PACs contributed or spent on campaigns.[20] Independent expendi-

---

[18]John C. Conybeare and Peverill Squire, "Political Action Committees and the Tragedy of the Commons," *American Politics Quarterly* 22 (April 1994), pp. 154–174.
[19]"PAC Activity in 1994 Elections Remains at 1992 Levels," pp. 18, 32. The organization also makes independent expenditures for and against candidates (especially presidential candidates), but a close analysis of their expenses reveals that most of this money actually goes for fundraising costs too. See Ronald Gunn, "A New Political Pragmatism? The National Right to Life Committee," in Robert Biersack, Paul S. Herrnson, and Clyde Wilcox, eds., *Risky Business?* (Armonk, N.Y.: M. E. Sharpe, 1994), p. 135.
[20]"PAC Activity in 1994 Elections Remains at 1992 Levels," p. 11.

tures on congressional campaigns have actually decreased since the mid-1980s.[21]

There are a number of reasons why independent campaign expenditures are not more popular with PACs. First, most PACs do not have the staffs that could manage such an effort. Second, PACs that have parent groups that lobby on Capitol Hill are hesitant to be so closely identified with a candidate because they may permanently alienate an opponent who might win. Few PACs with parent lobbies are willing to preclude any kind of relationship with an incumbent. Third, independent spending has something of an unsavory image; many think such expenditures are unfair since there are no spending limits. Fourth, independent campaigns that stand a chance of having an impact are quite expensive. Most PACs have modest sums to contribute to all candidates, and they feel it is more strategic to spread that money around rather than spend it all in one or two races.

Bundling   A handful of PACs "bundle" contributions to a specific candidate and then send them on to him or her. A spokesman for the Council for a Livable World, which uses this tactic extensively, explains, "We'll send a letter to contributors, saying please send [us] a check to 'Joe Smith's' campaign for Congress. One hundred percent of that money goes directly to the candidate." The advantage to PACs is that since the checks are made out to the candidate and never pass through a PAC's account, the total is not subject to the $5,000 gift limit. Thus, a PAC can send on a bundle of checks that total a considerable amount and earn the deep gratitude of the candidate. EMILY'S List, a nonconnected PAC that supports pro-choice Democratic women candidates, has been particularly successful in bundling contributions. The group claims that it channeled $8.2 million in contributions in the 1994 campaign. Members must send $100 to the organization itself and pledge to contribute a minimum of $100 to at least two Democratic women backed by EMILY'S List.[22]

In-Kind Contributions   An in-kind contribution is a gift other than cash given to a candidate. The value of the contribution is counted as

---

[21]Frank J. Sorauf, *Inside Campaign Finance* (New Haven: Yale University Press, 1992), p. 181.
[22]EMILY'S List solicitation, July 14, 1995; and Terri Susan Fine, "When EMILY WISHes Upon a Star, Do Her Dreams Come True," paper delivered at the annual meeting of the American Political Science Association, New York City, September, 1994.

if it were a regular cash contribution in reports filed with the Federal Election Commission, but such gifts may actually be more helpful to candidates than a check. For example, the National Committee for an Effective Congress (NCEC) puts the bulk of its money available to candidates into its Campaign Services Program.[23] Using its expertise and taking advantage of economies of scale, it provides liberal congressional candidates with services that would be more difficult or more expensive for the campaigns to purchase on their own. One such form of assistance is NCEC's precinct targeting effort, which uses sophisticated computer technology and know-how to isolate precincts that, for example, contain high percentages of split-ticket voters. "We have a greater impact on a campaign by doing this [kind of thing]," says one NCEC staffer.

DOES MONEY MATTER?

It is much easier to document the amount of money being contributed than to account for its influence. We have no way of knowing for sure whether any group's contribution made a difference in an election. Likewise, interpreting the influence of money on votes in Congress is always a matter of inference.

Elections

Although the effect of any one group's contribution is difficult to measure, the influence of aggregate spending on congressional outcomes has been examined. Political scientist Gary Jacobson concludes after careful statistical analysis that campaign contributions are very important to the electoral chances of a nonincumbent. "In contests between incumbents and challengers, the critical variable is the amount spent by the challenger."[24] The amount spent by incumbents has less consequence for them because they enter elections with a decided advantage in public recognition. Increased spending by incumbents can af-

---

[23]See Paul S. Herrnson, "The National Committee for an Effective Congress: Liberalism, Partisanship, and Electoral Innovation," in Biersack, Herrnson, and Wilcox, *Risky Business?*, pp. 39–55.

[24]Gary C. Jacobson, *Money in Congressional Elections* (New Haven: Yale University Press, 1980), p. 51.

fect that recognition only marginally, if at all, but money is absolutely vital if the challenger is to become known to the electorate.[25]

Although money given to challengers is much more likely to affect their chance of winning an election, the largest share of PAC money goes to incumbents. Among all candidates seeking a House or Senate seat during the 1993–1994 period, PACs gave $137.6 million to congressional incumbents, $18.8 million to challengers of incumbents, and $32.9 million to those fighting for an open seat.[26] This is not surprising given the propensity of incumbents to win reelection. In the House, members choosing to run for reelection usually win at the rate of 90 percent or more. Senate elections are more volatile, with the rate of reelection for incumbents ranging from below 60 percent to above 90 percent.[27] PACs would be foolish to ignore this trend in making their contribution decisions.

For a large number of PACs, influencing elections is secondary to improving a group's access to members of Congress. Even when they prefer the challenger, PACs commonly donate instead to incumbents to enhance their relationship with them. PACs defend this practice as being a matter of pragmatism. Even if the incumbent is antagonistic toward the group's goals, some PACs will contribute anyway just to keep lines of communication open. Given that most PACs have modest budgets and are limited in the number of candidates they can give to, challengers to incumbents tend to receive low priority. Said one PAC director, "We're realists. If a member of Congress has a consistent voting record against us . . . [but] his district isn't apt to turn him out, we're not going to throw our money down a rat hole."

Committee chairs and party leaders are in an especially good position to receive campaign donations because of their crucial role in the legislative process. They can sometimes determine whether a bill or amendment will even be considered. Members on committees with

---

[25]Jacobson, *Money in Congressional Elections,* p. 53. On incumbent spending, see, *contra,* Donald P. Green and Jonathan S. Krasno, "Salvation for the Spendthrift Incumbent: Reestimating the Effects of Campaign Spending in House Elections," *American Journal of Political Science* 32 (November 1988), pp. 884–907; and the rejoinder, Gary C. Jacobson, "The Effects of Campaign Spending in House Elections: New Evidence for Old Arguments," *American Journal of Political Science* 34 (May 1990), pp. 334–362.
[26]"PAC Activity in 1994 Elections Remains at 1992 Levels," p. 5.
[27]Norman J. Ornstein, Thomas E. Mann, Michael J. Malbin, eds., *Vital Statistics on Congress, 1995–1996* (Washington, D.C.: Congressional Quarterly, 1994), pp. 60–61.

well-endowed interest group constituencies are similarly blessed. The House Ways and Means Committee, for example, is a magnet for PAC money because it has jurisdiction over tax legislation. Each committee, however, has its constituency. PACs representing accountants have poured money into the campaigns of members of the House Commerce Committee because, among other things, they want securities lawsuits restricted to limit accountants' exposure in fraud cases. In the 1994 election, committee member Billy Tauzin received $70,000 just from accounting firm PACs and professional associations like the American Institute of Certified Public Accountants.[28]

The propensity of PACs to back incumbents has continued strong over the years. As Figure 7.2 illustrates, challengers and open-seat candidates actually got a higher share of PAC money in 1978 than in 1994. One might guess that when there is sharp movement toward one of the parties in a congressional election, as in 1994, changes in PAC contributions are related in some way to the political upheaval. Even though the Republicans picked up 52 seats in the 1994 election, PACs were much less change-oriented than the American public. Although there was a rise in funds channeled to open-seat candidates, PACs demonstrated once again that they are the incumbents' best friend. As one study noted, "The best available data do not implicate PACs in the political cataclysm of 1994."[29]

Beyond an incumbent's inherent advantage in rasing money, the behavior of PACs can make the incumbent's victory a self-fulfilling prophecy. By determining that specific incumbents are likely to win and thereby withholding support from challengers, PACs further undermine the challengers' chances. Once deemed unlikely to win, a challenger's chances are worsened because of the critical need for contributions to make the campaign viable. The impact of PACs on the electoral fortunes of challengers is compounded by the groups' herd instincts. One representative of a business PAC said in an interview, "The majority of people watch the big ten [business PACs]. If they haven't given, none will." It should also be stressed that a substantial portion of PAC money goes to incumbents whom the groups are en-

---

[28]Jeffrey Taylor, "Accountants' Campaign Contributions Are About to Pay Off in Legislation on Lawsuit Protection," *Wall Street Journal,* March 8, 1995.

[29]Theodore J. Eismeier and Philip H. Pollock III, "Of Time and Political Action Committees," paper delivered at the annual meeting of the Midwest Political Science Association, Chicago, April, 1995, p. 12.

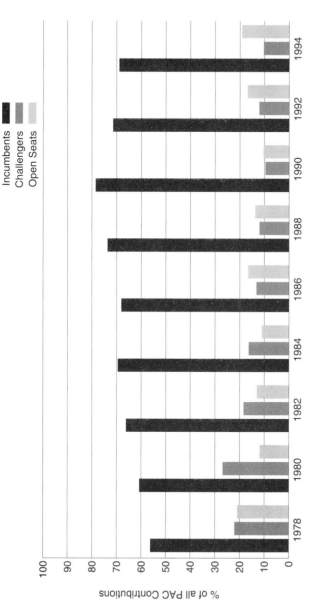

Figure 7.2   PAC Contributions by Type of Candidate

Source: Twenty-Year Report (Washington, D.C.: Federal Election Commission, 1995), p. 29.

thusiastic about and want to protect. By giving early in the campaign cycle and helping incumbents build formidable war chests, PACs can discourage attractive challengers from appearing in the first place.

Although most PAC contributions go to incumbents, because access is the commodity that PACs value most, the amount of money donated to challengers and open-seat candidates is hardly insignificant. This money is spread over a smaller number of races because there are fewer competitive or open seats. In this era of sophisticated polling and political analysis, the campaigns where the money will do the most good are widely identified and monitored closely. As we will explore later, PACs are well versed on which candidates are running ahead and are guided by this knowledge when targeting donations.

Of the four major categories of PACs, corporations are the most likely to support incumbents, with 76 percent of money donated going to those running for reelection. PACs in the trade/membership/health category give only slightly less to incumbents. Even nonconnected PACs, whose donors are surely the most ideological of contributors to political action committees, give 62 percent to incumbents.[30] The bottom line about PACs is that they are agents of the status quo.

Public Policy

The problem of interest groups and campaign finance is not new. Some PACs were active, of course, prior to the FECA amendments. More importantly, corporations and their broader industries were represented outside the PAC system by large, individual contributions from executives in various businesses. The oil industry did not have to wait for the FECA amendments to have a say on Capitol Hill. One turning point was the 1940 elections, when a young Texas congressman, Lyndon Johnson, aggressively sought out wealthy oilmen and channeled their money into the hands of his Democratic colleagues across the country.[31]

Nevertheless, PACs are now the instrument through which interest groups get their money to candidates. Does all the money they

---

[30]"PAC Activity in 1994 Elections Remains at 1992 Levels," p. 5.
[31]Robert Caro, *The Path to Power* (New York: Random House, 1982), especially pp. 606–664.

contribute influence public policy? After reviewing the available research, one scholar concluded, "Empirical evidence about the influence of PAC contributions on congressional voting is filled with ambiguity and apparent contradiction."[32] A number of studies show that PAC contributions do not seem to influence congressional voting decisions or only influence them in rather marginal ways.[33] However, there is other research which shows that PAC money appears to have influenced votes. One study of tobacco PACs and congressional voting determined that "Tobacco industry contributions to members of the U.S. Congress strongly influence the federal tobacco policy process."[34] The authors divided all House members into three tiers according to the amount of campaign contributions received from tobacco lobbies. Those members of the House who were in the top tier of contributions received were 14.4 times more likely to vote against an amendment prohibiting subsidies for a tobacco export program than those in the bottom tier. This pattern was evident on a range of tobacco-related legislation. When other factors were taken into account (statistically controlled), the correlation between votes and tobacco contributions remained firm.

Despite the apparent link between tobacco PAC donations and votes on the floor of the House of Representatives, this study is far from definitive. The Representatives who receive the largest tobacco contributions may be those who are the most reliable supporters of tobacco legislation and, thus, are being rewarded by the tobacco PACs for their past support of the industry. Determining the causality of votes is a central problem in research on PACs. How do we know that contributions actually *caused* a member to vote one way or another? For their part, legislators claim that donations are rewards rather than indirect bribes. In reference to the alleged influence of PAC donations, Republican Representative Jack Fields of Texas said bluntly, "I haven't

---

[32]John R. Wright, "PACs, Contributions, and Roll Calls: An Organizational Perspective," *American Political Science Review* 79 (June 1985), p. 401.
[33]See, for example, Janet M. Grenzke, "PACs in the Congressional Supermarket: The Currency Is Complex," *American Journal of Political Science* 33 (February 1989), pp. 1–24.
[34]Stephen Moore, Sidney M. Wolfe, Deborah Lindes, and Clifford Douglas, "Epidemiology of Failed Tobacco Control Legislation," *Journal of the American Medical Association* 272 (October 19, 1994), p. 1171.

changed my philosophy in the 15 years I've been in Congress. My philosophy has always been free enterprise and to support whatever creates jobs, and those who want to contribute to me are free to do so."[35]

Another difficulty in assessing PAC influence is understanding how contributions affect agendas. Policy alternatives may never be considered because of the dependence of legislators on the contributions of industry PACs with legislation before their committees. Measuring how the expectations within a committee are shaped and nurtured by campaign contributions may not be possible. Policy ideas that are never proposed may be just as much a function of PAC influence as the proposals that are actively championed by lobbies and taken up by Congress.

Despite the methodological difficulties in such research, there is work by both journalists and political scientists which makes a strong case that PAC contributions influenced members of Congress on specific policy questions. One study, for example, found that contributions had an effect on mobilizing sympathetic legislators to actively push the group's position in committee.[36] Another study of committee voting found that by themselves PAC contributions did little to influence policy decisions. However, PAC contributions facilitated access by lobbyists, and contact with lobbyists was linked to the way members of the committee acted on the legislation.[37] Both of these carefully nuanced studies suggest that the real impact of PACs in terms of access and policy decisions comes at the committee level rather than on the floor. Since few PACs have the funds to try to influence the entire membership, and since policy is generally made in committee rather than on the floor, it makes perfect sense for lobbies to direct their contributions to members who sit on the right committees.

PAC influence is probably greatest on legislation that is not highly visible. Why did Walt Disney and other movie studios receive a transition rule in the 1986 tax bill giving them a lucrative temporary exemption from a change in the investment tax credit? It's hard to believe that PAC money contributed by the movie industry to selected legislators

[35]Taylor, "Accountants' Campaign Contributions."

[36]Richard L. Hall, "Buying Time: Moneyed Interests and the Mobilization of Bias in Congressional Committees," *American Political Science Review* 84 (September 1990), pp. 797–820.

[37]John R. Wright, "Contributions, Lobbying, and Committee Voting in the U.S. House of Representatives," *American Political Science Review* 84 (June 1990), pp. 417–438.

had nothing to do with it.[38] One survey of corporate lobbyists found that 90 percent described a tax loophole benefiting their company or industry as an example of an issue they won.[39]

In fairness, members of Congress are more than willing to act on behalf of their constituents without PACs. Many constituency groups that do not make campaign contributions enjoy good access to their legislators. Still, legislators do not have the time to work strenuously on behalf of all constituency groups that approach them (and with whom they agree). It seems inevitable that their choice of how to spend their time will be affected by PAC contributions. As one lobbyist put it, congressmen may forget who gives, but "their schedulers don't."[40] Legislators compound this problem not only by pressuring PACs to give a donation, but also by asking lobbyists to raise funds for them. Whether lobbyists feel comfortable doing this is beside the point because if they refuse, says one Washington lawyer, "Chances are you are not going to get your phone calls returned. Maybe once, but you are not going to be on anyone's short list."[41] Members of Congress who ask lobbyists and PACs to help them are surely prepared to reciprocate.

The role of PACs in the campaign finance system is routinely defended by lobbyists as a means of providing them with access to those who make policy decisions. "The whole system is built on access," says one lobbyist. Some may argue that access cannot be divorced from influence because the policymaking process is not neatly divided into an access stage and a hermetically sealed policy formulation stage that excludes group participation. If access had no value in influencing policy, why would it be so important for lobbies to possess it? When lobbyists were pressed and asked if access was really a form of influence, they were divided in their responses. Some rejected the idea that access was anything more than an opportunity to talk to legislators. The PAC director of a professional association said, "We just want our day in court. . . . Access is just a chance to say our piece." An official of a drug company PAC took offense at any notion that access is influence: "[Contributions] help your ability to have a dialogue with people but that does not mean that you are buying a vote."

---

[38]Brooks Jackson, "Congress, Wined and Dined by Jack Valenti, Writes a Rule Giving Hollywood a Tax Break," *Wall Street Journal,* June 17, 1987.
[39]Clawson et al., *Money Talks,* p. 95.
[40]Jeffrey H. Birnbaum, *The Lobbyists* (New York: Times Books, 1992), p. 165.
[41]Birnbaum, *The Lobbyists,* p. 165.

Influence does not have to be thought of as crude vote buying, and some PAC officials acknowledged that influence was, in fact, what they were after in making donations to members of Congress. The spokesperson for a health association PAC said bluntly, "Influence is an extension of access. Influence gives you a leg up on people who don't have it." An insurance company's PAC director defined his job as using contributions to gain influence: "The more influence that I have, the better the job I'm doing for my employers and customers."

TARGETING AND COOPERATION

For all the millions of dollars that are collectively given by the PACs, donations are still doled out in small increments, from a few hundred dollars to $5,000. For each PAC, large or small, decisions must be reached on whom to give to and how much they should receive. The decisions that groups make reflect their own needs and judgments as well as judgments of the broader political community in Washington.

Decisions on endorsements and donations are usually handled by a small group of people within each PAC. Although the PAC may have only a single administrator, that person typically shares decision-making authority with a board. Yet the board's role is often symbolic. One study concludes that "the PAC staff not only often influences candidate se-lection, it many times completely determines it."[42] This description of decision making at the American Dental Association PAC outlines a formalized process involving the group's board, but where decisions are bound by rather general criteria:

> We have a board of sixteen members that represent our nationwide con-stituents. The board evaluates the criteria of incumbents, challengers, and those running for open seats. The board looks to see if these people have a relationship with our constituents and how they have dealt with them in the past. If an incumbent is on a committee with an assignment over den-tal issues and they have been accommodating to us and their staff has been helpful to the members back home, we are likely to support them. However, it is hard to find dental specific assignments. We have to go into committees for this. We are very bipartisan and we look at all candidates. For example, even if a member does not have jurisdiction over one of our

---

[42]Larry J. Sabato, *PAC Power* (New York: Norton, 1984), p. 41.

issues, but they have a good relationship with the members at home, we will support them.

For most PACs, most decisions about whom to back are relatively easy because the groups are simply reaffirming their support for incumbents. Some of the PACs with a strong orientation toward incumbents make little effort to use their money strategically to influence close races. They hold little, if any, money back, to make donations in the contests that appear to be going down to the wire. Instead, they want to gain the gratitude of the incumbent by giving early to help him or her build up a commanding war chest. A health lobbyist said his PAC's strategy was to take "the opportunity to shine while others are still waiting."

The more difficult decisions involve contributions to challengers, open-seat candidates, and even incumbents locked in tight races. A group holding back $20,000 or $30,000 for close races wants to make sure it invests that money wisely. Is a particular race really close or a foregone conclusion? Much of the information comes from other like-minded PACs. One trade association PAC official said, "The Washington, D.C.-based PACs are a close-knit community. Most people associated with the PACs know each other from other political work."

Communication between those affiliated with various interest groups and their PACs leads not only to trading information on which candidates are doing well but also to requests for assistance to particular candidates. One bank lobbyist said it was common for him to get calls from trade associations and PACs saying, "We have a candidate. Come meet him." The PACs and their parent organizations will hold a meeting or reception for a candidate and invite other PAC representatives to come. Since there are literally hundreds of candidates who may approach a PAC, systematically evaluating each one would be a considerable task for organizations that are typically small. Consequently, most PACs do not rely on a questionnaire or formal interview when they size up new candidates. "It's a casual thing," said the head of a corporate PAC.

Since most PACs have neither the resources nor the incentives to thoroughly assess new candidates or closely analyze the competitiveness of all the House and Senate contests, they must rely on other organizations when they need additional information. The two most important channels through which PACs acquire campaign and candidate information are the congressional committees of the two national parties and a small group of large and well-respected PACs. As discussed in Chapter 3, the Republican National Committee and the Democratic National Committee have PAC liaison staffers who work with the congressional campaign committees to help sympathetic PACs direct their money where the party most needs it.

The second source of information and direction for PAC managers are "lead PACs." Three lead PACS dominate: BIPAC, COPE, and NCEC. BIPAC, the Business-Industry Political Action Committee, is highly respected among Washington lobbyists for trade groups and corporations. It's fundamentally a Republican organization and is especially useful to other PACs by identifying those new candidates who are most pro-business. The AFL-CIO's COPE works to guide the donations of 48 labor PACs. The organization prepares a "marginal list" to identify labor sympathizers who are in relatively close races. This, in turn, will generate $50,000 to $200,000 in donations by PACs who follow COPE's advice.[43] As noted earlier, the liberal National Committee for an Effective Congress does sophisticated election analysis that it shares with candidates it endorses. It also holds meetings to brief liberal PACs in Washington about what it knows.

PACs are not allowed to formally coordinate their giving, but by sharing information about how races are shaping up and whom they like, or by holding receptions for candidates, PACs with similar interests act to achieve the same goal without violating the law.

CONCLUSION

Change in campaign finance law that came with the Federal Election Campaign Act Amendments of 1974 led to sharp growth in participation by interest groups in the electoral process. This explosion has been a mixed blessing at best. PACs give people a means of participating in the electoral system, though this participation may be only the few minutes it takes to write a check. What this participation does, however, is give people a tangible means of trying to influence the issues they care about most. Donors assume that their contributions improve the chances that their views will be heard on Capitol Hill. PACs also

---

[43]Clyde Wilcox, "Coping with Increasing Business Influence: The AFL-CIO's Committee on Political Education," in Biersack, Herrnson, and Wilcox, eds., *Risky Business?*, pp. 24–25.

bring badly needed campaign funds into the electoral system. It is easy for reformers to call for an end to PACs, but it has proved difficult to find an alternative source of funds that all can agree on.

Unfortunately, PACs are symptomatic of a disturbing and growing attitude that says, "Without campaign contributions, my interests will not be heard as well in Congress." When some groups in a policy area begin to contribute, other groups may feel they have no choice but to organize a PAC to try to keep their opponents from gaining an advantage in Congress. The price for this "equal representation" of PACs is that whatever policy actions Congress takes, large segments of the American people will believe that the "other side" bought the decision with their campaign contributions.

The Federal Election Campaign Act and its amendments were intended to reform a campaign system that had raised profound questions about the integrity of the political process. Undisclosed donations by fat-cat donors were seen as incompatible with the proper workings of a democracy. Strict disclosure requirements, public financing of presidential elections, increased incentives for individual giving, and an expanded role for interest groups were all part of this broad effort at reform. Expanding the role of interest groups in campaign finance has not, however, restored public confidence in the integrity of the political process. Rather, it has heightened concern about the role of interest groups in a democracy.

Chapter
8

Washington Lobbying

*I*t might seem best for an interest group to approach a lobbying campaign with a coordinated strategy to influence public opinion, activate group members, and have their lobbyists meet with public officials continually. Such an idealized approach is not generally possible; financial resources are limited, members can be called to action only so many times each year, and most organizations have only a few lobbyists who must juggle a number of issues simultaneously.

With limited organizational resources, lobbyists must develop advocacy plans with great care. Lobbyists' work is complicated by the ideological differences often found between themselves and those they wish to influence. Sometimes, neither Congress nor the executive branch is likely to give the group what it wants, and it may turn to the courts instead. Yet going to court is expensive, and issues may be sacrificed because the organization cannot afford to add litigation to its already strained budget.

How do lobbyists and leaders of interest groups make such decisions in planning the structure of lobbying campaigns? After we examine how Washington representatives lobby the three branches of government, we will analyze how interest groups plan their strategy and make their advocacy decisions.

CONGRESS

With most of the work done in Congress done in committees, it's no surprise that most of the work of legislative lobbyists is done there too. Usually the substantive decisions that Congress makes on questions of public policy are made either prior to formal committee deliberations or during the "markup" of a bill by committee members. Trying to change legislation on the floor of either house through amendments is a chancy strategy. Says one corporate lobbyist, "You have to start at the bottom. You have to start at the subcommittee level. . . . If you wait until it gets to the floor, your efforts will work very seldom."

That Congress relies on its committees works to the advantage of interest groups. It enables them to concentrate their lobbyists' work on relatively few legislators and staffers. Since most interest groups employ small professional staffs, communicating effectively with even half of the offices on Capitol Hill may not be possible. Committee-based policymaking is advantageous to interest groups not just because of the committees' more manageable size but also because it facilitates building personal relationships. As one corporate lobbyist noted, "Once you have established a good reputation, they will call on you." In time and with regular contact, lobbyists have the opportunity to prove that their information is reliable and that they can be of help to the committee in developing outside support for pending legislation.

Such relationships are usually begun and nurtured at the staff level. Committee staffers are more immediately accessible and can put lobbyists' ideas directly into drafts of legislation or bring the ideas to the attention of their bosses if they so choose. Staff members do not act out of line with the general policy preferences of the representatives and senators they work for. Yet within this general constraint, their influence can be quite significant. In an interview, a lobbyist for a large manufacturer said bluntly: "If you have a staff member on your side, it might be a hell of a lot better than talking to the member." When NAFTA was emerging as a significant political issue, a Mexican business alliance paid for 76 congressional aides to come to Mexico to meet with government officials and businesspeople. The business coalition's expectation was that these staffers would influence their bosses' attitudes.[1]

---

[1] Bob Davis, "Mexico Mounts a Massive Lobbying Campaign to Sell North American Trade Accord in U.S.," *Wall Street Journal*, May 20, 1993.

When interest groups turn from trying to influence a committee to trying to influence a floor vote, they must develop a plan for reaching legislators they do not regularly deal with. If a number of interest groups share a point of view, they are likely to divide the task, each group dealing with those members of Congress it is most familiar with. When another trade accord, the General Agreement on Tariffs and Trade came before the Congress in 1994, the Business Roundtable coordinated lobbying by member groups. Boeing took responsibility for working the congressional delegation from Washington; Monsato worked members from Missouri and tried to mobilize other chemical companies; and Warner Lambert focused on the New Jersey delegation and other pharmaceutical manufacturers.[2]

Congressional Hearings

The most visible part of an interest group's effort to influence pending legislation takes place at congressional hearings. On the list of those called to testify at hearings are officials from interest groups involved with the issue at hand. Interest group leaders like to testify because it bestows status on them and their organizations, because it shows members that their group is playing an important part in the legislative process, and because it helps to legitimize their further participation.

Virtually every interest group testifies at one time or another. One survey showed that 99 percent of the lobbyists interviewed said their organization testified before Congress.[3] Participation is high because the costs of testifying are relatively low. Testifying is regarded as window dressing for the more substantive lobbying efforts made by the organization.[4] Still, hearings do offer an opportunity for media coverage, and interest groups give a lot of thought to whom they want to put forward to testify. When a House Judiciary subcommittee held hearings on a bill to ban certain kinds of second- and third-trimester abortions, a small drama was staged by the interest groups on both sides. The organizations opposing abortion brought forward physicians who used charts and models of fetuses to demonstrate how inhumane the proce-

---

[2]Peter H. Stone, "GATT-ling Guns," *National Journal,* July 2, 1994, p. 1573.
[3]Kay Lehman Schlozman and John T. Tierney, *Organized Interests and American Democracy* (New York: Harper & Row, 1986), p. 150.
[4]Jeffrey M. Berry, *Lobbying for the People* (Princeton: Princeton University Press, 1977), pp. 223–225.

dures under discussion were. Groups trying to protect abortion rights countered with the tearful testimony of a woman who needed a late abortion because her child would have been born with serious deformities and would have died soon afterward.[5]

Interest groups see more potential for influencing public policy by persuading committees to hold hearings in the first place. Even though a group's own testimony may be of little consequence, the hearings themselves can bring a great deal of publicity to an issue. In the early years of the food stamp program, representatives of the hunger lobby helped to stimulate congressional hearings designed to bring public attention to the severity of hunger and malnutrition in the United States. The hearings received substantial press coverage, and testimony by doctors and nutritionists helped to create public sympathy for expanding the food stamp program.

The Personal Encounter

Lobbying that tries to influence public opinion by catalyzing letters or focuses on work with committee staff is aimed ultimately at influencing congressional votes. Yet no tactic is considered more effective by lobbyists than personally presenting their case to a member of Congress in a private meeting.[6] Other approaches can give a lobbyist entree and create a perception of popular support for a policy, but a personal meeting is an opportunity to press the case home and make the legislator understand the virtue of the group's position.

Because lobbyists perceive meeting with a senator or representative as so important, and the time they are usually allotted for their sessions is so short, professional lobbyists go into such an encounter with a clear idea of what they hope to accomplish and how they can most effectively make their case. Washington representatives recognize that the session is not an end in itself but part of a lengthier effort to establish a relationship with the legislator and his or her office. In working toward this goal, lobbyists are conscious of their "presentation of self":

---

[5]Jerry Gray, "Emotions High, House Takes on Abortion," *New York Times,* June 16, 1995.
[6]See Lester W. Milbrath, *The Washington Lobbyists* (Chicago: Rand McNally, 1963); Harmon Zeigler and Michael Baer, *Lobbying* (Belmont, Calif.: Wadsworth, 1969); and Berry, *Lobbying for the People.*

the verbal and nonverbal means of expressing themselves, which collectively create an impression of the persons they are.[7] The most important part of the impression lobbyists try to convey about themselves is that they are persons of character. If the messenger is suspect, the message will be suspect. A labor lobbyist said, "The most important thing is your trust and integrity." Another lobbyist elaborated: "It's a relationship that we try to build. They know why we're there."

In trying to create favorable personal impressions, lobbyists do not neglect substance in favor of small talk designed to show what nice people they are. There is surely some of that, but lobbyists regard information as the primary means for displaying their intelligence, political common sense, and overall character. Members of Congress don't need lobbyists as friends, and Washington-based lobbyists know that being seen as a good source of information is their entree back into the office. A lobbyist who represents small business people said that in meetings "providing information is the most effective tool. People begin to rely on you." Stressing a substantive presentation, a chemical company lobbyist said his philosophy was, "You'd better bring good ideas and some facts, and they'd better be accurate."

The emphasis lobbyists place on providing concrete factual information to legislators leads them to push their organizations for an ongoing stream of research. It makes little difference to them if their data comes from researchers on the Washington staff, from other personnel in the parent organization, or from outside sources. Lobbyists use the research to respond directly to the most pressing concerns of legislators. Coretech, a coalition of corporations and universities wanting renewal of a research and development (R&D) tax credit, recognized that one of its problems was that some studies demonstated that the tax credit didn't actually stimulate much additional research and development. Coretech hired two economists from the Brookings Institution to study the issue. Their report showed that the R&D credit resulted in a 7 percent increase in research and development. When Coretech's lobbyist, Stuart Eizenstat met with Representative Michael Andrews and the Congressman expressed doubt that the R&D credit did anything, "Eizenstat almost leaped out his chair with his well-rehearsed answer" citing the Brookings study.[8]

---

[7]Erving Goffman, *The Presentation of Self in Everyday Life* (New York: Doubleday, 1959). See also, Richard F. Fenno, Jr., *Home Style* (Boston: Little, Brown, 1978).

[8]Jeffrey H. Birnbaum, *The Lobbyists* (New York: Times Books, 1992), pp. 86–89.

For many years, the accepted view of a lobbyist's interaction with members of Congress was Bauer, Pool, and Dexter's conclusion from their study of foreign trade legislation in the 1950s that *"The lobbyist becomes in effect a service bureau for those congressmen already agreeing with him, rather than an agent of direct persuasion."*[9] Few lobbyists today see their role as strictly one of supplying information to their strongest supporters in the House and the Senate. That is still a vital part of their job, but in interviews they clearly state that another important aspect of their job is trying to persuade undecided legislators to back their group's point of view. One public interest lobbyist said simply, "I try to educate them and to convince them that the position we are advocating is the correct one and the one they should support."

In their encounters with legislators, lobbyists from large membership organizations have the advantage of being able to discuss the effect of the proposed bills on the members within the legislator's constituency. Some lobbyists claim that this is the type of information that members of Congress are most interested in. A Washington representative for the National Education Association describes his philosophy:

> You go in there and talk to him about the specific program in his district. He isn't much interested in a national program. He needs to be able to take credit for doing something positive for the folks back home. You do it on the basis of what it does for him in his district. Your materials must be designed to reflect the district's activities.

Even if a group doesn't have a lot of members back in each district or state, it still searches for a way to bring the problem "home." For example, a lobbyist for a small environmental group tells Florida legislators that they should be concerned about acid rain because "BMW won't import cars through Jacksonville because the acid rain ruins the paint on the cars." How convincing any information is regarding the constituency depends partly on the legislator's own reading of constituency opinion and intensity of interest. Interest groups understand this as well, which is why so many of them will spend significant resources trying to influence and activate their members and attentive publics. If the legislator sees little constituency support for the lobbyist's argument, the latter's case is weakened.

---

[9]Raymond A. Bauer, Ithiel de Sola Pool, and Lewis Anthony Dexter, *American Business and Public Policy* (New York: Atherton, 1963), p. 353.

Lobbyists may regard personal presentations to legislators as the most important part of their job, but it is still the culmination of much more extensive work with congressional staffers. When lobbyists meet with staffers, their approach is much the same: providing useful information and trying to add to their reputations as reliable sources of data. Every visit, every phone call, every research paper or issue brief they give to a staffer or legislator is part of their constant effort to build a trusting relationship. Most of all, lobbyists want that relationship to be a two-way street, where they not only have easy access to Capitol Hill offices but also are called on to supply those offices with information.

EXECUTIVE BRANCH

Few public policies are conclusively settled by legislative action. If an interest group is to maximize its effectiveness, it must be skilled in lobbying the executive branch as well. Many interest groups are oriented more toward lobbying a particular agency than they are toward legislative advocacy. The National Association of Broadcasters must constantly monitor the activities of the Federal Communications Commission, which steadily issues new regulations. By comparison, Congress passes broadcast legislation infrequently.

When agencies formulate general policies, they usually do so by administrative rule making. Rule making is designed to facilitate public input into the administrative process. Through the notice-and-comment procedure, draft regulations are published in the *Federal Register,* a compendium of all regulations issued each day. Interest groups take advantage of the comment period to write detailed analyses of the proposed administrative regulations. Of course, interest groups prefer to help write the regulations than to merely comment on them. One survey shows that about half the groups in the sample reported that they have helped to draft administrative regulations.[10] Another formal means that interest groups use in trying to influence administrative rule making is testifying at fact-finding hearings held by an agency to

---

[10]Kevin Hula, *Links and Choices: Explaining Coalition Formation Among Organized Interests,* doctoral dissertation, Department of Government, Harvard University, 1995, p. 139. The vast majority of interest groups report that they participate in some form in administrative rule-making proceedings. See Cornelius M. Kerwin, *Rulemaking* (Washington, D.C.: Congressional Quarterly, 1994), pp. 195–210.

provide data on regulatory actions it is considering. Interest groups can also file petitions requesting administrative action on a problem.

Interest groups recognize that if they are to exert real influence on administrative agencies, they must go beyond the formal opportunities available to them. As much as they can, lobbies mobilize political support to buttress their efforts. Groups also try to develop relationships with executive branch policymakers that allow them to express their interests through meetings and phone calls. Most executive branch lobbying is directed at administrative agencies, but some groups also try to influence the White House.

Administrative Agencies

The greatest difference lobbyists see between members of Congress and administrators is that the former are much more worried about the popularity of their actions with constituents back home. A corporate lobbyist describes the differences he sees in his work:

> A good many [in Congress] are idealists, but they have to get elected. They are concerned about their constituency and the media. . . . Agency [administrators] are usually more specialized in their field and they're purists. They are not concerned about the press or a constituency. You bring in your technical experts and you just defend your point of view.

Agency personnel are probably not as callous toward public opinion or interest group concerns as this lobbyist suggests, but the frustration he feels is very real. At the highest levels in the federal bureaucracy are the president's appointees, individuals who are strongly interested in the next election. Beneath the top political stratum are the career civil servants, who by virtue of their nonpartisan status are somewhat more insulated from constituency pressures. Depending on their group's point of view, lobbyists may find either or both sets of officials unsympathetic to their cause. Likewise, depending on the issue, they can find considerable support among agency policymakers for the position they are advocating.

As in working with Congress, lobbyists deal more frequently with staffers than with top officials. The career bureaucrats are not minor functionaries but can hold important positions from which they can significantly affect the agency's policies. They are likely to see themselves as technocrats, determined to make up their minds from their own reading of the scientific or social scientific record. Middle-level officials evaluating a drug for the Food and Drug Administration have scientific backgrounds and like to think that their decisions are based wholly on the scientific merits of test results and experimental usage. Yet FDA evaluators are in regular contact with drug company representatives on whom they must rely for test data. Exactly how much this interaction affects their decisions is not known. Writing about FDA medical officers, Paul Quirk says:

> Having frequent contacts with industry representatives, getting to know and perhaps like them personally, and seeing their anxiousness to have drugs approved obviously will tend to create some sympathy for industry viewpoints and interests. Such contacts on a regular basis over a period of years may strongly shape the attitudes of FDA officials.[11]

Although the political independence of civil servants can be troublesome for lobbyists, the worst-case scenario for them is the appointment of high-level administrators who are hostile to their groups. When President Reagan was elected, he appointed to the top positions in the Environmental Protection Agency people who shared his view that industry needed relief from burdensome regulations. Liberal environmental groups that support strong regulatory efforts to protect the environment were treated with open contempt by Reagan's first EPA administrator, Anne Gorsuch, and her aides. Gorsuch's deputy administrator, John Hernandez, reflected this attitude when he held meetings over three-and-a-half months to assess the dangers of certain chemicals. Of the 92 people he met with, most were from the chemical industry, and none were from an environmental group.[12]

If agencies are hostile toward an interest group's general political philosophy, lobbyists generally can do little to directly influence top agency administrators. They must instead try to work through public opinion or, more often, through members of Congress who share their point of view. Legislators on a pertinent committee, especially those high in seniority, can have clout with an agency even if they are of the "wrong" party or ideological persuasion. Agencies want to foster good relations with members of committees that formulate their budgets and oversee their operations. As a result, interest groups on the outs

---

[11] Paul J. Quirk, "Food and Drug Administration," in James Q. Wilson, ed., *The Politics of Regulation* (New York: Basic Books, 1980), p. 211.
[12]Philip Shabecoff, "Environment Aide's Industry Talks Criticized," *New York Times,* October 22, 1981; and "Spending Compromise Sought," *Boston Globe,* October 22, 1981.

with an agency will prevail upon their congressional allies to intervene in agency policymaking.[13]

Agency officials have strong incentives, however, to cooperate with groups that share at least some of their policy objectives. Administrators need to build outside support for their agencies, and strong clientele support can help them win larger budgets in Congress or protect them from would-be budget cutters at the Office of Management and Budget. It can also help them win approval for new policy initiatives. At the same time, administrators also value autonomy and balance their desire for outside support with their desire to make decisions themselves.

As with congressional advocacy, lobbyists know that their effectiveness is only as good as their credibility. In their personal presentations to administrators, many lobbyists see their approach being much the same as with legislators or their staffs. A lobbyist for a manufacturing firm said, "There's really not much difference. You are always trying to get them to see things your way." Some indicate, however, that their presentations are even more factual, with more data for administrators than for those on Capitol Hill. "Generally, we have to go into much more detail. . . . We have to go into much more depth," said one lobbyist.

There are times when the "facts" just don't work. Interest group politics is waged largely with competing sets of facts; no group in Washington has cornered the market on the truth. When Department of Treasury officials were formulating a sweeping tax plan in 1986, they were guided by a general principle that special tax advantages given to different groups should be dropped from the tax code so that all Americans could have their income tax rates reduced. Assistant Secretary of the Treasury Ronald Pearlman agreed to meet with lobbyists from various veterans groups who were concerned about Treasury's idea to start taxing veterans' disability payments. Their arguments seemed to fall on deaf ears and they were taken aback by Pearlman who asked, "Why should veterans' disability payments be treated differently than any other income?" By the end of the session Pearlman hadn't budged, but the lobbyists were able later to get an appointment to see Pearlman's boss, Secretary of the Treasury James Baker. When they met with

---

[13]Jeffrey M. Berry, *Feeding Hungry People: Rulemaking in the Food Stamp Program* (New Brunswick, N.J.: Rutgers University Press, 1984).

Baker, they showed him a copy of a full-page ad they were planning to run in major newspapers. The ad had a large picture of Chad Colley, a Vietnam veteran who is a triple amputee and served as commander of the Disabled American Veterans. Above the picture the ad said, "WHAT'S SO SPECIAL ABOUT DISABLED VETERANS? That's what a top Treasury official said to Chad Colley. . . " Baker knew the ad was political dynamite, and the offending provision was dropped from Treasury's tax plan.[14]

The ties between interest groups and agencies can become too close. A persistent criticism by political scientists is that agencies that regulate business are overly sympathetic to the industries they are responsible for regulating.[15] Critics charge that regulators often come from the businesses they regulate and thus naturally see things from an industry point of view.[16] Even if regulators weren't previously involved in the industry, they have been seen as eager to please powerful clientele groups rather than have them complain to the White House or to the agency's overseeing committees in Congress.

The relationship between agencies and interest groups is influenced by a number of major factors. As noted earlier, the ideology of the administration is a significant variable. Each interest group's constituency helps determine its ease of access.[17] Citizen groups especially depend on having sympathetic administrators in power to gain meaningful access. The climate of public opinion and the prominence of an agency are also important. Finally, norms of agencies guide civil servants in their interaction with lobbyists.

The White House

As the executive branch has grown, so too has White House involvement in cabinet and agency policymaking. A large White House staff gives the president the resources to control an expanding number of

[14]Jeffrey H. Birnbaum and Alan S. Murray, *Showdown at Gucci Gulch* (New York: Random House, 1987), pp. 79–80.

[15]See, for example, Marver H. Bernstein, *Regulating Business by Independent Commission* (Princeton: Princeton University Press, 1955); and Theodore J. Lowi, *The End of Liberalism* (New York: Norton, 1979).

[16]See, *contra*, Paul J. Quirk, *Industry Influence in Federal Regulatory Agencies* (Princeton: Princeton University Press, 1981).

[17]See Anne Schneider and Helen Ingram, "Social Construction of Target Populations: Implications for Politics and Policy," *American Political Science Review* 87 (June 1993), pp. 334–347.

policy decisions. One consequence of this is that more and more inter-est groups find themselves needing access to the inner circle at the White House.

"Contacts" are probably more important for White House lobby-ing than for any other type of interest group advocacy. The president's aides can be selective as to whom they choose to meet. Sometimes the aides may prefer not to meet with interest group representatives so as to insulate the president from responsibility for a potentially unfavor-able decision. Consequently, contact with someone close to the admin-istration in power is vital for an interest group that wants White House access. A high-ranking administration official who leaves before the president's tenure is up is especially attractive as a lobbyist for groups with serious problems with the government.

Occasionally, leaders from some sector of society such as business, labor, or women's groups may be brought to the White House for a pep talk from the president on what the administration is doing for them. This practice can help the president politically by showing a special concern for a particular segment of American society. At times, the president will even call interest group leaders into the Oval Office to give the impression of responsiveness to some constituency. During the height of the civil rights movement, Lyndon Johnson met a number of times with prominent African American leaders such as Martin Luther King, Jr., and Roy Wilkins of the NAACP. The photo opportu-nity for these meetings brought them to the attention of people around the country in their morning newspapers.

One means the White House uses to build support for administra-tion policies is its Office of Public Liaison. First institutionalized in 1970, its job is to reach out to various constituencies and develop good relations with them.[18] Typically, staffers are responsible for a segment of the population, such as Jews, blacks, women, or businesspeople, with whom the White House is concerned. The staffers serve as a point of contact for interest groups representing these constituencies. For lobbyists, the public liaison office is a channel for communicating their interests to the administration. If the administration is generally un-sympathetic to the policy demands of the groups, this access to White House liaison staffers may be mostly symbolic.

---

[18]Joseph A. Pika, "Reaching Out to Organized Interests: Public Liaison in the Modern White House," in Richard W. Waterman, ed., *The Presidency Reconsidered* (Itasca, Ill.: F. E. Peacock, 1993), pp. 195–214.

White House contacts with interest groups extend far beyond the Office of Public Liaison. Many officials find themselves in contact with lobbies, either because they feel politically obligated to respond to a group's entreaties or because they seek out a group wanting its support. A White House staffer might try to mobilize support by asking the leaders of certain interest groups to generate a letter-writing campaign among their rank and file directed at members of Congress. As with administrative agencies, access to the White House is heavily influenced by the political views of the groups. Only about 8 percent of Washington lobbies report that they have frequent and cooperative interactions with any part of the Executive Office of the President.[19]

The selective access granted by the White House to favored groups is illustrated by the Bush administration's Council on Competitiveness, chaired by Vice President Dan Quayle. The Quayle Council operated in secret and kept no records of its meetings with lobbyists. The purpose of the council was to give large corporations and business trade associations the opportunity to request that administrative regulations they disliked be overturned or modified. In short, the Quayle Council acted as an appeals court for business interest groups who didn't get their way with an agency or department. The vice president or his staffers intervened with the Environmental Protection Agency and other administrative offices on numerous occasions to force a rollback of regulations.[20]

The White House restricts access because it cannot possibly handle the onslaught of lobbying that would overwhelm it if access were freely granted. At the same time, it cannot afford to ignore large and important interest groups. The White House task force that developed the Clinton health proposal, which was led by Hillary Rodham Clinton and Ira Magaziner, tried to develop its far-reaching proposal without significant participation by health groups. Given the enormous implications of the proposal for the nation's health care system, health lobbies were quite anxious about what the task force was going to propose

---

[19]Mark A. Peterson, "The Presidency and Organized Interest Groups: White House Patterns of Interest Group Liaison," *American Political Science Review* 86 (September 1992), pp. 612–625.

[20]Jeffrey M. Berry and Kent E. Portney, "Centralizing Regulatory Control and Interest Group Access: The Quayle Council on Competitiveness," in Allan J. Cigler and Burdett A. Loomis, eds., *Interest Group Politics,* 4th ed. (Washington, D.C.: Congressional Quarterly, 1995), pp. 319–347.

and made considerable effort to gain access to Magaziner or Mrs. Clinton. In a ludicrous effort to placate the health lobbies, the White House held a public hearing for groups wanting to offer input to the task force and gave each organization a scant three minutes to speak.[21] Although there are many reasons for the defeat of the Clinton administration's proposal, one of them was the failure of the White House to build a strong, broad interest group coalition to support the plan.

THE COURTS

If an interest group is to maximize its influence in the policymaking process, it must stand ready to use litigation as one of its lobbying tactics. Because of the high cost of litigation, only the largest interest groups and public interest law firms have substantial legal staffs of their own. For the small Washington offices that predominate, having a skilled litigator on board is an unaffordable luxury. Furthermore, the lawyers employed full time by interest groups usually are more experienced in administrative lobbying than in litigation.

Though it is not customary for Washington lobbies to have experienced litigators on their staffs, court suits brought by interest groups are quite common. Most frequently, an outside law firm (usually a Washington firm) will be engaged to carry out a group's case. Even if a group has in-house counsel, the higher the stakes, the more likely that an outside firm will be hired. The major exception is the public interest law firm. Organizations such as the liberal Center for Law and Social Policy and the conservative Center for Individual Rights were created to represent broad classes of people such as environmentalists, consumers, or taxpayers. Such citizens have important collective interests but, as individuals, have too marginal an interest to warrant hiring an attorney on their own.

Policy Change

The primary purpose of litigation is to seek a policy change or to stop a change from taking place. After the FDA proposed an ambitious set of

---

[21]Robert Pear, "Clinton Health Team Agrees to Let Public Speak, Quickly," *New York Times,* March 25, 1993.

regulations designed to stop teenage smoking, cigarette manufacturers immediately sued the agency.[22] When an industry's profits are liable to be significantly reduced by a government policy, it becomes worth the cost of litigation for a trade association to challenge the policy in court. Interest groups not only use the courts as an appeals process for adverse decisions by other branches, but they also litigate when they feel that their lack of popular support makes it fruitless for them to lobby Congress or the executive branch. The courts, though hardly impervious to popular opinion, do not demand the same type of constituency support to institute a policy change as Congress or an administrative agency does.

Civil rights groups have long relied on the courts to fight discrimination. It was lawyers from the National Association for the Advancement of Colored People (NAACP) who litigated against the separate-but-equal doctrine that was subsequently overturned by the Supreme Court in its 1954 decision *Brown v. Board of Education.*[23] At the time, strong civil rights legislation had little support in Congress; only the courts offered a reasonable target for lobbying by minority groups.

It is hardly unusual for an interest group to be the sponsor of important cases that are decided by the Supreme Court. One study of 306 highly significant constitutional cases found that 163 (53 percent) of them had been sponsored by an interest group. The proportion of significant cases brought by lobbies has increased over time, reflecting the increasing utilization of the courts by interest groups.[24]

Part of the rise of interest group litigation comes from citizen groups, which have used legal advocacy as a means to advance their ideological positions. There are a number of reasons for this growing activism. First, as leaders of public interest groups founded during the late 1960s and early 1970s began to look for constructive ways to work for political reform, they were able to find substantial foundation support for public interest litigation. Second, the rules of standing (discussed in the next section) were liberalized during this time, giving citizen groups broader opportunities to bring cases before the federal

---

[22]Yumiko Ono, "Tobacco Firms Rush to Counterattack Despite Signs of Dissension in Ranks," *Wall Street Journal,* August 14, 1995.

[23]*Brown v. Board of Education,* 347 U.S. 483 (1954).

[24]Karen O'Connor and Lee Epstein, "The Role of Interest Groups in Supreme Court Policy Formation," in Robert Eyestone, ed., *Public Policy Formation* (Greenwich, Conn.: JAI Press, 1984), pp. 72–74.

courts. Third, the success of liberal citizen groups in using litigation has stimulated formation of conservative citizen groups oriented toward legal advocacy. Sponsored mainly by contributions from corporations and foundations, groups like the Washington Legal Foundation and the Pacific Legal Foundation have become advocates for a variety of conservative causes.[25] A number of these groups focus on issues involving freedom of religion. The American Center for Law and Justice, with an annual budget of $8 million and a staff of 13 lawyers, has brought numerous legal actions that have forced schools to allow their facilities to be used by Christian student groups.[26]

For interest groups the greatest drawback to litigation is its high cost. To see a case through its initial adjudication in a federal court and a subsequent appeal, an interest group must contemplate costs that can easily reach six figures. The Women's Equity Action League lost an important case because, when faced with an appeal, the group could not afford $40,000 for copies of the trial transcript and had to abandon the suit.[27] Interest groups recognize the potential costs and hesitate to enter into litigation unless they see a reasonable chance for success and feel they will be able to carry a suit through an appeal and possibly on to the Supreme Court. Because the cost of litigation is so high, it is the wealthier lobbies like large corporations and trade associations that are the least likely to be deterred by the price of litigation.[28]

Standing

An important constraint on interest groups going to court is "standing." For an interest group to get a case heard before the courts, they must be an appropriate party to it. The courts' traditional test is that plaintiffs must show some direct injury to have standing. In the mid-1960s the federal courts began to expand the rules for standing, giving interest groups more latitude to litigate. One major case was *Office of Communication of the United Church of Christ* v. *FCC.* The church group

---

[25]Lee Epstein, *Conservatives in Court* (Knoxville: University of Tennessee Press, 1985).
[26]Gustav Niebuhr, "Conservatives' New Frontier: Religious Liberty Law Firms," *New York Times,* July 8, 1995; and W. John Moore, "The Lord's Litigators," *National Journal,* July 24, 1995, pp. 1560–1565.
[27]Karen O'Connor, *Women's Use of the Courts* (Lexington, Mass.: Lexington Books, 1980), p. 118.
[28]Jack L. Walker, Jr., *Mobilizing Interest Groups in America* (Ann Arbor: University of Michigan Press, 1993), p. 173.

had filed a petition before the FCC asking that the license to operate a television station in Jackson, Mississippi, be denied to the current operators because their programming and hiring policies were racist. The FCC denied the petition on the grounds that the station's viewers had not been tangibly injured. A federal court of appeals overturned the FCC denial, saying that standing could not be restricted to those with an economic interest in the case. The court declared that viewers of the station had legitimate standing.[29]

Not only was access expanded for citizen groups, but it was liberalized for corporations and trade associations as well. In another important case, *Association of Data Processing Service Organizations* v. *Camp,* the Supreme Court considered whether this trade group for data processors could challenge the authority of the Comptroller of the Currency to allow banks to provide data-processing services. The association did not prevail in the lower courts because of legal precedent holding that parties had no standing if their injury was caused by competition. The Supreme Court overturned the decision, setting forth a new doctrine saying there was a valid "zone of interests" for regulated industries that warrants standing in cases where there was a claim of injury, even if that injury resulted from increased competition.[30]

These and other cases significantly increased the ability of interest groups to take their grievances before the courts and expanded the range of conflicts between interest groups that the federal courts are called on to adjudicate. The courts, however, can move to make standing more restrictive too. In recent years a more conservative Supreme Court has been reluctant to ease the restrictions on standing. In a case brought by the Americans United for Separation of Church and State, the Supreme Court ruled that the group did not have standing to sue to stop the government from giving a surplus army hospital to a small Christian college. The Court ruled that members of the group did not suffer any personal injury other than displeasure with the action and thus did not have the right to fight the property transfer in court.[31]

---

[29]*Office of Communication of the United Church of Christ* v. *FCC,* 359 F. 2d 944 (D.C. Cir., 1966).

[30]*Association of Data Processing Service Organizations* v. *Camp,* 397 U.S. 150 (1970). See Karen Orren, "Standing to Sue: Interest Group Conflict in the Federal Courts," *American Political Science Review* 70 (September 1976), pp. 723–741.

[31]*Valley Forge Christian College* v. *Americans United for Separation of Church and State,* 454 U.S. 464 (1982).

Another means that interest groups use to try to influence the courts is the *amicus curiae* (friend of the court) brief. In suits to which they are not a direct party but have a very real interest in the outcome, interest groups will often file such a document with the court. A group must obtain consent from the parties to the suit or from the court before submitting the brief, though this is not difficult to do since the courts usually grant such requests. *Amicus* briefs may offer an additional legal interpretation to those being used by the disputants in the case. In the historic *Bakke* case, which called on the Supreme Court to rule on affirmative action quotas for the first time, 57 *amicus* briefs were filed.[32] (The Court subsequently rendered a confusing decision with 6 different opinions.) *Amicus* briefs seem most effective when filed prior to the Supreme Court's decision as whether to consider an issue on appeal or to let the lower court's ruling stand. *Amicus* briefs filed by lobbies at this stage may clarify for judges what is at stake in the case for various interests in society.[33] Once the court agrees to hear a case, it's difficult to discern the impact of *amicus* briefs on how the matter is decided.

Appointments

Interest groups also can try to influence the direction of the courts by attempting to affect selection of federal judges. This task is difficult because the norm is that the Justice Department or administration officials do not meet with interest group representatives to discuss possible selections. Only the American Bar Association, which evaluates professional qualifications of nominees (and sometimes potential nominees), is consistently active in the selection process.

Once a nominee is selected, interest groups may decide to try to persuade the Senate not to confirm that person because they regard the nominee as somehow unfit to serve on the bench. Traditionally, the Senate has been reluctant to reject presidential appointees, and interest groups hesitated to expend their scarce resources opposing candidates they did not like but who were going to be confirmed anyway.

---

[32]*Regents of the University of California* v. *Bakke,* 438 U.S. 265 (1978). See Gregory A. Caldeira and John R. Wright, "Organized Interests and Agenda Setting in the U.S. Supreme Court," *American Political Science Review* 82 (December 1988), p. 1111.
[33]Caldeira and Wright, "Organized Interests and Agenda Setting," p. 1123.

The Supreme Court nomination process, however, has become increasingly politicized, and presidents carefully weigh the anticipated reactions of interest groups before putting a candidate forward. The rise of citizen groups, with their emphasis on ideology, is a major reason for this change. Civil rights groups played a key role in building the case against two of President Nixon's nominees for the high court, both of whom were rejected.

When President Reagan nominated appeals court Judge Robert Bork to a seat on the Supreme Court in 1987, liberal groups launched an all-out attack on the highly conservative judge. A newspaper ad sponsored by the National Abortion Rights Action League claimed that as a Supreme Court justice, Bork might try "to wipe out every advance women have made in the twentieth century." People for the American Way paid for anti-Bork TV ads narrated by actor Gregory Peck. Liberal groups also worked hard to galvanize grassroots opposition to Bork so that senators would hear from large numbers of constituents.[34] The ferocity of the liberal assault on Bork stunned his supporters, and after his nomination was rejected by the Senate, conservative citizen groups vowed that they would not let this happen to another conservative candidate for the Court.

Tantalizingly close to a solid conservative majority on the Supreme Court, conservative groups felt betrayed when President Bush appointed David Souter to replace the retiring liberal justice William Brennan. Fearing a fight in the Senate, Bush chose the obscure, nondescript Souter who had little public record on controversial issues. When an enraged Thomas Jipping, a lobbyist for the conservative Free Congress Foundation, cornered Bush Chief of Staff John Sununu at a reception for Souter's swearing-in, Sununu told Jipping that "The next one" would be a true-blue conservative. Sununu added, "It will be a knock-down, drag-out, bloody-knuckles, grassroots fight."[35] Truer words were never spoken.

When Justice Thurgood Marshall announced his retirement, President Bush nominated Clarence Thomas, whom he had earlier appointed to a federal appeals court, to take Marshall's place. Thomas

---

[34]Stuart Taylor, Jr., "Bork Fight: Tactics Supplant Issues," *New York Times,* August 6, 1986; and Stuart Taylor, Jr., "Debate Continues on Accusations of Distortion in Ads Against Bork," *New York Times,* October 21, 1987.

[35]Jane Mayer and Jill Abramson, *Strange Justice* (Boston: Houghton Mifflin, 1994), p. 13.

was very popular on the right because of his fervent conservatism, and citizen groups sympathetic to his candidacy mobilized immediately to make sure his nomination didn't get "borked." Liberal citizen groups, however, fearing what Thomas's vote would do on the Court, began looking for ways to discredit him. Two of these groups, the Alliance for Justice and People for the American Way, played a critical role in leading Democratic Senate staffers to Anita Hill, a law professor at the University of Oklahoma who had worked for Thomas at the Equal Employment Opportunity Commission.[36] Hill would eventually come forward and testify at Thomas's Senate confirmation hearings that she had been sexually harrassed by Thomas on numerous occasions. A titantic struggle ensued, and conservative groups went all out to get Thomas confirmed. Some of these conservative groups sponsored television ads that attacked the character of two of the Democratic senators on the Judiciary Committee for their own ethical transgressions. One of the groups, Citizens United, sent 2 million pieces of direct mail in support of Thomas and called its 112,000 members to ask them to call their senators.[37] In a close vote, Thomas was confirmed.

STRATEGIC DECISION MAKING

A variety of specific tactics have been described, each with its unique strengths and weaknesses. With limited staffs and funds, interest groups must be careful to use their lobbying resources efficiently. As interest groups consider the policy problem at hand, they ask what tactics and longer-term strategies will yield the greatest influence at the lowest cost?

The decision-making process for selecting tactics and strategies resembles in many ways the decision-making process for selecting issues. As we pointed out in Chapter 4, many decisions for an interest group are hardly decisions at all because the issue that emerges so matches the group's purpose that there is no question of whether or not to act on it. The AFL-CIO does not have to deliberate on whether it should

---

[36]Mayer and Abramson, *Strange Justice,* pp. 225–233.
[37]Christine DeGregorio and Jack E. Rossotti, "Campaigning for the Court: Interest Group Participation in the Bork and Thomas Confirmation Processes," in Cigler and Loomis, *Interest Group Politics,* p. 221; and Mayer and Abramson, *Strange Justice,* p. 200.

lobby on proposed legislation affecting the minimum wage. Likewise, the organization doesn't have to decide whether or not it will try to lobby members of Congress personally on such a matter. The group would not need a staff of Washington lobbyists unless it was going to use them on issues critical to its members. Thus, the most important factor in determining what tactics a group chooses is the issue under consideration.

A second major influence determining an interest group's tactics has to do with its advocacy design.[38] The small size of the typical lobbying office limits the range of specializations among its professional staffers. If an office's lobbyists are primarily skilled in legislative lobbying, the interest group must decide whether hiring an outside law firm to lobby an administrative agency when pertinent regulations are being formulated is worth the additional resources. As already noted, a potential lawsuit will be thoroughly analyzed to assess whether the chance of success and the potential benefits warrant the heavy cost of hiring an outside firm. In general, a Washington office will be very quick to respond with tactics appropriate to the staff the organization employs full time. Tactics requiring the expertise of outsiders, however, will be considered more deliberately.

Tactical decision making is also influenced by changes in the political environment. As new opportunities or constraints arise, a group may rethink its basic approach. After Bill Clinton's election, it looked like some type of reform of the health care system would be enacted. Although philosophically much closer to the Republicans, the Chamber of Commerce vowed cooperation with the new president and said it had an open mind on many key aspects of health care reform. As public support dwindled and the Clinton plan faltered, the Chamber became openly hostile and abandoned trying to work with the administration.[39]

Many Washington lobbyists are like fire fighters, reacting to what is thrust upon them and not able to adhere to plans as to how they are going to allocate their time and effort. Yet it is still true that interest groups occasionally try to plot long-term strategy. With little control

---

[38]Berry, *Lobbying for the People,* pp. 262–264; and Russell J. Dalton, *The Green Rainbow* (New Haven: Yale University Press, 1994), pp. 208–209.
[39]David Rogers, "Business Delivers Another Blow to Health Plan," *Wall Street Journal,* February 4, 1994.

over how the nation's political agenda develops, an interest group recognizes that its planning is highly problematic. Nevertheless, groups do try to implement plans to reorient their strategy toward advocacy.

A group's approach to judging its influence on government is predicated on the assumption that it can fairly evaluate what works and what doesn't. When asked directly about this, Washington lobbyists generally indicate that there is little difficulty in determining lobbying success. A lobbyist for a women's group said that she knew her group was effective "when someone gets very angry because you've stepped on his toes." Usually, it's a simple evaluation of whether or not the group got some of what it was after. A farm lobbyist described his group's assessment this way: "If we've decided on eleven policies that we wanted to get through, then we look at those policies at the end of the year. We ask ourselves if we got something accomplished or did we get our butt kicked?" A banking lobbyist answered similarly: "The proof of the pudding is in the results."

While Washington lobbyists express a high degree of certainty in evaluating lobbying success, political scientists are considerably more cautious, finding it very difficult to evaluate the effectiveness of interest groups' advocacy campaigns. In carrying out such analyses, political scientists face formidable obstacles in developing scientifically valid measures of influence. A multiplicity of actors are always trying to influence the development of a policy. Groups begin lobbying efforts with unequal resources and with significantly different degrees of sympathy on the part of policymakers toward their points of view. Moreover, some policy options are never considered by government officials because they anticipate negative reaction from powerful interests or have been socialized into accepting "truths" about the proper role of government. Considerable influence may thus be wielded by some sectors of society though that power is not directly observable in lobbying campaigns.[40] Finally, when research is carried out it is handicapped by policymakers who are not fully forthcoming about being swayed by interest group pressure.

The rather striking differences between lobbyists' and political scientists' confidence in being able to evaluate advocacy effectiveness can

---

[40]Peter Bachrach and Morton S. Baratz, "Two Faces of Power," *American Political Science Review* 56 (December 1962), pp. 43–54; and John Gaventa, *Power and Powerlessness* (Urbana: University of Illinois Press, 1980).

be explained by a number of factors. First, lobbyists probably exaggerate the impact of their own organizations. Despite the many actors who may have been involved, a successful policy outcome is interpreted as validation of the group's effectiveness. A more dispassionate observer would not assume that an outcome matching an interest group's preferences is proof of that group's effectiveness. Second, a lobbyist is likely to define success in terms of what happened to particular alternatives that participants bargained over as a law or regulation was being formulated. Scholars look at a broader context and try to assess the underlying forces that make some alternatives more or less acceptable before the bargaining begins. Third, many topics in political science are subjected to the exacting scrutiny of complex statistical tests or are approached through formal analysis built upon mathematical equations. With such emphasis placed on rigor in the discipline, such indicators as we "stepped on his toes" or we got "our butt kicked" are too vague to impress political scientists.

CONCLUSION

The diversity of tactics used by interest groups may give the mistaken impression that a wide range of choices are open to a group when it contemplates how it is going to approach government. The issue at hand, the stage it is at in the policymaking process, and the organizational constraints of the group limit the choices. Many such decisions are automatic, and no alternatives other than the tactic eventually used are given serious consideration.

Groups do stop to evaluate whether an approach is working or can work if adopted. Sometimes these questions will be asked as part of a broader examination of how the group is doing and whether its fundamental strategy ought to be changed. At other times, it considers the potential of a tactic as it considers whether to take on (or continue) with an issue. For the larger, wealthier groups, the choices are more extensive, while the smaller groups with few lobbyists and a limited budget must restrict themselves to basic, inexpensive advocacy campaigns.

The most valued tactic of all is not so much a tactic as it is a relationship. Lobbyists would prefer not to be the aggressor, bringing pressure to bear on particular targets. The best of all possible worlds is to be in constant contact with policymakers, continually giving them information about the problems facing the group. When issues do have to be resolved, it can be done through quiet, informal negotiations between the principals. This type of arrangement requires a great deal of cooperation between lobbies and policymakers. Our next step, then, is to analyze patterns of cooperation and conflict among interest groups and between interest groups and policymakers.

Chapter
9

The Rise of Issue Networks

*C*ontemplating the frustrations that Republican presidential nominee General Dwight Eisenhower might find in the presidency, Harry Truman remarked, "He'll sit here and he'll say, 'Do this! Do that!' *And nothing will happen.*"[1] It's no wonder that a president can't simply snap his fingers and get the Congress, agencies, and interest groups to go along with him. When he wants to make a significant change in policy, he's likely to encounter many competing interests that prefer other policy options.

If someone as powerful as the president finds Washington politics frustrating, think of the task facing a single interest group. The Washington office may consist of only a handful of staffers. That office, in turn, represents just one interest group in a town that has thousands. The group's day-to-day activities are not newsworthy, and they rarely command much attention from the *Washington Post* or the *New York Times*.

How, then, does an interest group get things to happen? A basic strategy is to try to pyramid its resources. If it can find willing partners, a group will seek to form a *coalition* with other interest groups. Coalitions will usually reflect the immediate strategic interests of various lobbies who all want to influence the same policy in the same way. Over time, any one group is likely to coalesce with groups they have worked with in the past and who lobby in the same general issue area.

---

[1]Richard Neustadt, *Presidential Power* (New York: John Wiley, 1980), p. 9.

The many interest groups who share expertise in a policy domain and who frequently interact constitute an *issue network*. In simpler times, when fewer lobbies worked the corridors of power in Washington, policymaking in an issue area was often consensual in nature and involved only a limited number of groups, legislators, and administrators in a *subgovernment*. In contrast, contemporary issue network politics tends to be highly complex and conflictual. The end result of the growth in groups, lobbying resources, and coalition formation is more pressure on the institutions of government to respond to demands for policy change.[2]

In this chapter we look at the basis of interest group cooperation and conflict. In particular, we are concerned with the rise of issue networks and the way in which interest group politics has been changed by the emergence of these dense policymaking communities. Moreover, we want to understand the relationship between issue networks and democratic policymaking. Do they enhance or inhibit a broad representation of interests before government? A first step, though, is to examine just why interest groups cooperate in the first place.

COALITIONS: EVERYDAY POLITICS

Coalitions are everywhere in Washington. Lobbyists form them instinctively out of practical necessity. One survey of lobbyists found that approximately 80 percent agreed with the statement that "Coalitions are the way to be effective in politics."[3] As one lobbyist put it, "If you're not a good coalition maker, you're not going to survive for long in D.C." Forming a coalition is always a step lobbyists consider in developing an advocacy campaign. Says another lobbyist, "The first thing we do when an issue comes up is sit down and contact people. We find out who our friends are and who our enemies are on the issue and then we form coalitions. I do it every day, on every issue."

---

[2]Frank R. Baumgartner and Jeffrey C. Talbert, "Interest Groups and Political Change," in Bryan D. Jones, ed., *The New American Politician* (Boulder, Colo.: Westview, 1995), pp. 92–108.

[3]Kevin Hula, *Links and Choices: Explaining Coalition Formation Among Organized Interests,* doctoral dissertation, Department of Government, Harvard University, 1995, p. 103.

Coalitions offer a number of advantages. Principally, they offer a means of expanding scarce resources. One interest group may have only two lobbyists; ten interest groups with the same number of lobbyists can provide 20 operatives for the coming battle. The Washington office of an interest group is often stretched thin with a number of issues to follow, so a coalition may enable it to take on a new issue without seriously diminishing its coverage of another. Coalition partners provide other types of resources besides lobbyists. The constituency of each group broadens the coalition's expertise on the issues and subissues before policymakers. When a bill affecting milk prices came before the Congress, "the Coalition to Reduce Inflated Milk Prices won considerable attention because different coalition members were able to address industrial production costs, noncompetitive U.S. prices, dairy surplus conditions, abuses in surplus distribution programs, and antitrust concerns related to the regulation of milk co-ops."[4]

Coalitions also extend the information net. A group added to a coalition is an extra set of eyes and ears and will expand the intelligence gathering that is crucial to any lobbying effort. Finally, a coalition adds to the credibility of an advocacy campaign. The formation of a coalition indicates that a group isn't an isolated maverick and that there is some breadth of support for its position. As the Washington representative for a pharmaceutical manufacturer noted, "Your chances for success are really much greater if you [form a coalition]. If you go in to see a congressman or staff member with other people who support your position, it's a lot easier to get their support."

Interest group coalitions are not inevitable, and it is not uncommon to uncover a group going it alone. On any given issue, a lobbying organization may not find other groups that are highly concerned and in agreement with it. For some groups, few other organizations are natural allies. This is true of the National Cable Television Association, where "most of the time we go it alone. We rarely seek out a group." Interest groups are more likely to go it alone when they are lobbying an administrative agency rather than Congress.[5] Regulations are typically narrower in scope and may affect organizations in unique ways.

The most common pattern is that an issue will affect a number of groups, and natural allies will be clearly evident to the individual lobby-

---

[4]William P. Browne, *Private Interests, Public Policy, and American Agriculture* (Lawrence: University Press of Kansas, 1988), p. 185.
[5]Hula, *Links and Choices*, pp. 139–144.

ists. One corporate lobbyist said of advocacy in his industry, "I mostly work in coalitions. . . . In forest products, very seldom do you have an issue that only affects one corporation. An issue might affect just two or three, but not just one." As an issue begins to take shape, the search for coalition partners intensifies. A lobbyist for the National Coal Association describes how he put together a coalition to fight provisions in a bill governing fuel use that could hurt his industry:

> First, I met with gas consumers—they were industrial users—and got their support. If the bill passed, they would get cut off if there was a gas shortage. Second, I met with the railroads. Coal is the railroads' number one product—you can't move gas by rail. They have a direct interest in making sure that legislation isn't passed that favors gas over coal. . . . We also brought in labor unions. Gas isn't labor-intensive; coal is a very labor-intensive industry, so labor will support us. I called these meetings separately. There was no reason to include the consumer group with the railroads because their issues are different.

Most coalitions are ad hoc arrangements. They exist for the specific purpose of working on a single issue and dissolve when that issue reaches some resolution or when the coalition partners no longer feel the effort is worthwhile. When the Justice Department encouraged the Supreme Court to deny legal standing to associations that wish to file suits on behalf of individual members, eight interest groups coalesced to oppose the effort. The American Medical Association, the NAACP, the AFL-CIO, the Chamber of Commerce, the Sierra Club, the Alliance for Justice, the Chemical Manufacturers Association, and the National Association of Manufacturers filed a brief asking the Court not to accede to the Justice Department's request. This unusual partnership of groups was limited to this one issue of standing, and had no longer-term purpose.[6]

Ad hoc coalitions maximize flexibility. They are easy to enter and easy to leave. As will be discussed, organizations prefer not to commit financial support to a permanent coalition because they lose control of those scarce resources and cannot apply them to new and more pressing issues. Sometimes, however, advocates believe that an ad hoc alliance will not be sufficient and money must be committed to a permanent coalition. The Leadership Conference on Civil Rights is an unusually large and successful permanent coalition. It was founded in

---

[6]Stuart Taylor, Jr., "Coalition Opposes Access Curb," *New York Times,* March 19, 1986.

1950 and has grown to over 185 member organizations. Throughout its history the Leadership Conference has played a key role in developing strategy over civil rights legislation. Although the breadth of the coalition is a strength when the member organizations are in agreement, the diversity of the Leadership Conference has also led to considerable internal conflict. Over the years organizations representing blacks, Hispanics, Jews, labor, and women have quarreled over what issues the coalition ought to pursue.[7]

For an ad hoc coalition that primarily draws on the time and effort of lobbyists, bigger is not always better. Ten groups joined together on an ad hoc basis is much better than one group working on its own. Yet a hundred groups in an ad hoc coalition may not be much improvement over ten groups. The larger a coalition grows, the more peripheral members it attracts and the more effort is required to manage the coalition. Large coalitions also mean that each group is less accountable for its effort (or lack thereof). In a small coalition, an organization that does little work on that coalition's issues will be conspicuous.

Common Bedfellows, Strange Bedfellows

The old saw, politics makes strange bedfellows, aptly describes coalition politics among interest groups. Coalitions frequently encompass unlikely sets of partners. The American Civil Liberties Union, although often seen as liberal, has formed separate alliances with the tobacco industry, the American Bankers Association, and the National Conservative Political Action Committee. It joined with the ultraconservative National Rifle Association to stop the Justice Department from putting raw, unsubstantiated data into a national computer network. The ACLU regards such computerized databases as a violation of civil liberties, while the National Rifle Association regards this kind of national network as a step toward unlawfully denying its members the right to bear arms.[8]

For all the strange and even bizarre coalitions that form in Washington, the beginning point for any group seeking to form a coalition is

---

[7]Dick Kirschten, "Not Black-and-White," *National Journal,* March 2, 1991, pp. 496–500.

[8]Robert Pear, "Tactical Alliances and the A.C.L.U.," *New York Times,* November 5, 1986; and Kirk Victor, "Strange Alliances," *National Journal,* August 15, 1987, pp. 2078–2079.

still its usual allies. The American Podiatric Medical Association commonly allies with groups representing dentists and psychologists. Repeatedly these groups have found themselves fighting to be included in coverage by insurance plans. The services that podiatrists, dentists, and psychologists provide are not always seen as crucial parts of insurance coverage or worth a more costly premium. Because issues have so often touched upon the common interests of these groups, a pattern of frequent cooperation has developed.

A group's regular allies tend to come from the policy area that it primarily works in; this is where it is most in contact with other lobbies.[9] It is not only that common interests continue to bring the same groups into contact with each other but that trust and friendships develop over time among lobbyists. As they gain experience working with each other, their contact is likely to increase as they rely on each other to gather information. The lobbyists, legislators, and administrators in a policy area who communicate with each other form an issue network. It is in these networks, which will be discussed more fully later in this chapter, that coalitions breed and multiply. A new coalition effort among frequently teamed partners can easily be initiated with a few phone calls. Thus the costs of forming a coalition, notably the lobbyists' time, are kept down.

But many coalitions extend beyond a small circle of friends. Issues can cut across a wide variety of groups, prompting alliances of lobbies from many different policy areas. It's understandable that groups that normally have little to do with each other, but do not work in contradictory ideological directions, can come together to work on an issue. What may be puzzling, however, is when groups that are usually in opposition to each other lay down their weapons and declare a truce while they join together on a particular issue. When the liberal ACLU and the conservative NRA put their differences aside and join together in a coalition, one may wonder if interest groups follow any principles in choosing their allies. Clearly, the norm among interest groups in Washington is that *no one is too evil to work with.* "We may be sworn enemies on one issue and work together on others," said one trade group lobbyist. Chrysler, for example, usually finds itself at odds with environmentalists. Yet when the Reagan administration proposed ending fuel economy standards after Chrysler had spent $450 million

---

[9]John P. Heinz, Edward O. Laumann, Robert L. Nelson, and Robert H. Salisbury, *The Hollow Core* (Cambridge, Mass.: Harvard University Press, 1994), pp. 254–258.

meeting those standards, the company chose to work with environmental groups to preserve them while other car companies fought them.

Why is it that interest groups have so little trouble working with their enemies when it suits their needs? Quite simply, it is because lobbying is a profession guided by pragmatism. "We're not fussy [about whom we work with]," a communications industry lobbyist noted bluntly. Short-term results, getting things done, are the day-to-day imperatives. There is not much credit to be gained with the corporate headquarters, member organizations, or rank-and-file members by staying pure in their choice of allies. To be sure, there are a few exceptions to the no-one-is-too-evil-to-work-with norm. Radical feminists and conservative Christian groups who are active in the fight against pornography could strengthen their efforts by coalescing, but they have generally worked separately on the issue rather than together.[10] This is an unusual case though, and few lobbies have moral qualms about whom they work with. Lobbies are generally much more interested in getting action out of Washington rather than in reserving a special place in heaven for the pure and righteous.

Sharing Resources

Coalitions flourish because they are a means of expanding and coordinating the resources needed for an advocacy effort. A member group enters a coalition with the knowledge that it will be expected to devote some resources to achieving the goals set by the partners. In practical terms, lobbyists must at least cooperate in splitting up the work. In some cases, financial contributions are also expected.

One resource that coalitions can share is their contacts and their constituency base. A corporate lobbyist says he and his allies divide the contacts this way: "We'll do it based on who knows which member better, who has a facility in his district, [and] the impact of the issue in his district." For large trade groups, the most effective coalition work is really internal. If a trade association can mobilize its member companies to participate in a lobbying campaign, it greatly improves its ability to gain access to the offices of many members of Congress. When the Chemical Manufacturers Association lobbies, it can draw on the 185 member companies that are involved in that industry. These compa-

---

[10]Jean Bethke Elshtain, "The New Porn Wars," *New Republic,* June 25, 1984, pp. 15–20.

nies are located all over the country and can play a critical role in a lobbying campaign by contacting their own representatives and senators.

Dividing up the lobbying is far easier than deciding to share the costs of a court suit or a research study. Groups do not want to spend money unless an issue is a high priority for them. When there is support for a financial assessment within an ad hoc coalition, the alliance must decide how to assign contributions. Since ad hoc coalitions are by nature voluntary, informally run groups, only peer pressure can force a group to contribute.[11] A lobbyist for a consumer products company noted that uneven contributions are common. "In terms of providing funding for studies, the biggest responsibility falls on the company with the highest stake in the outcome. Maybe one company will give $15,000 and another company will give nothing."

The scarcity of financial resources is not the only reason why groups do not do more to share costs or develop more permanent coalitions. Organizations have egos, and the more resources an interest group devotes to coalition activities, the less it has for doing things in its own name. Although interest group leaders can shamelessly claim credit for a policy victory that rightly belongs to a large coalition, few lobbying offices are satisfied with a constant diet of coalition politics. A group's organizational ego makes it want to shine on its own some of the time and to gain the reputation of being able to make things happen in Washington.

In sum, lobbying organizations commonly form coalitions in Washington but are likely to do so under well-defined circumstances. The chances of success increase when

1. The coalition is clearly intended to be of a temporary, ad hoc nature.
2. The coalition is limited to one specific issue.
3. The issue is of some immediacy with a good chance of government action.
4. The coalition is run informally and each group contributes lobbying by its own personnel rather than giving money to a separate coalition staff.

---

[11]See Marie Hojnacki, "Organized Interests as Coalition Members," paper delivered at the annual meeting of the American Political Science Association, Chicago, September, 1995.

5. The coalition's members are part of an issue network in which the lobbyists have experience working with each other.
6. Participants believe there is "turn taking" in the leadership for the ad hoc coalitions that grow from their issue network.
7. The coalition itself is not likely to take on so much public visibility that any successes in lobbying will be entirely credited to it rather than being shared with the separate member organizations.

FROM SUBGOVERNMENTS TO ISSUE NETWORKS

Coalitions operate within a broader pattern of interest group interaction. As noted above, interest groups commonly search for coalition partners among other members of their issue network. Issue networks, which are characterized by their dense environment of competing interest groups, bear little resemblance to an earlier model of interest group–government relations that was strongly embraced by political scientists. Indeed, few approaches for analyzing the American political system endured as long or as well as that of the policy subgovernment.

In simple terms a subgovernment consists primarily of interest group advocates, legislators and their aides, and key agency administrators who interact on an ongoing basis and control policymaking in a particular area. Its central belief seems indisputable: policymaking takes place across institutions. Thus government decision making can be best understood by looking at how key actors from different institutions and organizations interact with each other.

The subgovernment model can be traced back to Ernest Griffith's description of policy whirlpools in *Impasse of Democracy*.[12] The term *whirlpools* didn't have much staying power, but other terms that gained currency include *iron triangles, triple alliances, cozy little triangles,* and *subgovernments.* Whatever the label, the basic idea was the same: A small group of actors dominate the development of policy in a given field. Policymaking is consensual, with quiet bargaining producing agreements among affected parties. Partisan politics does little to dis-

---

[12]Ernest Griffith, *Impasse of Democracy* (New York: Harrison-Hilton Books, 1939). See John T. Tierney, "Subgovernments and Issue Networks," paper presented at the annual meeting of the American Political Science Association, New Orleans, August, 1985, p. 28.

turb these relatively autonomous and stable arrangements. Douglass Cater's description of the sugar subgovernment is instructive:

> Political power within the sugar subgovernment is largely vested within the Chairman of the House Agriculture Committee who works out the schedule of quotas. It is shared by a veteran civil servant, the director of the Sugar Division in the U.S. Department of Agriculture, who provides the necessary "expert" advice for such a complex marketing arrangement. Further advice is provided by Washington representatives of the domestic beet and cane sugar growers, the sugar refineries, and the foreign producers.[13]

The subgovernment model proved popular with political scientists for a number of reasons. First, it provided an escape from the confines of institutional analysis. Research on the Congress or the bureaucracy could not capture the full nature of the policymaking process without going well beyond the boundaries of those institutions. Second, much scholarship in political science focuses on an individual policy domain. To those who wanted to study a particular issue area, the idea of subgovernments offered a conceptual framework to guide their research. Third, the subgovernment idea could be communicated easily to students and scholars alike. The model was based on straightforward, convincing case studies; those who read the relevant works were not required to make leaps of faith or to agree to any problematic assumptions. Fourth, the idea of subgovernments offered a critical perspective on the performance of American government. The closed nature of the policymaking system and the central role played by key interest groups in each area made subgovernments an inviting target for those who found fault with the direction of public policy. The public interest was not served because not all important interests were represented at the bargaining table.

Since the research on subgovernments was built around case studies, it is not clear how much government policymaking took place in these closed, consensual systems. By the late 1970s political scientists began to doubt that subgovernments characterized the policymaking process. However representative they once were, many subgovernments had crumbled, and a new model of interest group–government relations was needed. An alternative conception was offered by Hugh Heclo who argued that policymaking is best described as taking place

---

[13]Douglass Cater, *Power in Washington* (New York: Vintage Books, 1964, p. 18.

within much larger issue networks. If we look "for the closed triangles of control," says Heclo, "we tend to miss the fairly open networks of people that increasingly impinge upon government."[14]

Heclo defines an issue network as "a shared-knowledge group" that ties together large numbers of participants with common technical expertise.[15] Unlike the simple and clearly defined nature of subgovernments, issue networks are difficult to visualize and rather ill defined. Participants move in and out easily, and it is "almost impossible to say where a network leaves off and its environment begins."[16] Networks are not radically different from subgovernments in their membership, since lobbyists, legislators, legislative aides, and agency administrators still make up the vast majority of participants. White House aides, consultants, and prominent, knowledgeable individuals can also be found in their midst, however. Rather, what is distinctive about issue networks is their size and accessibility to new participants. A large network can be made up of dozens and even hundreds of interest groups, a number of executive branch offices, and different congressional committees and subcommittees. Even a smaller network allows for broader and more open participation than a subgovernment.

A Pattern of Conflict

Despite some evocative imagery, Heclo's model was rather imprecise and did not offer strong empirical evidence on interest group behavior. His model was compelling, however, and as studies were completed, issue networks gained currency as an alternative to the increasingly discredited subgovernment model. Not all patterns of interest group–government relations fit the issue network model, especially in policy areas that are relatively narrow in focus and involve a limited number of groups.[17] Still, the basic premise of the subgovernment model is now

---

[14]Hugh Heclo, "Issue Networks and the Executive Establishment," in Anthony King, ed., *The New American Political System* (Washington, D.C.: American Enterprise Institute, 1978), p. 88.

[15]Heclo, "Issue Networks and the Executive Establishment," p. 103.

[16]Heclo, "Issue Networks and the Executive Establishment," p. 102.

[17]James A. Thurber, "Dynamics of Policy Subsystems in American Politics," in Allan J. Cigler and Burdett A. Loomis, eds., *Interest Group Politics,* 3rd ed. (Washington, D.C.: Congressional Quarterly, 1991), pp. 319–343.

invalid. In other words, *the significant interest groups and key government officials in an issue area do not usually work in a consensual fashion to develop public policy.*

Instead, the research shows that interest groups are typically in open and protracted conflict with other lobbies working in their policy area. One study based on a survey of Washington lobbies found that over 70 percent of the citizen groups and for-profit groups (professional and trade associations) indicated that they face opposition by other lobbies. The figures were around 45 percent for nonprofit groups and 40 percent for organizations with mixed memberships from the profit and not-for-profit sectors.[18] Another study found pervasive conflict between business organizations and citizen groups. Seventy percent of corporations and 66 percent of trade associations said that the growing number of citizen groups had made their lobbying tasks harder. Less conflict was found among business groups themselves.[19]

A third large-scale study found that in four different policy domains, about 75 percent of interest group representatives cited lobbies that were adversaries.[20] The researchers analyzed agriculture, health, labor, and energy policymaking and in each area identified 20 "policy events," such as a committee vote on a bill or the issuance of new regulations by an agency. The typical pattern of interest group alignment for these events was a substantial division among the participating lobbies.[21]

Research also establishes that partisan change is a key factor in determining interest group access to policymakers. Subgovernments were said to be relatively autonomous from the electoral process. Presidents come and go, but subgovernments live on forever. This is not what Mark Peterson and Jack Walker found in their surveys of interest groups in 1980 and 1985:

> When Reagan replaced Carter in the White House, there was a virtual revolution in the access enjoyed by interest groups in Washington. In the

---

[18]Jack L. Walker, *Mobilizing Interest Groups in America* (Ann Arbor: University of Michigan Press, 1991), p. 129.

[19]Kay Lehman Schlozman and John T. Tierney, *Organized Interests and American Democracy* (New York: Harper & Row, 1986), pp. 283–287.

[20]Heinz et al., *The Hollow Core*, p. 252.

[21]Heinz et al., *The Hollow Core*, pp. 313–367.

past, many groups may have been able to maintain their contacts with the bureaucratic agencies of the federal government through politically isolated subgovernments or iron triangles, no matter what the outcome of the election, but it was difficult to build such safe enclaves around a group's favorite programs during the 1980s.[22]

Clearly the Reagan administration profoundly affected the Washington interest group community with its highly ideological agenda and its successful effort to cut budgetary sacred cows. Earlier, the election of Jimmy Carter in 1976 also had significant impact on interest group access to the executive branch. The large number of liberal citizen groups in Washington were a major beneficiary of his administration. Activists from these organizations filled important administrative positions and gave generous access to public interest lobbyists. These same groups had found the doors to the Nixon administration's bureaucracies tightly shut. When Bill Clinton took office after 12 years of Republican control of the executive branch, lobbyists for liberal citizen groups rejoiced because a number of their colleagues were appointed to key agency positions. Environmentalists, for example, cheered the selection of Bruce Babbitt, who had headed the League of Conservation Voters, as Secretary of Interior. He was joined at Interior by George Frampton, former president of the Wilderness Society, who became the assistant secretary for Fish and Wildlife. Also at Interior, Brooks Yeager of the National Audubon Society became director of policy analysis, and John Leshy of the Natural Resources Defense Council became the department's solicitor. With friends in high places, environmental lobbyists had improved access and more sympathetic ears to listen to them.

In sum, the simple, stable structure of subgovernments gave way to a much different kind of policy community. Individual lobbying organizations constantly search for coalition partners in an effort to pyramid resources so that they can better contend with their interest group adversaries. A lobby's relations with government can be significantly af-

---

[22]Mark A. Peterson and Jack L. Walker, "Interest Group Response to Partisan Change: The Impact of the Reagan Administration upon the National Interest Group System," in Allan J. Cigler and Burdett A. Loomis, eds., *Interest Group Politics*, 2nd ed. (Washington, D.C.: Congressional Quarterly, 1986), p. 172.

fected by who is in the White House; this is especially true for citizen groups whose ideological character make them vulnerable to changes in administrations. These changes in interest group politics are considerable. Why did they happen?

Again, the Advocacy Explosion

The most important source of change affecting policymaking communities has been the proliferation of interest groups. The arguments in Chapter 2 do not need repeating; our goal here is to explore how the growth in the number of lobbies and the increasing diversity of advocacy organizations affected the policymaking process.[23] In this respect the impact of the advocacy explosion was probably most profound in the way it altered the relations between groups and agencies. For example, the Department of Agriculture, long the bureaucratic center of many subgovernments, was transformed by a "proliferation of groups" that "destabilized the agricultural subsystem."[24] As new groups emerged and demanded to be heard, subgovernments weren't able to wall themselves off from those who wanted to be included in policymaking. Subgovernments flourished in the absence of competing interest groups, not in spite of them.

Most new groups approaching subgovernments had resources that made it difficult for the subgovernments to exclude them. Even if an administrative agency was antagonistic to a new group because of its ideological leanings, there were always legislators who held the same views and were willing to help. Particularly notable in this respect was the growth in the number of citizen groups. When these highly conservative or liberal groups found an administrative agency of the opposite persuasion, they worked with allies in Congress to attack agency decisions they disagreed with.[25] One study concluded, "Once these new

---

[23]See Jeffrey M. Berry, "Citizen Groups and the Changing Nature of Interest Group Politics in America," *Annals of the American Academy of Political and Social Science* 528 (July 1993), pp. 30–41.
[24]William P. Browne, "Policy and Interests: Instability and Change in a Classic Issue Subsystem," in Cigler and Loomis, *Interest Group Politics,* 2nd ed., p. 187.
[25]Jeffrey M. Berry, *Feeding Hungry People: Rulemaking in the Food Stamp Program* (New Brunswick, N.J.: Rutgers University Press, 1984).

groups of the Left and Right became permanent fixtures in Washington, the conditions that had nurtured the decentralized system of subgovernments were fundamentally altered."[26]

With the growing number of interest groups came a greater variety of interests. The new groups were not just carbon copies of those that already existed. A representative from the National Association of Realtors described the changes for his industry:

> If you go back a few years ago, you would have to say that if the National Association of Realtors and the [National Association of] Home Builders spoke, that was the whole industry speaking. Now there are more groups, such as low income housing groups, real estate developers, residential real estate developers, etc. . . . Members of Congress have to listen to all these groups.

Each new group brings with it a different set of priorities and will aggressively seek out policymakers on its own as well as frequently enter into coalitions with other groups. The expanding number of advocacy organizations heightens the competition between them because it is difficult for policymakers to find solutions for large numbers of client groups that make all of them winners.

Competition often shades into open conflict. This is most apparent between traditional adversaries, such as business versus labor or business versus liberal public interest groups. Conflict among businesses in the same industry also characterizes a number of policy domains. One important change that has fostered such conflict is the movement toward deregulation. Scholarly analyses of regulatory practices encouraged a view that much of the federal government's regulatory efforts led to inefficiency, unnecessary protection for privileged companies, stifling of competition, and a bad deal for consumers. The hold of industries such as trucking, airlines, and telecommunications over regulatory policy was shattered by the intellectual appeal of deregulation proposals, nurtured first in academe and in think tanks and then pushed by sympathizers in the legislative and executive branches.[27]

As regulatory barriers that parcel out markets to different types of business enterprises weaken, firms begin to push for further regulatory

---

[26]Thomas L. Gais, Mark A. Peterson, and Jack L. Walker, "Interest Groups, Iron Triangles, and Representative Institutions in American National Government," *British Journal of Political Science* 14 (April 1984), p. 166.
[27]Martha Derthick and Paul Quirk, *The Politics of Deregulation* (Washington, D.C.: Brookings Institution, 1985).

changes. This has happened in the broad area of financial services. As some regulatory practices have been changed to stimulate competition, various industry sectors have pressed for even more changes. Banks, insurance companies, and brokerage houses all want to encroach on each other's turf. Substantial conflict can exist even within one sector, as in banking. Large money center banks, small banks, and savings and loans do not see eye-to-eye on all issues.

New competition has come not only from traditional segments of the financial services community trying to steal business from each other but from entirely new players entering the picture. When Microsoft announced its intention to purchase Intuit, producers of Quicken, a program for managing home finances on a personal computer, observers realized that Microsoft wanted more than just another popular piece of software. Rather, the software giant was trying to position itself to become a major player in financial services. In Microsoft's mind, why should banking be left to banks? (The federal government subsequently filed antitrust objections to the sale, and the deal was halted.[28]) In short, the expanding number of interest groups in conflict with each other has transformed policymaking in financial services.

Although the advocacy explosion was the primary reason for the collapse of subgovernments, change in the structure of government contributed to this transformation of interest group politics as well. The institutional arrangements within the Congress and the executive branch that helped to sustain subgovernments were altered by reforms and changing norms.[29] During the period when subgovernments were declining, the trend in Congress was toward decentralization of its structure of authority. An important part of this was a growth in the number of subcommittees, which in turn meant more overlapping jurisdictions. For example, 110 different committees and subcommittees claim some jurisdiction over programs of the Environmental Protection Agency.[30] As one observer pointed out, decentralization means that "the scope of conflict changes continually, usually expanding, as

---

[28]G. Christian Hill, Don Clark, and Viveca Novak, "Microsoft Drops Bid for Intuit—A Victory for Antitrust Agency," *Wall Street Journal,* May 22, 1995.
[29]Jeffrey M. Berry, "Subgovernments, Issue Networks, and Political Conflict," in Richard A. Harris and Sidney Milkis, eds., *Remaking American Politics* (Boulder, Colo.: Westview, 1989), pp. 239–260.
[30]Robert F. Durant, "The Democratic Deficit in America," *Political Science Quarterly* 110 (Spring 1995), p. 37.

legislation passes from one stage to the next. Deals and accommodations devised at one stage cannot be adhered to later because negotiations must be reopened at each stage."[31]

More recently, there have been signs of recentralization in the House of Representatives. When Newt Gingrich took over as Speaker in 1995, he was able to instill more party discipline and reduce the autonomy of committee chairs. This may enhance the power of lobbies particularly valued by the leadership but will not lead to a reversal of issue network politics and the reemergence of subgovernments. It could mean, however, that the overlapping jurisdictions of committees that once enabled competing interest groups to play one committee against another will not be as significant a factor as they once were.

The growth of the executive branch also contributed to the fall of subgovernments. Policymaking became dispersed across more agencies and bureaus, and the authority of many such organizations was reduced as different units began working in the same broad policy area. The autonomy of individual bureaucracies was reduced further as the White House began trying to increase its control over the sprawling executive branch. Recent presidents have used the Office of Management and Budget or other parts of the Executive Office of the President to oversee regulatory policymaking. Over time, the structure of the executive branch and the growth of interest group politics has made agency policymaking more complex and conflictual.

THE QUALITIES OF ISSUE NETWORKS

Issue networks are as complex as subgovernments were simple. To provide a concrete illustration of issue network politics, a case study of the telecommunications industry will be offered below. Before proceeding to this specific case, however, some of the general qualities of issue networks should be outlined.

A network can be defined as "a specific type of relation linking a defined set of persons, objects, or events."[32] In terms of interest groups

---

[31]Steven S. Smith, "New Patterns of Decisionmaking in Congress," in John E. Chubb and Paul E. Peterson, eds., *The New Direction in American Politics* (Washington, D.C.: Brookings Institution, 1985), p. 221.

[32]David Knoke and James Kuklinski, *Network Analysis,* Sage Series on Quantitative Applications in the Social Sciences, no. 28 (Beverly Hills, Calif.: Sage, 1982), p. 12.

and government, what does this mean? The "type of relation" is primarily one revolving around the exchange of information.[33] A fundamental axiom of Washington politics is that "information is power," and issue networks provide ways in which information may be gathered and disseminated quickly and inexpensively. As noted in the discussion of coalitions, no one interest group has the means of gathering or monitoring all the information it needs to operate at maximum effectiveness. It is always the case that other groups will have better relationships with some of the key policymakers, have superior knowledge of some aspect of the problem at hand, or will hear about new developments first.[34]

Interest groups develop relationships with other groups where they freely exchange information under a norm of reciprocity. That is, if one group gives information to a second, the second group is expected to give the first group information when the second acquires it. This does not apply when the groups find themselves on different sides of an issue, as commonly happens to even the best of friends. Information is exchanged in simple and straightforward ways through phone calls, chance meetings (like those at Capitol Hill receptions), and more formal meetings. Finding out what amendment the subcommittee chair is thinking of offering, or what transpired in a conversation between an agency head and a White House adviser, is information critical to a lobbyist.

The "set of persons, objects, or events" are those who exchange information in some recurring fashion in a particular policy area. They are individuals who speak for organizations, notably interest groups, congressional committees, and executive branch agencies. Not all of these individuals exchange information with all others in their network. Within a large network, there are likely to be clusters of lobbies grouped according to issue focus. People in government are eager to exchange information with lobbyists because it helps them to understand what policy alternatives are most politically acceptable and what kind of lobbying strategy is being planned to try to influence them. It is a form of intelligence gathering, and they may gain information that they can't otherwise acquire at a reasonable cost of time or money.[35] As

[33]Karen S. Cook, "Network Structures from an Exchange Perspective," in Peter V. Marsden and Nan Lin, eds., *Social Structure and Network Analysis* (Beverly Hills, Calif.: Sage, 1982), pp. 177–199.

[34]See, generally, Hula, *Links and Choices.*

[35]John Mark Hansen, *Gaining Access* (Chicago: University of Chicago Press, 1991).

issues develop, policymakers develop alliances with various groups and keep in touch with them on a regular basis to share information.

It is evident that issue networks are characterized by high degrees of conflict and cooperation. Political scientists have begun to explore the structure of issue networks to see what kinds of cleavages may divide these policymaking communities and to try to identify the different kinds of roles groups might play in network politics. Examining the structure of networks is important because it can offer insight into the distribution of power among interest groups.[36] Understanding how individual networks operate is the first step toward comparing networks and building models of the different kinds of issue networks that may exist.

Issue networks can be further defined by the following properties:

Hollow Cores   The research that has been done on issue networks shows some common patterns in their internal structure. In their study of four large policy domains, Heinz and his colleagues found that none of the four had a central lobbying group that acted as a broker among most of the other groups in the network. In the energy field, for example, there is no one trade association or large corporation that is at the center of all communication among energy groups. No one lobby coordinates all the major interest group activity, hence there is a "hollow core" in the middle of the network.[37] This is not only the case because policy differences and ideological divisions exist within a network, but because there are so many issues and organizations that no one group could provide such consistent leadership.

Multiple Niches   Another structural characteristic of networks is that most individual groups are narrowly focused. They generally operate within issue niches, interacting primarily with those groups representing similar interests.[38] For example, one agricultural lobbyist commented: "In agriculture it tends to be commodity groups working

---

[36]David Knoke, *Political Networks: The Structural Perspective* (New York: Cambridge University Press, 1990), pp. 1–27; and Barry Wellman, "Structural Analysis: From Method and Metaphor to Theory and Substance," in Barry Wellman and S. D. Berkowitz, eds., *Social Structures: A Network Approach* (New York: Cambridge University Press, 1988), pp. 19–61.

[37]Heinz et al., *The Hollow Core*, pp. 275–308.

[38]William P. Browne, "Organized Interests and Their Issue Niches: A Search for Pluralism in a Policy Domain," *Journal of Politics* 52 (May 1990), pp. 477–509.

closely together. We have to. We're not all that different." These different groups representing dairy, soybean, peanut, wheat, cotton, cattle, and other such interests rely largely on each other.

The Importance of Being Expert   Much of the glamour and glitz of Washington lobbying is generated by the handful of lobbyists who have unusual access to those in power because of their high-powered reputations or political connections of some kind. For the foot soldiers of the lobbying profession, however, having extensive knowledge about one's issue area is critical to ongoing access to policymakers. It is not that being an expert in earlier times was not helpful. Rather, as policymaking has become more complex and competition from other interest groups in the same area has increased, expertise has become a more significant means by which lobbyists qualify themselves as participants in the policymaking process.

Expertise is something more than familiarity with the issues. All lobbyists have a sound knowledge of the issues they work on. Expertise is a very high degree of knowledge about a policy area, including enough technical sophistication to gain the respect of those in government who are themselves specialists in the policy area. A lobbyist on issues such as toxic wastes, nuclear energy, or acid rain cannot get far without some working knowledge of the scientific issues at the root of the controversies.

Sloppy Boundaries   One criticism that can be made of the issue network model is that the lack of precisely defined boundaries can make a network seem like an amorphous blob. The membership and overall shape of networks are fluid; a new organization can enter a network by developing a relationship with just one other organization already in it. Becoming a critical player in a network may be difficult, but finding other organizations to exchange information with is not. Boundaries are sloppy because issue areas overlap considerably and because there is no central authority capable of excluding new participants.

Yet even within these broad generalizations, there is reason for caution. As the case study of telecommunications will demonstrate, networks do not always operate by the norms of well-defined niche politics. And although the research demonstrating that issue networks have hollow cores is very persuasive, the research was restricted to rather large policy domains. It's conceivable that in smaller networks, centrally located groups play more of a consistent leadership role.

THE TELECOMMUNICATIONS NETWORK

At a hearing of the House Telecommunications Subcommittee in 1976, freshman Representative Tim Wirth (D-Colorado) was surprised at the large turnout for the session. He asked the witness from AT&T who was testifying to identify his colleagues sitting in the audience. After five minutes the AT&T executive had identified those in only one corner of the room. A reporter noted that a frustrated Wirth asked, "'Will everyone associated with AT&T just stand up?' Everyone in the audience stood up, all 150 of them."[39]

Today, a hearing on telecommunications would draw a crowd too, but they wouldn't all be from AT&T. The telecommunications industry has been radically transformed, and AT&T, which was once the world's largest corporation and monopolized the telephone industry, is a considerably smaller company facing competition in all aspects of its business. The days when policy was made quietly by AT&T lobbyists, the Federal Communications Commission (FCC), and the congressional subcommittees are as much a relic as party-line telephone service. Policymaking in this area is now a free-for-all, and Washington is full of lobbyists and lawyers representing competing telecommunications companies. "Every day you see a new office popping up," says one telecommunications lobbyist.

Ma Bell Dies

How did all this happen? The history is complex, and only a thumbnail sketch can be offered here.[40] Our narrative focuses on how the breakup of the system led to the creation of an issue network organized around various commercial niches in the telecommunications industry and how that network then evolved into a different kind of structure.

---

[39]Monica Langley, "AT&T Sends a Horde of Lobbyists to Fight a Phone-Bill Proposal," *Wall Street Journal,* November 4, 1983.

[40]For a full history of the AT&T breakup, see Steve Coll, *The Deal of the Century* (New York: Atheneum, 1986); and Peter Temin with Louis Galambos, *The Fall of the Bell System* (New York: Cambridge University Press, 1987). On the earlier history of AT&T's relations with government, see Alan Stone, *Public Service Liberalism* (Princeton: Princeton University Press, 1991).

The first major step toward the breakup of the Bell system monopoly came with the 1968 *Carterfone* decision. The FCC, which regulates the communications industry, ruled in *Carterfone* that "terminal equipment" could be sold by companies other than AT&T. As a result, individuals and businesses could buy a telephone from anyone and, presumably, enjoy the price and performance benefits of competition. A year later, Microwave Communications, Inc. (now known as MCI) won FCC approval to offer private long-distance lines between businesses in Chicago and St. Louis through microwave technology. Yet because the microwave transmissions still had to be connected to the local phone systems, AT&T would have to let MCI rent access to its lines. AT&T, outraged at the FCC's decision, was uncooperative, and negotiations with MCI dragged on. AT&T feared, correctly, that allowing MCI a foot in the door was an invitation to wholesale competition in long-distance services. MCI aggressively pushed forward, lobbying the FCC and eventually filing a complaint with the antitrust division of the Justice Department. Ma Bell was under siege.

The Justice Department began an investigation in 1973. In a decision that shocked the business community, it filed an antitrust suit against AT&T in 1974, charging it with monopolizing various parts of the telecommunications industry. Meanwhile, MCI had begun offering regular long-distance service rather than just its business-to-business private lines. AT&T counterattacked with an effort to get Congress to pass a law that would forbid competition in the long-distance business. Despite an extraordinary effort by AT&T, the bill didn't come close to passage. Although the Justice Department suit lay dormant during the mid-1970s, it was actively pursued toward the end of the decade. In January of 1981, the trial of *United States* v. *American Telephone and Telegraph* began in the courtroom of federal district judge Harold Greene.

As the trial proceeded, it became clear that AT&T stood a good chance of being handed a devastating decision by Judge Greene. Meanwhile, AT&T's lobbying of the White House to get the Justice Department to stop prosecuting the case had failed. Reading the handwriting on the wall, AT&T entered into negotiations with the Justice Department to break up the Bell system. It could at least horse-trade with Justice; there was no lobbying Judge Greene, who could deal them a much worse hand. In January of 1982, a basic agreement was reached, and the trial, which was still going on, was stopped.

In the out-of-court agreement, AT&T agreed to give up local telephone service. Seven new regional companies ("Baby Bells"), such as

Pacific Telesis in the West and NYNEX in the Northeast, were created to take over local phone service. AT&T retained long-distance services, though it had to face competition from other companies. AT&T was also able to keep control of two of its prized possessions—Bell Labs, its research arm, and Western Electric, its manufacturing division. AT&T also won the right to enter the computer industry, an important goal of the company. It had long had the technological know-how, but as a regulated monopoly it had not been allowed to sell computers. This substantially sweetened the deal for AT&T, which was losing three-quarters of its assets in the settlement.

One of the political consequences of the AT&T breakup and the competition that had earlier come to the phone industry was a spectacular growth in telecommunications advocacy. Just about anybody with expertise on telecommunications could land a lucrative position with one of the newly established Washington offices of firms in the industry. All seven regionals set up lobbying offices to protect their interests against AT&T. The one part of AT&T that did not shrink was its political arm: After reorganizing its Washington operations in the wake of the breakup, it had 55 lobbyists on board.[41] For lawyers with the right experience, the AT&T breakup was a cause for celebration. "Washington D.C.'s 'telecommunications bar' boomed like a Nevada silver town."[42]

In the wake of the divestiture agreement there was substantial competition in many sectors of the industry, and both consumers and businesses enjoyed the benefits of expanded product choice and competitive pricing. Other sectors, notably basic local phone service, were not competitive markets. A large, fractious issue network developed as new companies freely entered some markets, and political alliances changed rapidly from issue to issue. Ad hoc coalitions quickly formed and then dissolved, often putting strange bedfellows together on one matter while they fought each other bitterly on another.

Telecommunications was not turned into an integrated market by the consent agreement. Federal district court Judge Harold Greene retained jurisdiction over questions left unclear by the out-of-court set-

---

[41]Michael Wines, "Ma Bell and Her Newly Independent Children Revamp Lobbying Networks," *National Journal,* January 28, 1984, pp. 148–152.
[42]Coll, *The Deal of the Century,* p. 365.

tlement and over petitions to expand competition by companies wanting to overturn parts of the initial agreement. As indicated by Figure 9.1, by 1988 the basic structure of the network was composed of distinctive industry niches. Most of the conflict within the network was generated by one industry niche wanting to gain Judge Greene's permission or congressional approval to move into a market it was prohibited from participating in. The businesses that held some regulatory advantage would vigorously defend their turf. For example, the consent decree forbid the seven Baby Bells from manufacturing telecommunications products. AT&T, concerned that the Baby Bells were going to get around this provision by designing products and then simply having another company manufacture them, pressed Judge Greene to rule that the consent decree's intent for the Baby Bells included a ban on design as well as manufacturing. Greene ruled in favor of AT&T and other manufacturers and against the regional phone companies.[43]

There is no agreed upon way to map out an issue network in Washington. In Figure 9.1 the two most important policymaking bodies, the Federal Communications Commission and Congress, are arbitrarily placed in the center. Other parts of government (such as the Office of the Special Trade Representative in the White House) are participants in the network as well. At the time, the various industry niches included long-distance carriers, regional phone companies, small telephone companies, computer and electronics firms, and domestic and foreign manufacturers. Labor unions, consumer groups, and various trade associations are also part of the telecommunications policy community.

In 1988 the telecommunications issue network was still primarily focused on telephone equipment and services. People in telecommunications certainly anticipated some integration of the telephone industry with the computer and cable TV industries, and many issues at the time concerned future opportunities that the large-scale integration of these fields would bring. Nevertheless, around this time the network was largely animated by conflict between different industries trying to encroach on each other's telephone service and equipment markets.

---

[43]Bob Davis, "AT&T Case Judge Berates Regulators, Reaffirms Manufacturing Ban on Bells," *Wall Street Journal,* December 4, 1987, p. 2.

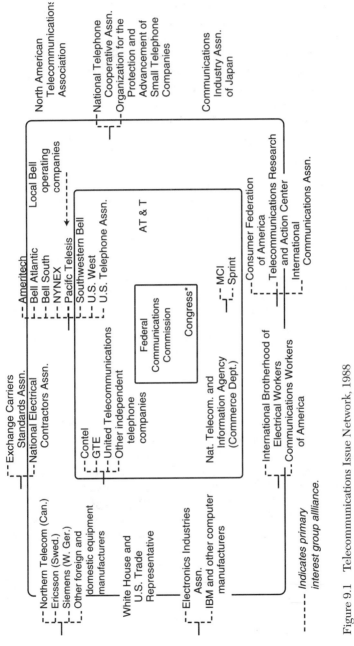

Figure 9.1   Telecommunications Issue Network, 1988

*The primary congressional actors in 1988 were the Subcommittee on Telecommunications and Finance, House Committee on Energy and Commerce, and the Subcommittee on Communications, Senate Committee on Commerce, Science, and Transportation.

Market Integration

By 1994, in the space of only six years, the telecommunications issue network had been thoroughly transformed.[44] Although there is still conflict between different industries, it is no longer the defining characteristic of network politics. As Figure 9.2 illustrates, the political relationships among major companies in the network is not based on a primary manufacturing or service identity. Indeed, what is most conspicuous about the evolution of the telecommunications issue network is the large-scale integration of different companies into business alliances that provide a range of products and services to consumers. In some cases, this integration extends to foreign companies that have working agreements or cross-ownership ties with American firms.

The scope of some of these business alliances is staggering. For example, Time Warner, a publishing and entertainment colossus in its own right, has strategic alliances with many other key players in telecommunications. U.S. West, a Baby Bell, has a major ownership interest in Time Warner, which in turn has ownership interests in Turner Broadcasting (cable TV networks and a movie library), 3DO (a computer software company), and Teleport (a provider of phone lines). It has business agreements with Oracle and Microsoft (computer software companies) and TCI (the nation's largest owner of local cable TV companies). This set of alliances reflects the dominant strategy in the telecommunications industry: the future belongs to those companies who can provide all the key services of the information superhighway. And what are those key services? In simple terms, it is basic telephone service, cellular or wireless service, long distance, access to computerized databases, cable TV, electronic mail, an Internet gateway, and connections to a variety of consumer services (banking, travel reservations, shopping, and so on).

To position themselves to be a player in the telecommunications industry of the future, companies such as Time Warner are making sure they have all the pieces to compete. Despite the heavy competition today and the substantial diversity of interests within the network, telecommunications executives feel that the industry is moving toward

---

[44]See Jeffrey M. Berry, "The Dynamic Qualities of Issue Networks," paper delivered at the annual meeting of the American Political Science Association, New York, September, 1994.

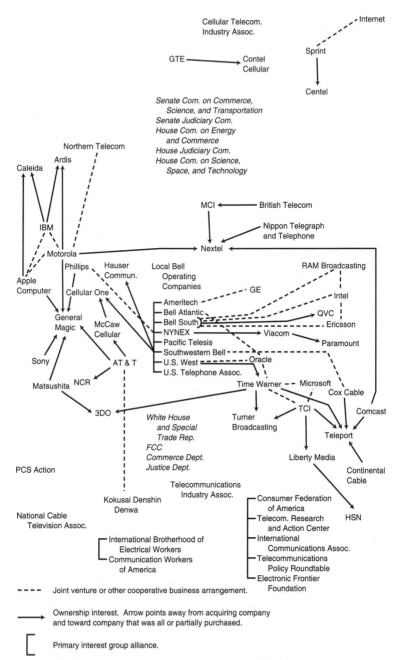

Figure 9.2   Telecommunications Issue Network, 1994

Note: Current as of March 1, 1994.

Source: Jeffrey M. Berry, "The Dynamic Qualities of Issue Networks," paper delivered at the annual meeting of the American Political Science Association, New York, September 1994, p. 12a. Reprinted by permission.

a limited set of business alliances who are able to provide all the services that consumers want.

Whatever the future of telecommunications, the integration of companies pursuing this strategy has had profound political implications for participants in this issue network: predictable lobbying fault lines are disappearing, leadership within the network is changing, and there is extreme uncertainty because of the movement toward full deregulation of telecommunications.

Two Models

In examining telecommunications interest groups at two points in time, we see two very different models of an issue network. The 1988 model was characterized by well-defined industry niches, and interest group coalitions were built largely around these industry clusters. Competition existed within separate industry sectors, but many regulatory restrictions prevented certain companies (most notably AT&T and the Baby Bells) from freely entering particular markets. For short-hand purposes, we shall refer to the 1988 system as the *industry niche model.*

The 1994 model is characterized by business alliances that cross different markets. Mergers, joint working arrangements, and cross-ownership are common relationships connecting different kinds of telecommunications firms. By 1994 the regulatory framework for telecommunications was crumbling, and policy was moving rapidly toward open competition in most markets. Bell Atlantic, a Baby Bell, won permission to compete with cable television by offering programming through its phone lines. Time Warner gained regulatory approval in New York State to offer basic telephone service. All the Baby Bells formed partnerships with movie studios. We shall refer to the 1994 system as the *full market integration model.*

Since the time the research was done on the 1994 system, mergers, acquisitions, and new business alliances have continued at a dizzying pace. In February of 1996, new telecommunications legislation passed Congress and was signed into law by President Clinton. The law provides for sweeping deregulation of the long-distance, local telephone service, and cable-TV markets, allowing companies in any one of these industries to fully compete in the others. Below, we'll speculate on where this issue network might be headed in light of these changes. The question that must be first addressed is why did such a transformation take place? Why did an industry niche network evolve into a full market integration network?

There are a number of reasons. First, and foremost though, enormous technological change has occurred in the telecommunications field. When the consent agreement was signed, no one could have foreseen all the new technologies that would emerge. Everyone knew change was coming, but there was no adequate regulatory apparatus in place to continually redraw the boundaries to determine which companies could offer what services. Entrepreneurs came to conceive of this industry as one with limitless opportunities for combining markets. The shrewdness and imagination of business leaders like John Malone (TCI), Raymond Smith (Bell Atlantic), Gerald Levin (Time Warner), and others outran the capacity of the regulatory system to govern telecommunications.

Telecommunications is certainly not unique in being deeply affected by rapid technological change. Regulation of many industries has been affected by new inventions and changes in technology. What does seem unusual about telecommunications is the breadth of integration between so many important business sectors, most notably, telephones, television and movies, and computers.

There is not enough research to know how characteristic of Washington policymaking either of these models are. Moreover, there are surely other models of issue networks that can be found in Washington. There is certainly no reason to believe that all industries evolve into a full market integration network. Agriculture, for example, is an industry that has had its share of scientific breakthroughs and technological change; yet it remains an industry niche network.[45] The inference one would have to draw from the research that is available is that the industry niche model is more commonly found than the type of integration seen today in telecommunications.[46]

It is important to understand issue networks not only because it is helpful to have models to guide our thinking about complex policymaking environments, but because such analysis is useful for clarifying our thoughts about the role of interest groups in a democratic society. Is

---

[45]See Browne, "Organized Interests and Their Issue Niches."
[46]See Heinz et al., *The Hollow Core.*

one of the models outlined here more conducive to democratic policy-making than the other? This is a complicated question, but at least a few considerations can be brought up here.[47]

One advantage of the contemporary telecommunications network is that the expanding breadth of the interest groups involved in policymaking enlarges the range of constituencies represented. A recent effort of the Baby Bells to enter some new markets generated conflict that involved over 300 corporations and other interest groups.[48] Everyone is affected by telecommunications policy, and an extensive array of interest groups involved in policymaking is surely desirable. In an industry niche network, the range of groups participating is more restricted. An added benefit of such broad interest group participation is that it increases the chances that policy problems will get reconceptualized in new and different ways.

Although this full market integration network has broadened participation in telecommunications policymaking, trends in the industry warrant some concern. As the regulatory barriers in telecommunications fall and corporate alliances position themselves in every part of the field, competition could give way to oligopoly. As consumers find advantages to purchasing all their telecommunications services through one vendor, those companies that are not part of the huge alliances that are developing will have a tougher time competing. The capital entry requirements of trying to build a new telecommunications alliance that serves all relevant markets are immense. A planned merger between Bell Atlantic and TCI, which eventually collapsed, was valued at as much as $32 billion.[49] Predicting the course of such a rapidly changing industry is hazardous at best, but it is certainly plausible that such corporate alliances could come to dominate the market. If so, it is equally plausible that government would step in and increase its regulatory control. If this occurs, a new type of issue network will evolve and present us with a different kind of policymaking model than the two discussed here.

---

[47]A more thorough discussion on networks and democratic policymaking can be found in Berry, "The Dynamic Qualities of Issue Networks."

[48]Kirk Victor, "Road Warriors," *National Journal,* March 20, 1993, p. 680.

[49]The exact value of the merger was unclear because how much of TCI would be merged into Bell Atlantic was never finally determined. John Huey and Andrew Kupfer, "What *That* Merger Means for You," *Fortune,* November 15, 1993, pp. 82–94.

CONCLUSION

In surveying the relationship of interest groups to other lobbies and government policymakers, both stability and change can be observed. Interest groups still coalesce with each other for the same reasons they always have. They need to share resources (staff, money, and contacts) because each group is limited in the amount of advocacy it can engage in and in its ability to influence the federal government. Coalitions also enhance the credibility of a group's position.

Change has come as well in the way lobbies interact with others in their political environment. For years political scientists argued that policymaking through subgovernments was characteristic of the way Washington works. This may have been true of an earlier time, but it is not accurate today. With the sharp increase in the numbers of interest groups, policymaking communities changed dramatically. One way to conceive of the interaction of large numbers of interest groups and government officials is to think of these organizations and people as a network. Issue networks facilitate communication between people working in the same policy area.

The decline of subgovernments and the rise of issue networks raise some important questions for political scientists and how they view interest group politics. When the subgovernment model was widely accepted, political scientists were highly critical of the relationships at the core of the policymaking process. To scholars, subgovernments suggested a privileged position for a small number of groups in each policy area. For those political scientists who thought that pluralist theory offered a far too generous assessment of American democracy, the subgovernment model offered a considerably different view of interest groups. At the heart of pluralist thinking is the belief that democratic ends are reached through the bargaining and compromise of affected interests in an open political system. Subgovernments represented agency capture by clientele groups, highly restricted participation, stability that preserves the status quo, and centralized decision making. Subgovernments were evidence that a group-based policymaking system is deeply flawed and does not promote democratic government.

Issue networks suggest something else entirely. The policymaking process is seen as more open, more decentralized, more conflictual, more dynamic, and more broadly participatory. In short, issue networks come much closer to fulfilling the pluralist prescription for democratic politics. This is not to say that they are a perfect mechanism for promoting true pluralist democracy. Despite their expanded participation, issue networks do nothing to ensure that all affected interests are represented at the bargaining table. Lacking a centralized decision-making process, issue network politics may also favor the status quo by making compromise more difficult to achieve when there are sharply divergent views. In the last analysis, though, issue networks come closer to fitting our expectations of democratic policymaking than do subgovernments.

Chapter
10

Bias and Representation

*T*he central issue of interest group politics is the bias of representation. Since some sectors of society are better represented by lobbies
than others, we must ask if the advantages gained by such representation are a threat to the integrity of the democratic process.

The sector of American society that is best represented by interest
groups is big business. Controversy has long surrounded the involvement of business in the political process, and claims of undue corporate influence are a continuing refrain in American political debate.
The charges against business are quite serious. Political journalist
William Greider, for example, says that the increasing political activity
of business "is the centerpiece in the breakdown of contemporary
democracy."[1] In his masterful *Politics and Markets,* social scientist
Charles Lindblom concluded that "The large private corporation fits
oddly into democratic theory and vision. Indeed, it does not fit."[2]

Judging whether or not business possesses a level of influence that
is inimical to democracy is extremely difficult because we have no
agreed upon standard for measuring interest group power. Defining
power in academic journals is one thing; trying to apply the definition
in the real world of Washington politics is quite another. Indeed, politi-

---

[1] William Greider, *Who Will Tell the People* (New York: Simon and Schuster, 1992),
p. 331.
[2] Charles E. Lindblom, *Politics and Markets* (New York: Basic Books, 1977), p. 356.

cal scientists have generally shied away from trying to resolve the thorny measurement issues involved in calculating how much political power is exercised by groups in a policy conflict.[3]

Even without the ideal measuring instruments, there is much to be gained by trying to determine what kinds of advantages are held by business and by other types of interest groups. Such an analysis can help us to clarify the types of issues that members of Congress must address in writing legislation that regulates interest group behavior. This includes such policies as campaign finance, lobbying laws, and the policymaking procedures that facilitate or hinder interest group access to government. Here we will look at three questions about interest groups and the bias of representation. First, what kinds of resources are available to business, and how do those resources compare to other sectors of the interest group universe? Second, does business have a special relationship with government, allowing it to influence public policy in ways not available to other interest groups? Third, are there ways that other types of interest groups are advantaged in the contemporary American political system? The chapter will close with some thoughts as to how the biases in interest group representation might be reduced.

CORPORATE WEALTH AND POLITICAL ADVOCACY

The resources available to business are so immense that it is easy to conclude that corporations can dominate any policy issue if they choose to utilize those resources. Yet equating wealth and status with political power is dubious. In the words of one scholar, "One cannot *assume* that the disproportionate possession of certain resources (money, organization, status) leads to the disproportionate exercise of political power. Everything depends on whether a resource can be converted into power, and at what rate and at what price."[4] How does business try

---

[3]See Jeffrey M. Berry and Kevin Hula, "Interest Groups and Systemic Bias," paper delivered at the annual meeting of the American Political Science Association, Washington, D.C., August, 1991.

[4]James Q. Wilson, "Democracy and the Corporation," in Ronald Hessen, ed., *Does Big Business Rule America?* (Washington, D.C.: Ethics and Public Policy Center, 1981), p. 37.

to convert its wealth into power? What resources does it draw upon in trying to influence public policy?

Representation

Washington lobbying is very much a day-to-day activity; influence is achieved through continuous work in the trenches. Simply being in Washington, monitoring what is going on, is important. In this sense, business is greatly advantaged because, in terms of who is represented by Washington lobbyists, the bias toward business is overwhelming. An analysis by Kay Schlozman and John Tierney of 6,600 organizations that maintain some presence in Washington is revealing. Of those interest groups that maintain an office in Washington, approximately half are corporations or business trade associations. When organizations that are represented by a law firm, public relations firm, or other hired hand are added to the pool, the tilt toward business is even more evident. Roughly 70 percent of all the organizations having representation in Washington through an office of their own or through hired representatives were corporations (including foreign companies) or business trade groups.[5]

At the very least, keeping a lobbyist in Washington puts a company in the information loop of the policymaking process and reduces its uncertainty about what actions government might take.[6] If a corporate office is just a small listening-post operation, company executives will still be kept abreast of developments and, as the need arises, can hire more help from the pool of lobbyists-for-hire in Washington. A corporate lobbyist from a two-person office described their function this way, "I type a lot of memos and send them to corporate headquarters. I inform them of a new bill, the status of legislation, results of a meeting, whatever they need to know about what's going on here." But lobbyists are more than passive conveyors of Washington intelligence. In the daily interaction of issue network politics, lobbyists help to create expectations about acceptable policy alternatives, exchange studies and other information that influence the way problems are defined, and create the coalitions that may negotiate with government officials.

---

[5]Kay Lehman Schlozman and John T. Tierney, *Organized Interests and American Democracy* (New York: Harper & Row, 1986), p. 67.
[6]John P. Heinz, Edward O. Laumann, Robert L. Nelson, and Robert H. Salisbury, *The Hollow Core* (Cambridge, Mass.: Harvard University Press, 1993), pp. 1–3.

The value of representation is obvious. What's important is not simply that there are more lobbyists for business than for other parts of society, but that large corporations are represented in so many important ways. Take, for example, the Weyerhaeuser Company, a timber and paper products concern headquartered in Tacoma, Washington. First, it is represented by a modest Washington office for government relations staffed by two professionals and a secretary. Second, it is a member of two trade groups, the National Forest Products Association and the American Paper Institute. Third, it belongs to large business peak associations and works in coalitions with the Chamber of Commerce, the Business Roundtable, and the National Association of Manufacturers. Fourth, it draws upon corporate personnel from headquarters, including the company CEO, who frequently travel to Washington to meet with members of Congress.

Weyerhaeuser is not a typical American corporation. With $9.5 billion in annual sales and $580 million in earnings it is far larger than most. But in terms of political representation, it is typical of corporations its size. It is the largest American companies that are most advantaged in the degree to which they are represented in Washington. Small and mid-size firms are represented primarily by trade groups. Some very large firms don't have their own office in Washington, preferring to work with trade groups, keeping lawyers or other lobbyists on retainer or hiring them when the occasion arises, and sending personnel from headquarters to Washington when an issue heats up. Nevertheless, whether it has a Washington office or not, the large American corporation speaks loudly with many tongues in the policymaking process.

Deep Pockets

As the case of Weyerhaeuser indicates, large corporations "backstop" the Washington office with help from headquarters. Resources are made available as needed, avoiding unnecessary staffing in Washington and promoting a close working relationship between top corporate executives and government affairs specialists. Says one corporate lobbyist, "I have all the backup I could want. I have everything I need. If I call headquarters and say I need something, I'll usually get it." A lobbyist from a telecommunications company emphasized the cooperation between Washington and headquarters: "If we need additional employees, the only question is, 'Who?' If we need money, they say go ahead and spend it."

One advantage in having headquarters personnel backstop lobbying campaigns is that it helps to maximize the use of technical expertise in advocacy endeavors. Executives brought to Washington to talk to legislators or their staffers or to administrators can speak with great authority about the consequences of policy alternatives. The use of executives in lobbying also helps to keep the Washington office talking to corporate headquarters about what the company needs and what is politically possible in Washington. One corporate lobbyist noted, "As legislation froths up to the top, we need substantial interplay with senior management [who might] say, 'Section 7 kills us in our strategic plan,' and I wouldn't know that."

It is best to conceive of Washington offices of large businesses as a coordinating mechanism for the parent corporation's advocacy. It utilizes executives from corporate offices when their efforts can be useful; it helps to direct campaign contributions if the company has a PAC; it draws on corporate funds to make donations to ad hoc coalitions and other advocacy groups; it hires law firms and public relations firms as the need arises; it works with trade associations that the parent company belongs to; it may donate corporate funds in the form of "soft money" to one or both of the two major political parties; and it may contribute money to think tanks and other organizations that are doing research seen as favorable to the company's interests. Hence, the size of a corporation's Washington office may bear little relationship to the resources it has at its disposal. Stated another way, if an environmental citizens group has an annual budget of $500,000 for its lobbying office, that's basically what it has available for advocacy. If a Washington office of a major corporation has an annual budget of $500,000, that's not what it has available for advocacy. Rather, it has an elastic budget covered by the deep pockets of its corporate parent.

The advantage that business has in being able to purchase multiple forms of representation is illustrated by a recent attack against the Food and Drug Administration (FDA). After the Republican takeover of Congress in 1994 brightened prospects for streamlining the FDA's drug approval process, business attacked on a number of different fronts. Drug companies that regard the FDA's drug testing regulations as too expensive and too slow formed one salient of the offensive. Large and well-respected companies like Amgen, Burroughs Welcome, Genzyme, Glaxo, Johnson & Johnson, and Searle made the issue a priority. The Pharmaceutical Research and Manufacturers of America, the well-endowed trade association for drug manufacturers, worked with its member companies to push for a regulatory overhaul. A second trade group, the Biotechnology Industry Organization, worked on reforms of particular concern to biotech firms. Still another trade association, the Health Industry Manufacturers Association, joined the assault, as did the Dietary Supplement Coalition. The Washington Legal Foundation, a conservative public interest law firm supported by business, spent money on print ads criticizing the FDA. Citizens for a Sound Economy, a pro-business group, worked to mobilize public support for reform. Finally, the Progress and Freedom Foundation, a think tank close to Speaker of the House Newt Gingrich and supported by business, was another participant.[7] Although some consumer groups have worked to protect the FDA, their resources do not compare with the collective resources of so many corporations, trade associations, and ideological groups promoting free-market economics.

Politicizing the Corporation

Business has always had substantial advantages in its resources, but it has not always made the best use of them in trying to influence the governmental process. In recent years, however, business has done much more to draw upon the money, status, and political connections at its disposal. Some who are critics of business argue that corporations don't have to worry about their skill or devotion to Washington lobbying. They argue that the interests of business are simply too important for government to ignore.[8] To those in government, business is the most important among all types of interest groups. Still, even though government is hypersensitive to the overall well-being of the economy, it is not equally concerned about the well-being of every corporation. Nor is there assurance that Congress and regulatory agencies will always make wise decisions about each industry. Lobbying matters, and it matters a lot.

Studies of business involvement in politics have documented a transformation of how corporations organize themselves for political action. Bauer, Pool, and Dexter's comprehensive study of foreign trade legislation during the 1950s found the business community's lobbying

---

[7]Peter H. Stone, "Ganging Up on the FDA," *National Journal,* February 18, 1995, pp. 410–414.
[8]Lindblom, *Politics and Markets.*

on this issue to be relatively unimpressive, with many companies directly affected by the proposed legislation surprisingly passive. The authors concluded that whether a business communicated to government was related not to self-interest or ideology but rather to whether or not the company had a staff structure "which facilitated or blocked the production of messages."[9] There had to be men and women inside the firm whose role it was to make sure messages concerning government policy were sent out.

It is unclear why in years past corporations did not do more to create organizational roles and units through which they could have more aggressively responded to political problems and opportunities. Business was represented through trade groups and peak associations, but far fewer firms than today had their own offices in Washington. Moreover, firms did not usually go very far to try to integrate a public-affairs perspective in senior management decision making or to engage in a broad range of public-affairs activities. In the 1970s, however, business advocacy surged as the challenges of the changing world economy, growing competition in many industries, lobbying by public interest adversaries, and pressures first for regulation and then for deregulation led corporations to better use their assets to enhance their political influence.[10] Yet despite this general mobilization of corporate resources, change in firms that had been politically inactive was sometimes hard. Firms didn't simply have to start applying more resources to political advocacy; they often had to change their corporate culture.

Changing any corporation's culture is a difficult and incremental process. During the 1970s people in business viewed government as the enemy and believed policymakers didn't understand how to preserve the free-market system. A survey conducted by *Fortune* in 1976 revealed that 35 percent of CEO's thought that government was American business's biggest problem.[11] The prevailing attitude by senior management was that government relations was a disdainful activity,

---

[9]Raymond A. Bauer, Ithiel de Sola Pool, and Lewis Anthony Dexter, *American Business and Public Policy* (New York: Atherton, 1968), p. 229. For a more recent analysis of the institutional context of corporte advocacy, see Cathie Jo Martin, "Nature or Nurture? Sources of Firm Preference for National Health Reform," *American Political Science Review* 89 (December 1995), pp. 898–913.

[10]David Vogel, *Fluctuating Fortunes* (New York: Basic Books, 1989).

[11]Vogel, *Fluctuating Fortunes*, p. 145.

performed by lightweights exiled to the Washington office or by hired guns from law firms. As business's external environment changed, that attitude was a luxury few companies could afford.

As attitudes changed, new corporate practices followed and were often institutionalized through formal reporting relationships or reorganizations.[12] New positions were created or old jobs upgraded at headquarters for individuals to respond to requests, advice, and instructions from the Washington office. Today, direct and regular personal interaction between the Washington office and headquarters is the norm. One auto company lobbyist described the relationship in his firm this way: "The vice president in the D.C. office reports to the vice chairman and the chairman of the company. The decision-making process is very close between D.C. and Detroit. The vice president goes to Detroit every week and talks to them at least ten times a day." Another corporate lobbyist summed up the attitude that was successfully instilled in his company as, "Get into politics or get out of business."

Politicizing the corporation has been a major achievement for business. By creating norms and institutional practices that make politics the concern of all senior management, business has made better use of the resources at its disposal.

A SPECIAL RELATIONSHIP

In the wake of business's expanded influence during the 1970s, the election of Ronald Reagan in 1980 brought an administration into power that was unusually sympathetic to corporate interests. For 12 years the Reagan and Bush administrations pushed policies that greatly benefited business. After two years of Democrat Bill Clinton, the Republican capture of the Congress in the 1994 elections promised more pro-business and antiregulatory policies.

Some would argue, however, that to focus on what business gets out of one administration over another is to miss the point. Business, in Charles Lindblom's words, enjoys a "privileged position" in American politics. Business prosperity is so vital to the nation's well-being that

---

[12]Seymour Lusterman, *The Organization and Staffing of Corporate Public Affairs* (New York: Conference Board, 1987).

corporate America maintains unique advantages in the political system. Lindblom says that for governmental officials, "businessmen do not appear simply as the representatives of a special interest, as representatives of interest groups do. They appear as functionaries performing functions that government officials regard as indispensable."[13] Even though business doesn't win every battle, it always wins the war because if it doesn't get its way, Lindblom concludes, "recession or stagnation is a consequence."[14] Thus both legislators and the administration in power are especially eager to please those in the business community because they don't want to suffer the electorate's wrath after an economic downturn.

Lindblom's notion of a "privileged position" goes to the heart of the question concerning the power of business. Should business be viewed simply as a strong set of interest groups with the most lobbyists and the most money to use? Or, as Lindblom claims, does business's critical importance to our well-being give it unique advantages in the governmental process? This question may be addressed from many directions, but the analysis here will be limited to two lines of inquiry. First, we'll examine the type of access business leaders have to government officials. Second, we turn to the question of whether America is ruled through a power elite led by an inner circle of business leaders.

Access

It has already been established that business is unusually well represented, and that the presence of so many lobbyists in the employ of business is significant in the everyday policymaking of Washington. Organizations with representatives in issue networks help shape policy over the long term. But a fair evaluation of representation in Washington would go beyond counting lobbyists. An underlying question is, "Who gets to see whom?" There is a qualitative difference between seeing a middle-level bureaucrat about a particular regulation and having a private audience with the assistant secretary responsible for that broad policy area. Most lobbyists have good access to congressional staffers, but they can't always get to see committee and subcommittee chairs when they need to.

---

[13]Lindblom, *Politics and Markets,* p. 175.
[14]Lindblom, *Politics and Markets,* p. 187.

This may seem to be a pretty low-level test for assessing business influence. If business is truly a dominant power, need it be concerned about getting better access to subcommittee chairs? The answer is an unequivocal yes—it is significant. Access beyond what normally accrues to Washington representatives is a critical measure of influence because it indicates that an interest group gets a hearing not available to others. If business as a class consistently gets more access to high-ranking government officials, then it does have a special relationship that places its policy concerns at a higher level of importance than the concerns of others. The vast sums of money that PACs donate to congressional campaigns are an indication of the high premium interest groups place on access. In the real world of Washington politics, special access is what interest groups strive for.

By this criterion, business does well. Although the wealth of corporations may give them the most lobbyists along with deep pockets for backstopping Washington offices, their access is built on more than that. The high status of companies, their importance to the welfare of the district or state, and the personal connections of their executives yield a high degree of access to key policymakers. In a survey of leaders from various segments of American society, respondents were asked if they had talked to a member of Congress a few times a year or more. Among business leaders, who were primarily corporate executives rather than lobbyists, fully 86 percent talked to a member of Congress at least a couple of times a year. Thus almost all the corporate leaders in the sample were able to converse directly to legislators on at least an intermittent, if not regular, basis. It is important to point out, however, that the figures were relatively high for the leaders of other sectors of the interest group community too. The comparable figures were 75 percent for black leaders, 68 percent for labor leaders, 62 percent for farm leaders, and 57 percent for feminist leaders. For the public at large, only 15 percent reported talking to a member of Congress at least a couple times a year.[15] The door to the office of a member of Congress is generally open to leaders of important constituencies, but it's open a tad wider to business.

The access of business leaders has not escaped the notice of corporate lobbyists, and the most important request they make for backstopping from headquarters is for the company's chief executive officer to

---

[15]Sidney Verba and Gary Orren, *Equality in America* (Cambridge, Mass.: Harvard University Press, 1985), p. 69.

come to Washington. In the first hundred days of the Congress in 1995, when the House Republicans were pushing their Contract with America, there wasn't a lobbying group in Washington that didn't want an audience with Speaker Gingrich. He personally met with representatives of only a small number of groups, but getting an appointment wasn't a problem for Genzyme CEO Henri Termeer who came to Washington to talk to the Speaker about the needs of the biotech industry.

Since CEO's only come to Washington a limited number of times, it is the corporate lobbyists who must do the day-to-day work to influence the specific policies adopted by government. Recent history teaches us that the access of business lobbyists is excellent when the Democrats are in power and even better when the Republicans are in power. As noted in Chapter 8, during President Bush's administration, business lobbyists could appeal agency regulations they didn't like to the Council on Competitiveness, headed by Vice President Dan Quayle. The only interest groups the Quayle Council granted audiences to were corporations and business trade associations.[16] After the Republicans captured the Congress in 1994, the majority staffers on committees not only gave business lobbyists an unusual amount of access, but actually had them write some of the legislation that was being proposed. When the Senate Judiciary Committee took up the task of rewriting some key environmental laws, it turned much of the job over to Hunton & Williams, a law firm with a specialty in representing electric utilities before regulatory agencies. Hunton & Williams wrote much of one particular bill, and when Democrat staffers were briefed, the firm's lawyers had to explain it to them because GOP staffers didn't appear to know the specifics of what had been put in the legislation.[17]

Republicans reject criticism of this kind of coziness by saying it is no different than the access granted by the Democrats to liberal groups like organized labor and environmental lobbies. There is some truth to this. When the Democrats control the White House, they appoint their interest group allies to key agency policymaking positions and ensure access for the groups that support the party. A key difference is that the

---

[16]Jeffrey M. Berry and Kent E. Portney, "Centralizing Regulatory Control and Interest Group Access: The Quayle Council on Competitiveness," in Allan J. Cigler and Burdett A. Loomis, eds., *Interest Group Politics*, 4th ed. (Washington, D.C.: Congressional Quarterly, 1995), pp. 319–347.

[17]Stephen Engelberg, "Business Leaves the Lobby and Sits at Congress's Table," *New York Times*, March 31, 1995.

Democrats give much better access to business than the Republicans give to labor and liberal citizen groups. The reason, again, is that business is different: the Democrats can't ignore the needs of private enterprise, but the Republicans usually feel they can disregard their liberal antagonists.

A Class United or A Class Divided?

One of the most persistent strains of social science thinking about government is that America is ruled by a small, wealthy, and powerful elite. A special relationship is said to exist between business and government because business is able to express its classwide interests through leaders who are close to those in government. The power elite is largely interchangeable, with top policymakers easily moving into business and vice versa.[18] This is a controversial theory because it suggests that democracy is illusory. The theory argues that business is unified and utilizes its vast resources and advantages to dominate government. If, on the other hand, business is divided and resources are used largely by one set of businesses to fight another set of businesses, then business as a whole will have greater difficulty in achieving the kind of dominance attributed to a power elite.

Contemporary scholars sympathetic to the power elite thesis direct much of their research toward documenting the interrelationships among those defined as "elite." They want to prove that this elite is not simply composed of individuals with great wealth who hold powerful positions, but that these people have considerable contact with each other and that this contact is instrumental in their ability to assess and define the interests of their class.

What is the composition of this class? What characteristics define its membership? "By a ruling class," writes G. William Domhoff, "I mean a clearly demarcated social class which has 'power' over the government (state apparatus) and underlying population within a given nation (state)."[19] "Clearly demarcating" the ruling elite is a rather arbitrary process, for no accepted boundary encircles this group. Social scientists have generally defined the ruling elite as those who hold the top positions in our most significant institutions. This can be limited

---

[18]See C. Wright Mills, *The Power Elite* (New York: Oxford University Press, 1956).
[19]G. William Domhoff, *The Powers That Be* (New York: Vintage, 1979), p. 12.

largely to individuals in government and business or might be more expansive and include those in the media, foundations, the military, and other important sectors of American society. One scholar identified 7,314 top elite positions in 12 different sectors, reasoning that these people were the most important individuals in this country because they

> Control more than one-half of the nation's industrial and financial assets, nearly half of all the assets of private foundations, and two-thirds of the assets of private universities; they control the television networks, the news services, and leading newspapers; they control the most prestigious civic and cultural organizations; and they direct the activities of the executive, legislative, and judicial branches of the national government.[20]

After identifying the individuals who are at the top of institutions, the next step is to show somehow that these people's interactions make them a cohesive class. A common approach is to document interlocking ties among the elite. For example, one study examined the ties between the members of the boards of directors of the nation's 25 largest newspaper companies and the nation's largest corporations, business policy groups, the boards of trustees at the most prestigious private universities, and the most exclusive social clubs. A member of the board of directors of the *New York Times* who is an executive at the Chase Manhattan Bank represents one interlocking tie. If that same board member is also on the board of trustees at Princeton, then that person is responsible for two ties. The 290 members of the boards of these newspaper companies yielded 447 ties to other elite institutions, though the companies owning the four most influential and respected newspapers in the country (the *New York Times,* the *Washington Post,* the *Wall Street Journal,* and the *Los Angeles Times*) accounted for about 40 percent of them. What are we to make of this? The author concludes that "these four papers speak not only for the directors and owners, but also for the inner group of the larger capitalist class."[21]

The assumption behind this type of analysis is that the interlocking ties produce class cohesion. In this instance, the boards of directors of newspaper companies are held to be a force that pushes the editorial

---

[20]Thomas R. Dye, *Who's Running America?,* 5th ed. (Englewood Cliffs, N.J.: Prentice-Hall, 1990), p. 169.
[21]Peter Dreier, "The Position of the Press in the U.S. Power Structure," *Social Problems* 29 (February 1982), p. 307.

management of these papers to adopt an ideology that is protective of elite interests. Many feel that interlocking ties don't represent anything of the sort. How can we know that such connections are actually mechanisms facilitating the maintenance of class interests? Even if we assume that these people talk about issues of concern to their class, that is not proof that influence is exerted in some way.

A vigorous defense of this methodology is given by Michael Useem in *The Inner Circle*, a book that attempts to show the dominance of a small ruling class of business elites in the United States and in Britain. For Useem, an "inner circle" of business elites "gives coherence and direction to the politics of business."[22] These corporate leaders are people who are on the boards of several major corporations and thus form an interlocking network. Their most important interaction does not concern what one company can do to help another. Rather, when not discussing the company on whose board they sit, they turn to broader business developments and governmental activity affecting business.

Members of the inner circle are distinguished from other business executives in that they have an abiding concern for the health of business generally and do not confine their political activities to working on behalf of their own companies' narrow interests. If all corporate leaders directed their political efforts only toward helping their own companies' immediate needs, their parochialism could damage the broader, long-term interests of all large corporations. Through their communication with other corporate leaders, this inner circle is able "to enter politics on behalf of consensually arrived at classwide interests."[23] There is no formal consensus, of course, but through the interlocking ties the communication that flows back and forth educates the inner circle as to the areas of agreement and concern.

This approach is suggestive, but not convincing. What's missing is the "smoking gun"—some direct evidence that this kind of communication leads to the exercise of power. When top corporate leaders get together at board meetings or elsewhere, they surely talk about what is good for all of big business. Yet such communication is not proof of a cohesive inner circle that acts effectively on behalf of a ruling class.

Most interest group scholars would argue that at some point in the policymaking process, classwide interests would have to be manifested

---

[22]Michael Useem, *The Inner Circle* (New York: Oxford University Press, 1984), p. 3.
[23]Useem, *The Inner Circle,* p. 58.

in advocacy efforts.[24] Classwide influence from an inner circle can't be assumed—business has too many conflicting interests, and it has forceful and resourceful critics among labor unions, citizen groups, and Democratic Party liberals. Political influence isn't exercised by osmosis—some people have to say to government "This is what we want." Those people and the organizations at their disposal must be prepared to articulate and support that message repeatedly throughout the policy-making process.

With considerable resources and energetic advocacy, the Chamber of Commerce, the National Association of Manufacturers, and the Business Roundtable are certainly organizations whose leadership qualifies as part of an ostensible inner circle. These organizations do work on broad issues facing business and try to educate those in government about the long-term needs of the free enterprise system. At the same time, these groups can be immobilized on policy debates because their broad memberships are divided. The 1986 tax reform bill is a case in point. The sweeping reform legislation was initially intended to create a "level playing field" by eliminating special tax provisions that helped some industries but not others. Many such provisions were left in the tax code, but the new law did remove or reduce some major tax advantages, such as ending the investment tax credit. These changes hurt heavy manufacturing industries such as aluminum, steel, and machine tools. At the same time, many service industries, like retailing, which did not enjoy major tax preferences, were helped by the law because it lowered the general corporate tax rate. Since it hurt some industries while helping others, the tax reform bill created a bitter split among big business leaders. Even the Business Roundtable, symbol of the clout of big business during the Reagan years, was fractured. "Part of the group went in one direction, part went in the other direction, and both lost," said Irving Shapiro, former DuPont CEO and past chair of the Roundtable. The National Association of Manufacturers and the Chamber of Commerce were immobilized as well.[25] Nothing could be more fundamentally important to business than an overhaul of the tax code, but on this issue the inner circle sat on the sidelines.

---

[24]See Dan Clawson, Alan Neustadtl, and Denise Scott, *Money Talks* (New York: Basic Books, 1992), pp. 161–190.
[25]Alan S. Murray, "Lobbyists for Business Are Deeply Divided, Reducing Their Clout," *Wall Street Journal,* March 25, 1987.

It would be too severe a test to demand absolute unanimity by big business on behalf of broad policy decisions. Nevertheless, if the advocacy efforts of business can be taken as a measure of the pursuit of classwide objectives, substantial unity is commonly absent. Nor do we see evidence of an inner circle of elites who consistently promote classwide interests against other sets of business leaders. Different areas of policy divide the top business elite in different ways. If decisions ultimately favor long-term classwide interests, these decisions may reflect one set of elites and their organizations prevailing over another set more than they reflect a cohesive inner circle working its will.

BEYOND BUSINESS

Although business is uniquely favored in the American political system, other interest group sectors are not without their own distinctive advantages. The governmental process is structured by many social, economic, and political divisions and biases that work to support the advocacy of some groups but not others.

Power of the People

The traditional counterweight to the resources of business is the power of the people. If policymakers have to choose between the equally intense preferences of business leaders and of ordinary citizens, they will most likely choose the option favored by ordinary citizens. The reason is simple: there are more ordinary citizens than business leaders and thus more votes to be gained. In the real world, issues are not so starkly drawn, and ordinary citizens do not usually form a coherent, unified political force.

Nevertheless, the power of numbers works in favor of some important interest group constituencies. It is not merely that large interest group constituencies have many voters to cast ballots in the next election, but that they are sources of workers in campaigns. As noted in Chapter 3, organized labor has traditionally provided Democratic candidates with campaign workers to staff the phone banks and walk the precincts. Although organized labor has shrunk in size, it is still an extraordinarily important resource for Democrats. The Christian Coalition gives little money directly to the Republicans, but many recent

GOP candidates have staffed their campaign organizations with volunteers from the local chapters of that group. When an interest group has a large number of members with impassioned views and has built an effective organizational structure that can quickly mobilize the rank-and-file, it will be greatly respected (and maybe even feared) by politicians. This is why the American Association of Retired Persons has been so effective over the years. It can mobilize a huge number of senior citizens who are deeply concerned about social security and medicare. Business, while it can contribute valuable campaign money through its PACs, does not have the same kind of energy or broad commitment by its employees. Middle managers at IBM are not going to organize to work on behalf of a congressional candidate on the basis of his or her views on the future of the computer industry. Not many interest groups have this kind of power of the people, but those who do are endowed with an extraordinary political resource.

Status

Another bias in the interest group system is that great disparities exist in the status of different constituencies. Society values some groups of people more than others. We respect the elderly much more than welfare mothers. These "social constructions" are the culturally defined characterizations or images of different groups.[26] How our culture comes to define certain populations in positive terms and others in negative terms is a complex process. Some distinctions, however, are clear. Those who are in the majority in terms of race, religion, and ethnicity have a higher status than minority groups. And those who are successful are more highly regarded than those who are less so.

These kinds of distinctions in status have important political consequences. Veterans are esteemed because of the extraordinary sacrifice that soldiers have made in this country's wars. Many government programs benefit veterans, including preferential hiring for government jobs. When veterans apply for a job with the federal government,

---

[26]Anne Schneider and Helen Ingram, "Social Construction of Target Populations: Implications for Politics and Policy," *American Political Science Review* 87 (June 1993), p. 334.

they are given extra points in the evaluation process. This gives them a leg up in getting positions in the bureaucracy. Thirty percent of all postal employees are veterans, twice the proportion of the population of veterans in the workforce. Few women are administrative law judges, a situation that one analyst blames on veterans' preferences that skew hiring toward men who have served in the armed services.[27] When an attack on programs designed to help minorities in the job market began after the 1994 election, this loud criticism of affirmative action never included veterans' preferences. Yet both sets of programs were designed to do the same thing: to give advantages to members of a particular group as they search for work. They are regarded quite differently, of course, because veterans are popularly viewed as a deserving population, while minorities are not.

Credibility

Another kind of respect is accorded in varying amounts to interest groups. Some organizations are seen as more credible than others because their views are perceived to be less self-interested. The organizations that have the most credibility with the American people and with the press are public interest groups and think tanks. Although studies by public interest groups are not universally accepted, they carry the aura of having been produced by people who have no economic gain to be made if the policies advocated were enacted. Leaders of public interest groups have understood the value of producing high-quality research that enhances their organization's image. They also understand how to package and market their research to the press. To maximize publicity, the Environmental Working Group timed the release of its report on farm subsidies to rich land owners to coincide with a Senate Agriculture Committee hearing. The report itself, "City Slickers," was a thorough computer analysis of where agriculture subsidies go. Amid all the data were some irresistible examples that made for good copy. For example, $1.2 million in farm subsidies, which are defended on the grounds that they save family farms, was sent to people who live within the zip code boundaries of Beverly Hills, 90210. The study was widely

---

[27]Ann Crittenden, "Quotas for Good Old Boys," *Wall Street Journal*, June 14, 1995.

reported in the press.[28] There is little chance that a study of farm subsidies produced by a farmers' lobby could have attracted anywhere near the attention.

Public interest groups are also helped by the need of journalists to report both sides of a story. If there is a proposal in Congress to help a particular industry, business lobbyists will aggressively seek to promote their position. But who should a journalist contact to learn why such a policy might harm consumers? Reporters contact others (academics, members of Congress), but public interest lobbyists are also a favorite source of sound bites. They are not merely convenient because of their location in Washington, but they are attuned to what the press needs and wants and they offer spokespersons who are articulate, highly expert, and ostensibly nonpartisan.

Think tanks possess the advantages of public interest groups in terms of credibility, but they are seen as more scholarly because of the type of personnel they hire and the type of research they undertake. A major reason why think tanks have flourished is precisely because they have such a high level of credibility. Organizations and individuals who want to push a particular point of view have contributed considerable sums of money to establish and maintain new think tanks.

REFORM

We end where we began, with Madison's dilemma. Our form of government allows people to organize and to lobby for their own selfish interests, even if the policies they advocate are contrary to the general well-being of the country. The increasing prominence of lobbying organizations in the governmental process has focused attention on the problems associated with interest group politics. If the system is ailing,

---

[28]Among the articles are John M. Broder and Dwight Morris, "Urban 'Farmers' Reap Rich Harvest of Crop Subsidies," *Los Angeles Times,* March 16, 1995; Stephen Engelberg, "Farm Aid to Chicago? Miami? Study Hits an Inviting Target," *New York Times,* March 16, 1995; Bruce Ingersoll, "As Congress Considers Slashing Crop Subsidies, Affluent Farmers Come Under Scrutiny," *Wall Street Journal,* March 16, 1995; Lynne Marek, "Subsidies to Absentee Farmers are Criticized," *Chicago Tribune,* March 16, 1995; and "Urban Residents Said to Reap $1.8B in Subsidies for Agriculture," *Boston Globe,* March 16, 1995. The story was also widely reported in the TV and radio news.

why not fix it? Madison's warning in *Federalist* No. 10 is sobering. Efforts to cure the "mischiefs of faction" warns Madison, could end up "destroying" our political freedom:

> Liberty is to faction what air is to fire, an aliment without which it instantly expires. But it could not be a less folly to abolish liberty, which is essential to political life, because it nourishes faction than it would be to wish the annihilation of air, which is essential to animal life, because it imparts to fire its destructive agency.[29]

Madison believed that the size and diversity of the country and the structure of our government would prevent any particular faction from oppressing all others. Madison's solution certainly has worked to make it harder for any one set of groups to dominate American politics. Nevertheless, his solution is not entirely adequate. At times in our history the government has stepped in to limit the power of groups and recent calls for lobbying reform strike a familiar chord in American politics. Lobbies are always a target for those frustrated with the performance of government. One might think that the public's high level of alienation toward government would have prompted serious reform years ago. Concern about interest group politics has stimulated an ongoing debate in Congress over a stream of bills designed to reform our campaign finance and lobbying laws. Little of this recent legislation has made it into law, though as noted in Chapter 5, some modest reforms were enacted in 1995.

Beyond the dilemma outlined in *Federalist* No. 10 and the partisan and ideological differences that are brought to the debate in Congress, there is an additional reason why it is so hard to agree on interest group reforms. What are the principles that should guide what is allowable interest group activity? And what is so harmful that we must violate *Federalist* No. 10's warnings and restrict the freedom of groups? Madison speaks of the ultimate consequence of faction-based politics as "oppression." This is a rather extreme condition, and surely a government must not wait to take action until circumstances suggest that such disaster looms. What principles, then, should be followed in deciding whether regulation of interest groups is just or an unwarranted violation of personal freedom? Let me offer three commonsense standards for regulating interest groups.

---

[29]*The Federalist Papers* (New York: New American Library, 1961), p. 78.

First, government should be vigilant in ensuring that interest group spending does not play an undue role in the political process. In the abstract, few disagree with this. Controversy comes from efforts to set specific limits on spending by groups. Still, government has long regulated what lobbies could spend money on. If corporate PACs could donate unlimited amounts to political candidates, that would so dominate campaign spending that the contributions by others would become largely symbolic. Just as free speech is no longer free speech if someone owns all the newspapers and TV stations, interest group politics is not fair when money spent by one sector crowds out the participation of others. If, for example, the government wanted to step in and abolish or significantly restrict soft money contributions by corporations to political parties, it would have every right to do so.

Second, government should protect the integrity of the political system. No one would take issue with this, but the devil is in the details. There are already many rules that govern the relationships between lobbyists and policymakers. As discussed in Chapter 5, policymakers who leave government to work for lobbies must observe a moratorium on contacts with their previous colleagues. Protecting the integrity of the system means more than rooting out the conditions that lead to favoritism because of a campaign contribution or a revolving-door connection to former colleagues in government. It also means making the political process as open as possible. The formal meetings of committees writing legislation or agencies holding hearings on proposed rules are already open. The problem emerges when policymakers from one party or the other meet privately only with their allies in the interest group community and exclude participation by others. When bargaining takes place in private and excludes groups with significant interests at stake, it diminishes the quality of policymaking and the integrity of representative democracy. It is naive to believe that policymakers can always act in the open with all interested groups participating. Nevertheless, when policymaking is truly exclusionary or based on favoritism, it is appropriate for government to restrict such behavior.

Third, government should ensure that disadvantaged sectors of society that are inadequately represented by interest groups receive support to improve their representation in the political process. For the poor, minorities, and the disabled, there are interest groups active on their behalf, but they are few in number and do not have the resources to fund the kind of advocacy efforts they need. Over the years the gov-

ernment has taken steps through grants and contracts to help groups
for the disadvantaged to organize, develop programs, and train leaders.
Such efforts reduce the inequities that are inevitable in any society.
Despite their good intentions, these programs are controversial because they have partisan implications. Republicans perceive, correctly,
that such programs help to empower constituencies partial to the Democrats. The GOP has repeatedly made efforts to "defund the left" by
trying to reduce the federal money available for advocacy organizations.[30] Not every such program may be worthwhile, but the Congress
must rise above partisan and ideological considerations. Interest group
politics is only defensible when all significant constituencies are represented by viable lobbying organizations.

The lobbying world is by and large an adversarial one.[31] Groups are
aligned against each other, and the type of prohibitions and rules described earlier are designed to keep policy fights reasonably fair. Another
way of trying to structure interest group politics is to make it "cooperationist" rather than adversarial.[32] If ways can be found to develop policy
through mediation of interest group differences, many of the problems
of interest group politics will be diminished. One such approach is negotiated rule making. This is a procedure sanctioned by the federal government that allows agencies to turn over the formulation of regulations to
panels of interest group representatives. The Negotiated Rulemaking
Act requires that these panels be balanced in their makeup, and that all
interests who "will be significantly affected" by the regulations will be
represented.[33] This is a particularly useful procedure when protracted
conflict between business and citizen groups would otherwise prevail.[34]

---

[30]Michael S. Greve, "Why 'Defunding the Left' Failed," *Public Interest* 89 (Fall 1987),
pp. 91–106; Jeff Shear, "The Ax Files," *National Journal,* April 15, 1995, pp. 924–927;
and Keith Bradsher, "House Seeking Data on Nonprofit Groups," *New York Times,* September 27, 1995.

[31]See Jane J. Mansbridge, *Beyond Adversary Democracy* (New York: Basic Books,
1980).

[32]Steven Kelman, "Adversary and Cooperationist Institutions for Conflict Resolution
in Public Policymaking," *Journal of Policy Analysis and Management* 11 (1992),
pp. 178–206.

[33]*Negotiated Rulemaking Act of 1989,* 101st Congress, 1st session, 1989, Senate Report
101-97, p. 16.

[34]Jeffrey M. Berry, "Citizen Groups and the Changing Nature of Interest Group Politics
in America," *Annals of the American Academy of Political and Social Science* 528 (July
1993), pp. 30–41.

It makes policymaking efficient and requires consensus among interest group participants.

Government can nurture cooperationist policymaking in other ways, and efforts should be made to develop additional procedures that encourage groups with different views to work together in a publicly-spirited search for policy solutions. At the same time, we should recognize that no set of government reforms is going to eliminate conflict in politics. Even though people may not be as inherently selfish as Madison assumed, self-interest will always be a part of politics. Thus, government must always be ready to rectify the balance between personal freedom and the need to prevent interest groups from seriously damaging the democratic process. Beyond government's actions to regulate campaign finance and the like, we need strong political parties that have clear agendas and are committed to carrying out the programs they campaign on. More needs to be done to strengthen our parties so that the votes of the many are more influential than the voices of interest groups.

Bibliography

Aberbach, Joel, and Bert Rockman. "Bureaucrats and Clientele Groups." *American Journal of Political Science* 22 (November 1978): 818–832.

Ainsworth, Scott. "Regulating Lobbyists and Interest Group Influence." *Journal of Politics* 55 (February 1993): 41–56.

Aldrich, Howard, and Udo Staber. "How American Business Organized Itself in the Twentieth Century." Paper delivered at the annual meeting of the American Political Science Association, Washington, D.C., August 1986.

Bachrach, Peter, and Morton S. Baratz. "Two Faces of Power." *American Political Science Review* 56 (December 1962): 947–952.

Baer, Denise L., and Julie A. Dolan. "Intimate Connections: Political Interests and Group Activity in State and Local Parties." *American Review of Politics* 15 (Summer 1994): 257–289.

Bauer, Raymond A., Ithiel de Sola Pool, and Lewis Anthony Dexter. *American Business and Public Policy.* New York: Atherton, 1968.

Baumgartner, Frank R., and Bryan D. Jones. *Agendas and Instability in American Politics.* Chicago: University of Chicago Press, 1993.

Baumgartner, Frank R., and Jeffrey C. Talbert. "Interest Groups and Political Change." In *The New American Politician,* edited by Bryan D. Jones. Boulder, Colo.: Westview Press, 1995.

Bednar, Nancy L., and Allen D. Hertzke. "The Christian Right and Republican Realignment in Oklahoma." *PS* 28 (March 1995): 11–15.

Bennett, James T., and Thomas J. DiLorenzo. *Destroying Democracy.* Washington, D.C.: Cato Institute, 1985.

Bentley, Arthur. *The Process of Government.* Chicago: University of Chicago Press, 1980.

Berry, Jeffrey M. *Feeding Hungry People: Rulemaking in the Food Stamp Program.* New Brunswick, N.J.: Rutgers University Press, 1984.

———. *Lobbying for the People.* Princeton, N.J.: Princeton University Press, 1977.

———. "Beyond Citizen Participation: Effective Advocacy Before Administrative Agencies." *Journal of Applied Behavioral Science* 17 (October 1981): 463–477.

———. "Citizen Groups and the Changing Nature of Interest Group Politics in America." *Annals of the American Academy of Political and Social Science* 528 (July 1993): 30–41.

———. "The Dynamic Qualities of Issue Networks." Paper delivered at the annual meting of the American Political Science Association, New York, September 1994.

————. "On the Origins of Public Interest Groups: A Test of Two Theories." *Polity* 10 (Spring 1978): 379–397.

————. "Public Interest vs. Party System." *Society* 17 (May–June 1980): 42–48.

————. "Subgovernments, Issue Networks, and Political Conflict." In *Remaking American Politics*, edited by Richard A. Harris and Sidney M. Milkis. Boulder, Colo.: Westview Press, 1989.

Berry, Jeffrey M., and Kent E. Portney. "Centralizing Regulatory Control and Interest Group Access: The Quayle Council on Competitiveness." In *Interest Group Politics*, 4th ed., edited by Allan J. Cigler and Burdett A. Loomis. Washington, D.C.: Congressional Quarterly, 1995.

Berry, Jeffrey M., Kent E. Portney, and Ken Thomson. *The Rebirth of Urban Democracy*. Washington D.C.: Brookings Institution, 1993.

Berry, Jeffrey M., and Deborah Schildkraut. "Citizen Groups, Political Parties, and the Decline of the Democrats." Paper delivered at the annual meeting of the American Political Science Association, Chicago, September 1995.

Biersack, Robert, Paul S. Herrnson, and Clyde Wilcox, eds. *Risky Business?* Armonk, N.Y.: M. E. Sharpe, 1994.

Birnbaum, Jeffrey H. *The Lobbyists*. New York: Times Books, 1992.

Birnbaum, Jeffrey H., and Alan S. Murray. *Showdown at Gucci Gulch*. New York: Random House, 1987.

Boerner, Christopher, and Jennifer Chilton Kallery. *Restructuring Environmental Big Business*. Occasional Paper No. 146, Center for the Study of American Business, Washington University, December 1994.

Bosso, Christopher. *Pesticides and Politics*. Pittsburgh: University of Pittsburgh Press, 1987.

————. "The Color of Money: Environmental Groups and the Pathologies of Fund Raising." In *Interest Group Politics,* 4th ed., edited by Allan J. Cigler and Burdett A. Loomis. Washington, D.C.: Congressional Quarterly, 1995.

Brown, Kirk F. "Campaign Contributions and Congressional Voting." Paper delivered at the annual meeting of the American Political Science Association, Chicago, September 1983.

Browne, William P. *Cultivating Congress*. Lawrence: University Press of Kansas, 1995.

————. *Private Interests, Public Policy, and American Agriculture*. Lawrence: University Press of Kansas, 1988.

————. "Mobilizing and Activating Group Demands: The American Agriculture Movement." *Social Science Quarterly* 64 (March 1983): 19–34.

————. "Organized Interests and Their Issue Niches: A Search for Pluralism in a Policy Domain." *Journal of Politics* 52 (May 1990): 477–509.

————. "Policy and Interests: Instability and Change in a Classic Issue Subsystem." In *Interest Group Politics,* 2nd ed., edited by Allan J. Cigler and Burdett A. Loomis. Washington D.C.: Congressional Quarterly, 1986.

Burstein, Paul. "What Do Interest Groups, Social Movements, and Political Parties Do? A Synthesis." Paper delivered at the annual meeting of the American Political Science Association, Chicago, September 1995.

Cater, Douglass. *Power in Washington.* New York: Vintage, 1964.

Choate, Pat. *Agents of Influence.* New York: Alfred Knopf, 1990.

Chubb, John E. *Interest Groups and the Bureaucracy.* Stanford, Calif.: Stanford University Press, 1983.

Cigler, Allan J., and Burdett A. Loomis, eds., *Interest Group Politics,* 4th ed. Washington, D.C.: Congressional Quarterly, 1995.

Clark, Peter B., and James Q. Wilson. "Incentive Systems: A Theory of Organizations." *Administrative Science Quarterly* 6 (September 1961): 129–166.

Clawson, Dan, Alan Neustadtl, and Denise Scott. *Money Talks.* New York: Basic Books, 1992.

Coll, Steve. *The Deal of the Century.* New York: Atheneum, 1986.

"Communication and the Congress." Washington, D.C.: Burson-Marsteller and the Institute for Government Public Information Research, 1981.

Conybeare, John C., and Peverill Squire. "Political Action Committees and the Tragedy of the Commons." *American Politics Quarterly* 22 (April 1994): 154–174.

Cook, Karen S. "Network Structures from an Exchange Perspective." In *Social Structure and Network Analysis,* edited by Peter V. Marsden and Nan Lin. Beverly Hills, Calif.: Sage, 1982.

Costain, Anne N. *Inviting Women's Rebellion.* Baltimore: Johns Hopkins University Press, 1992.

———. "Representing Women: The Transition from Social Movement to Interest Group." *Western Political Quarterly* 34 (March 1981): 100–113.

Costain, W. Douglas, and Anne N. Costain. "Interest Groups as Policy Aggregators in the Legislative Process." *Polity* 14 (Winter 1981): 249–272.

Crawford, Alan. *Thunder on the Right.* New York: Pantheon, 1980.

Dahl, Robert A. *Dilemmas of Pluralist Democracy.* New Haven, Conn.: Yale University Press, 1982.

———. *The New American Political (Dis)Order.* Berkeley: Institute for Governmental Studies, 1994.

———. A *Preface to Democratic Theory.* Chicago: University of Chicago Press, 1956.

———. A *Preface to Economic Democracy.* Berkeley: University of California Press, 1985.

———. *Who Governs?* New Haven, Conn.: Yale University Press, 1961.

———. "The Concept of Power." *Behavioral Science* 2 (July 1957): 201–215.

———. "Further Reflections on 'The Elitist Theory of Democracy.'" *American Political Science Review* 60 (June 1966): 296–305.

Dalton, Russell J. *The Green Rainbow.* New Haven, Conn.: Yale University Press, 1994.

Dalton, Russell, and Manfred Kuechler, eds. *Challenging the Political Order.* New York: Oxford University Press, 1990.

Derthick, Martha, and Paul J. Quirk. *The Politics Of Deregulation.* Washington, D.C.: Brookings Institution, 1985.

Dexter, Lewis Anthony. *How Organizations Are Represented in Washington.* Indianapolis: Bobbs-Merrill, 1969.

————. *The Sociology and Politics of Congress.* Chicago: Rand McNally, 1969.

Domhoff, G. William. *The Powers That Be.* New York: Vintage, 1979.

Dowie, Mark. *Losing Ground.* Cambridge: MIT Press, 1995.

Eastman, Hope. *Lobbying: A Constitutionally Protected Right.* Washington, D.C.: American Enterprise Institute, 1977.

Eismeier, Theodore J., and Phillip H. Pollock, III. *Business, Money, and the Rise of Corporate PACs in American Elections.* Westport, Conn.: Quorum Books, 1988.

Epstein, Edwin M. "Business and Labor Under the Federal Election Campaign Act of 1971." In *Parties, Interest Groups, and Campaign Finance Laws,* edited by Michael J. Malbin. Washington, D.C.: American Enterprise Institute, 1980.

Epstein, Lee. *Conservatives in Court.* Knoxville, Tenn.: University of Tennessee Press, 1985.

Evans, Diana. "PAC Contributions and Roll-Call Voting: Conditional Power." In *Interest Group Politics,* 2nd ed., edited by Allan J. Cigler and Burdett A. Loomis. Washington, D.C.: Congressional Quarterly, 1986.

Federalist Papers. New York: New American Library, 1961.

Fowler, Linda L. "How Interest Groups Select Issues for Voting Records of Members of the U.S. Congress." *Legislative Studies Quarterly* 7 (August 1982): 401–413.

Freeman, Richard B., and James L. Medoff. *What Do Unions Do?* New York: Basic Books, 1984.

Gais, Thomas L., Mark A. Peterson, and Jack L. Walker. "Interest Groups, Iron Triangles, and Representative Institutions in American National Government." *British Journal of Political Science* 14 (April 1984): 161–185.

Gamson, William. *Power and Discontent.* Homewood, Ill.: Dorsey Press, 1968.

————. *The Strategy of Social Protest.* Homewood, Ill.: Dorsey Press, 1975.

Garrow, David J. *Protest at Selma.* New Haven, Conn.: Yale University Press, 1978.

Garson, G. David. *Group Theories of Politics.* Beverly Hills, Calif.: Sage, 1978.

Gaventa, John. *Power and Powerlessness.* Urbana, Ill.: University of Illinois Press, 1980.

Gelb, Joyce, and Marian Lief Palley. *Women and Public Policies,* rev. ed. Princeton, N.J.: Princeton University Press, 1987.

Godwin, R. Kenneth. *One Billion Dollars of Influence.* Chatham, N.J.: Chatham House, 1988.

Gormley, William T., Jr. *The Politics of Public Utility Regulation.* Pittsburgh: University of Pittsburgh Press, 1983.

Greenstone, J. David. *Labor in American Politics.* New York: Knopf, 1969.

Greider, William. *Who Will Tell the People.* New York: Touchstone, 1993.

Grenzke, Janet M. "PACs in the Congressional Supermarket: The Currency Is Complex." *American Journal of Political Science* 33 (February 1989): 1–24.

Greve, Michael S. "Why Defunding the Left Failed." *Public Interest* 89 (Fall 1987): 91–106.

Guth, James L., John C. Green, Lyman A. Kellstedt, and Corwin E. Smidt. "Onward Christian Soldiers: Religious Activist Groups in American Politics." In *Interest Group Politics,* 4th ed., edited by Allan J. Cigler and Burdett A. Loomis. Washington, D.C.: Congressional Quarterly, 1995.

Hall, Richard L. "Buying Time: Moneyed Interests and the Mobilization of Bias in Congressional Committees." *American Political Science Review* 84 (September 1990): 797–820.

Hamm, Keith E. "Patterns of Influence Among Committees, Agencies, and Interest Groups." *Legislative Studies Quarterly* 8 (August 1983): 379–426.

Hansen, John Mark. *Gaining Access.* Chicago: University of Chicago Press, 1991.

Harris, Richard A. *Coal Firms under the New Social Regulation.* Durham, N.C.: Duke University Press, 1985.

Hayes, Michael T. *Lobbyists and Legislators.* New Brunswick, N.J.: Rutgers University Press, 1981.

Heclo, Hugh. "Issue Networks and the Executive Establishment." In *The New American Political System,* edited by Anthony King. Washington, D.C.: American Enterprise Institute, 1978.

Heinz, John P., Edward O. Laumann, Robert L. Nelson, and Robert H. Salisbury. *The Hollow Core.* Cambridge, Mass.: Harvard University Press, 1993.

Herman, Edward S. *Corporate Control, Corporate Power.* New York: Cambridge University Press, 1981.

Herrnson, Paul S. *Party Campaigning in the 1980s.* Cambridge, Mass.: Harvard University Press, 1988.

———. "The National Committee for an Effective Congress: Liberalism, Partisanship, and Electoral Innovation." In *Risky Business?,* edited by Robert Biersack, Paul S. Herrnson, and Clyde Wilcox. Armonk, N.Y.: M.E. Sharpe, 1994.

Hertzke, Allen D. *Representing God in Washington.* Knoxville: University of Tennessee Press, 1988.

Hrebner, Ronald J., and Ruth K. Scott. *Interest Group Politics in America.* 2nd ed. Englewood Cliffs, N.J.: Prentice-Hall, 1990.

Hula, Kevin. *Links and Choices: Explaining Coalition Formation Among Organized Interests,* doctoral dissertation, Department of Government, Harvard University, 1995.

Hunter, Floyd. *Community Power Structure.* Chapel Hill, N.C.: University of North Carolina Press, 1953.

Imig, Douglas. *Poverty and Power: The Political Representation of Poor Americans.* Lincoln: University of Nebraska Press, 1996.

Jackson, Brooks. *Honest Graft.* New York: Knopf, 1988.

Jacobson, Gary C. *Money in Congressional Elections.* New Haven, Conn.: Yale University Press, 1980.

Johnson, Paul E. "How Environmental Groups Recruit Members: Does the Logic Still Hold Up?" Paper delivered at the annual meeting of the American Political Science Association, Chicago, September 1995.

Kerwin, Cornelius M. *Rulemaking.* Washington, D.C.: Congressional Quarterly, 1994.

Key, V.O., Jr. *Politics, Parties, and Pressure Groups,* 5th ed. New York: Crowell, 1964.

Kingdon, John W. *Agendas, Alternatives, and Public Policies.* Boston: Little, Brown, 1984.

————. *Congressmen's Voting Decisions,* 2nd ed. New York: Harper & Row, 1981.

Knoke, David. *Political Networks: The Structural Perspective.* New York: Cambridge University Press, 1990.

Knoke, David, and James Kuklinski. *Network Analysis.* Beverly Hills, Calif.: Sage, 1982.

Knoke, David, and Edward O. Laumann. "The Social Organization of National Policy Domains." In *Social Structure and Network Analysis,* edited by Peter V. Marsden and Nan Lin. Beverly Hills, Calif.: Sage, 1982.

Knoke, David, and James W. Wood. *Organized for Action.* New Brunswick, N.J.: Rutgers University Press, 1981.

Kotz, Nick, and Mary Lynn Kotz. *A Passion for Equality.* New York: Norton, 1977.

Kumar, Martha Joynt, and Michael Baruch Grossman. "The Presidency and Interest Groups." In *The Presidency and the Political System,* edited by Michael Nelson. Washington, D.C.: Congressional Quarterly, 1984.

Laumann, Edward O., and David Knoke. *The Organizational State.* Madison: University of Wisconsin Press, 1987.

Lester, James P., and W. Douglas Costain. "The Evolution of Environmentalism." In *The New American Politician,* edited by Bryan D. Jones. Boulder, Colo.: Westview Press, 1995.

Liebman, Robert C., and Robert Wuthnow. *The New Christian Right.* New York: Aldine, 1983.

Lindblom, Charles E. *Politics and Markets.* New York: Basic Books, 1977.

Lipset, Seymour Martin, Martin Trow, and James Coleman. *Union Democracy.* Garden City, N.Y.: Doubleday Anchor Books, 1956.

Lipsky, Michael. "Protest as a Political Resource." *American Political Science Review* 62 (December 1968): 1144–1158.

Lowi, Theodore J. *The End of Liberalism,* 2nd ed. New York: Norton, 1979.

Luker, Kristin. *Abortion and the Politics of Motherhood.* Berkeley: University of California Press, 1984.

Lusterman, Seymour, *Managing Federal Government Relations.* New York: Conference Board, 1988.

———. *The Organization & Staffing of Corporate Public Affairs.* New York: Conference Board, 1987.

Luttbeg, Norman R., and Harmon Zeigler. "Attitude Consensus and Conflict in an Interest Group." *American Political Science Review* 60 (September 1966): 655–666.

McAdam, Doug. *Political Process and the Development of Black Insurgency.* Chicago: University of Chicago Press, 1982.

McCann, Michael W. *Taking Reform Seriously.* Ithaca, N.Y.: Cornell University Press, 1986.

McCarry, Charles. *Citizen Nader.* New York: Saturday Review Press, 1972.

McConnell, Grant. *Private Power and American Democracy.* New York: Alfred A. Knopf, 1966.

McFarland, Andrew S. *Common Cause.* Chatham, N.J.: Chatham House, 1984.

———. *Cooperative Pluralism.* Lawrence: University Press of Kansas, 1993.

———. *Public Interest Lobbies.* Washington, D.C.: American Enterprise Institute, 1976.

———. "Interest Groups and the Policymaking Process: Sources of Countervailing Power in America." In *The Politics of Interests,* edited by Mark P. Petracca. Boulder, Colo.: Westview Press, 1992.

McGrath, Phyllis S. *Redefining Corporate-Federal Relations.* New York: Conference Board, 1979.

MacKenzie, G. Calvin, ed. *The In-and-Outers.* Baltimore: Johns Hopkins University Press, 1987.

McQuaid, Kim. "The Roundtable: Getting Results in Washington." *Harvard Business Review* 59 (May–June 1981): 114–123.

Manley, John F. "Neo-Pluralism: A Class Analysis of Pluralism I and Pluralism II." *American Political Science Review* 77 (June 1983): 368–383.

Mansbridge, Jane J. *Why We Lost the ERA.* Chicago: University of Chicago Press, 1986.

Marsh, David. "On Joining Interest Groups." *British Journal of Political Science* 6 (July 1976): 257–272.

Martin, Cathie Jo. "Nature or Nurture? Sources of Firm Preference for National Health Reform." *American Political Science Review* 89 (December 1995): 898–913.

Meier, August, and Elliott Rudwick. *CORE: A Study in the Civil Rights Movement.* New York: Oxford University Press, 1973.

Meyer, David S., and Douglas Imig. "Political Opportunity and the Rise and Decline of Interest Group Sectors." *Social Science Journal* 30 (July 1993): 253–270.

Milbrath, Lester W. *The Washington Lobbyists*. Chicago: Rand McNally, 1963.

Mills, C. Wright. *The Power Elite*. New York: Oxford University Press, 1956.

Moe, Terry M. *The Organization of Interests*. Chicago: University of Chicago Press, 1980.

————. "A Calculus of Group Membership." *American Journal of Political Science* 24 (November 1980): 593–632.

————. "Toward a Broader View of Interest Groups." *Journal of Politics* 43 (May 1981): 531–543.

Moen, Matthew C. *The Transformation of the Christian Right*. Tuscaloosa: University of Alabama Press, 1992.

————. "The Devolutionary Era: A New Phase of Activism Linking Religious and Secular Conservatives in the 104th Congress." Paper delivered at the annual meeting of the New England Political Science Association, Portland, Maine, May 1995.

Moffett, George D., III. *The Limits of Victory*. Ithaca, N.Y.: Cornell University Press, 1985.

Moore, Stephen, Sidney M. Wolfe, Deborah Lindes, and Clifford Douglas. "Epidemiology of Failed Tobacco Control Legislation." *Journal of the American Medical Association* 272 (October 19, 1994): 1171–1175.

Mucciaroni, Gary. *Reversals of Fortune*. Washington, D.C.: Brookings Institution, 1995.

Mundo, Philip A. *Interest Groups: Cases and Characteristics*. Chicago: Nelson-Hall, 1992.

Nugent, Margaret Latus. "When Is a $1,000 Contribution Not a $1,000 Contribution?" *Election Politics* 3 (Summer 1986): 13–16.

O'Brien, David J. *Neighborhood Organization and Interest Group Processes*. Princeton, N.J.: Princeton University Press, 1975.

O'Connor, Karen. *Women's Organizations' Use of the Courts*. Lexington, Mass.: Lexington Books, 1980.

O'Connor, Karen, and Lee Epstein. "The Rise of Conservative Interest Group Litigation." *Journal of Politics* 45 (May 1983): 478–489.

————. "The Role of Interest Groups in Supreme Court Policy Formation." In *Public Policy Formation*, edited by Robert Eyestone. Greenwich, Conn.: JAI Press, 1984.

Olson, Mancur, Jr., *The Logic of Collective Action*. New York: Schocken, 1968.

————. *The Rise and Decline of Nations*. New Haven, Conn.: Yale University Press, 1982.

Orren, Karen. "Liberalism, Money, and the Situation of Organized Labor." In *Public Values and Private Power in American Politics*, edited by J. David Greenstone. Chicago: University of Chicago Press, 1982.

————. "Standing to Sue: Interest Group Conflict in the Federal Courts." *American Political Science Review* 70 (September 1976): 723–741.

Peterson, Mark A. "The Presidency and Organized Interest Groups: White House Patterns of Interest Group Liaison." *American Political Science Review* 86 (September 1992): 612–625.

Peterson, Mark A., and Jack L. Walker. "Interest Group Responses to Partisan Change." In *Interest Group Politics,* 2nd ed., edited by Allan J. Cigler and Burdett A. Loomis. Washington, D.C.: Congressional Quarterly, 1986.

Peterson, Paul. "The Rise and Fall of Special Interest Politics." In *The Politics of Interests,* edited by Mark P. Petracca. Boulder, Colo.: Westview, 1992.

Petracca, Mark P., ed. *The Politics of Interests.* Boulder, Colo.: Westview, 1992.

Pika, Joseph A. "Reaching Out to Organized Interests: Public Liaison in the Modern White House." In *The Presidency Reconsidered,* edited by Richard W. Waterman. Itasca, Ill.: F.E. Peacock, 1993.

Piven, Frances Fox, and Richard Cloward. *Poor People's Movements.* New York: Pantheon, 1978.

Plotke, David. "The Political Mobilization of Business." In *The Politics of Interests,* edited by Mark P. Petracca. Boulder, Colo.: Westview, 1992.

Policy Studies Journal. Symposium on Interest Groups and Public Policy 11 (June 1983).

Polsby, Nelson W. *Consequences of Party Reform.* New York: Oxford University Press, 1983.

———. "Interest Groups and the Presidency." In *American Politics and Public Policy,* edited by Walter Dean Burnham and Martha Wagner Weinberg. Cambridge, Mass.: MIT Press, 1978.

Pratt, Henry J. *The Gray Lobby.* Chicago: University of Chicago Press, 1976.

Public Affairs Offices and Their Functions. Boston: Boston University School of Management, 1981.

The Public Interest Law Firm. New York: Ford Foundation, 1973.

Public Interest Law: Five Years Later. New York: Ford Foundation, 1976.

Quirk, Paul J. *Industry Influence in Federal Regulatory Agencies.* Princeton, N.J.: Princeton University Press, 1981.

———. "Food and Drug Administration." In *The Politics of Regulation,* edited by James Q. Wilson. New York: Basic Books, 1980.

Rauch, Jonathan. *Demosclerosis.* New York: Times Books, 1994.

Ricci, David M. *The Transformation of American Politics.* New Haven, Conn.: Yale University Press, 1993.

Richardson, Jeremy J., ed. *Pressure Groups.* New York: Oxford University Press, 1993.

Rochon, Thomas, and Daniel Mazmanian. "Social Movements and the Policy Process." *Annals of the American Academy of Political and Social Science* 538 (July 1993): 75–87.

Rosenbaum, Walter A. "Public Involvement as Reform and Ritual: The Development of Federal Participation Programs." In *Citizen Participation in America,* edited by Stuart Langton. Lexington, Mass.: D.C. Heath, 1978.

Rosenthal, Alan. *The Third House*. Washington, D.C.: Congressional Quarterly, 1993.

Rothenberg, Lawrence S. *Linking Citizens to Government*. New York: Cambridge University Press, 1992.

Rothman, Stanley, and S. Robert Lichter. "Elite Ideology and Risk Perception in Nuclear Energy Policy." *American Political Science Review* 81 (June 1987): 393–404.

Sabato, Larry J. *PAC Power*. New York: Norton, 1984.

Sale, Kirkpatrick. *SDS*. New York: Vintage, 1974.

Salisbury, Robert H. "Are Interest Groups Morbific Forces?" Paper delivered to the Conference Group on the Political Economy of Advanced Industrial Societies, Washington, D.C., August 1980.

————. "An Exchange Theory of Interest Groups." *Midwest Journal of Political Science* 13 (February 1969): 1–32.

————. "Interest Groups." In *Handbook of Political Science*, Vol. 4, edited by Fred I. Greenstein and Nelson W. Polsby. Reading, Mass.: Addison-Wesley, 1975.

————. "Interest Representation: The Dominance of Institutions." *American Political Science Review* 78 (March 1984): 64–76.

————. "Washington Lobbyists: A Collective Portrait." In *Interest Group Politics*, 2nd ed., edited by Allan J. Cigler and Burdett A. Loomis. Washington, D.C.: Congressional Quarterly, 1986.

————. "Why No Corporatism in America?" In *Trends Toward Corporatist Intermediation*, edited by Philippe C. Schmitter and Gerhard Lehmbruch. Beverly Hills, Calif.: Sage, 1979.

Salisbury, Robert H., John P. Heinz, Edward O. Laumann, and Robert L. Nelson. "Who Works with Whom?" *American Political Science Review* 81 (December 1987): 1217–1234.

Schattschneider, E. E. *The Semisovereign People*. Hinsdale, Ill.: Dryden Press, 1975.

Schlozman, Kay Lehman. "Representing Women in Washington: Sisterhood and Pressure Politics." In *Women, Politics, and Change,* edited by Louise A. Tilly and Patricia Gurin. New York: Russell Sage, 1990.

Schlozman, Kay Lehman, and John T. Tierney. *Organized Interests and American Democracy*. New York: Harper & Row, 1986.

Schneider, Anne, and Helen Ingram. "Social Construction of Target Populations: Implications for Politics and Policy." *American Political Science Review* 87 (June 1993): 334–347.

Shaiko, Ronald G. "Greenpeace, U.S.A.: Something Old, New, Borrowed." *Annals of the American Academy of Political and Social Science* 538 (July 1993): 88–100.

Smith, James A. *The Idea Brokers*. New York: Free Press, 1991.

Smith, Martin J. *Pressure, Power, and Policy*. Pittsburgh: University of Pittsburgh Press, 1993.

Sorauf, Frank J. *Inside Campaign Finance*. New Haven, Conn.: Yale University Press, 1992.

———. *Money in American Politics*. Glenview, Ill.: Scott, Foresman/Little, Brown, 1988.

Stewart, Joseph, Jr., and Edward V. Heck. "The Day-to-Day Activities of Interest Group Lawyers." *Social Science Quarterly* 64 (March 1983): 173–182.

Stone, Alan. *Public Service Liberalism*. Princeton, N.J.: Princeton University Press, 1991.

Tarrow, Sidney. *Power in Movement*. New York: Cambridge University Press, 1994.

Thomas, Clive, and Ronald Hrebenar. "Changing Patterns of Interest Group Activity: A Regional Perspective." In *The Politics of Interests,* edited by Mark P. Petracca. Boulder, Colo.: Westview, 1992.

Thurber, James A. "Dynamics of Policy Subsystems in American Politics." In *Interest Group Politics,* 3rd ed., Allan J. Cigler and Burdett A. Loomis, eds. Washington D.C.: Congressional Quarterly, 1991.

Tierney, John T. "Organized Interests and the Nation's Capitol." In *The Politics of Interests,* edited by Mark P. Petracca. Boulder, Colo.: Westview, 1992.

Truman, David B. *The Governmental Process,* 2nd ed. New York: Knopf, 1971.

Useem, Michael. *The Inner Circle.* New York: Oxford University Press, 1984.

Verba, Sidney, and Gary Orren. *Equality in America.* Cambridge, Mass.: Harvard University Press, 1985.

Verba, Sidney, Kay Lehman Schlozman, and Henry E. Brady. *Voice and Equality.* Cambridge, Mass.: Harvard University Press, 1995.

Vogel, David. *Fluctuating Fortunes.* New York: Basic Books, 1989.

———. *Lobbying the Corporation.* New York: Basic Books, 1978.

———. "How Business Responds to Opposition: Corporate Political Strategies During the 1970s." Paper delivered at the annual meeting of the American Political Science Association, Washington, D.C., September 1979.

———. "The New Political Science of Corporate Power." *Public Interest* 87 (Spring 1987): 63–79.

———. "The Public-Interest Movement and the American Reform Tradition." *Political Science Quarterly* 95 (Winter 1980–81): 607–628.

Vose, Clement. *Caucasians Only.* Berkeley, Calif.: University of California Press, 1949.

Walker, Jack L., Jr. *Mobilizing Interest Groups in America.* Ann Arbor, Mich.: Univeristy of Michigan Press, 1991.

———. "A Critique of the Elitist Theory of Democracy." *American Political Science Review* 60 (June 1966): 285–295.

———. "The Origins and Maintenance of Interest Groups in America." *American Political Science Review* 77 (June 1983): 390–406.

Waltzer, Herbert. "Advocacy Advertising and Political Influence." Paper delivered at the annual meeting of the American Political Science Association, Washington, D.C., August 1986.

"The Washington Executive." Washington, D.C.: Boyden Associates, 1980.

Weaver, Kent R. "The Changing World of Think Tanks." *PS* 22 (September 1989): 563–578.

Wellman, Barry. "Structural Analysis: From Method and Metaphor to Theory and Substance." In *Social Structures: A Network Approach,* edited by Barry Wellman and S.D. Berkowitz. New York: Cambridge University Press, 1988.

West, Darrell M., Diane J. Heith, and Chris Goodwin. "Harry and Louise Go to Washington: Political Advertising and Health Care Reform." *Journal of Health Policy, Politics and Law* 21 (Spring 1996): 35–68.

Wilcox, Clyde. "Coping with Increasing Business Influence: The AFL-CIO's Committee on Political Education" In *Risky Business?,* edited by Robert Biersack, Paul S. Herrnson, and Clyde Wilcox. Armonk, N.Y.: M.E. Sharpe, 1994.

Wilson, Graham K. *Business and Politics.* Chatham, N.J.: Chatham House, 1985.

————. *Interest Groups.* Oxford: Basil Blackwell, 1990.

————. *Unions in American National Politics.* London: Macmillan, 1977.

Wilson, James Q. *Political Organizations.* New York: Basic Books, 1973.

————. "Democracy and the Corporation." In *Does Big Business Rule America?,* edited by Ronald Hessen. Washington, D.C.: Ethics and Public Policy Center, 1981.

Wright, John R. *Interest Groups and Congress.* Boston: Allyn & Bacon, 1996.

————. "Contributions, Lobbying, and Committee Voting in the U.S. House of Representatives." *American Political Science Review* 84 (June 1990): 417–438.

————. "PACs, Contributions, and Roll Calls: An Organizatioal Perspective." *American Political Science Review* 79 (June 1985): 400–414.

Zeigler, Harmon, and Michael Baer. *Lobbying.* Belmont, Calif.: Wadsworth, 1969.

Index

Authoritarism
Librat groups
Anomalies
pluralist

In coumental reparms